The Natural Traveler
Along North Carolina's Coast

The Natural Traveler
Along North Carolina's Coast

John Manuel

JOHN F. BLAIR, PUBLISHER   Winston-Salem, North Carolina

Published by John F. Blair, Publisher

Copyright © 2003 by John Manuel
All rights reserved under International and
Pan American Copyright Conventions

The paper in this book meets the guidelines
for permanence and durability of the
Committee on Production Guidelines for
Book Longevity of the Council on Library Resources

Cover photograph by John Manuel
Book design by Debra Long Hampton

Library of Congress Cataloging-in-Publication Data
Manuel, John.
The natural traveler along North Carolina's coast / by John Manuel.
        p.   cm.
Includes bibliographical references and index.
ISBN 0-89587-272-2 (alk. paper)
1. Atlantic Coast (N.C.)—Guidebooks. 2. Natural areas—North Carolina—Atlantic
Coast—Guidebooks. 3. Historic sites—North Carolina—Atlantic Coast—Guidebooks. 4.
Museums—North Carolina—Atlantic Coast—Guidebooks. 5. Atlantic Coast (N.C.)—
History, Local. 6. Natural history—North Carolina—Atlantic Coast. I. Title.

F262.A84M36   2003
917.56'10444—dc21
2003001042

Contents

The Sound Country

∾The Southern Coast

Preface

As with most people, my love of the North Carolina coast began at the beach. Trips with friends to Sunset Beach, Emerald Isle, and Topsail Island were the high points of many a summer and fall weekend. The combination of affordable oceanfront rental housing, soft sand, warm water, and great body-surfing offered by the North Carolina beaches is as good as anywhere on the East Coast. As a canoeist and adventurer, I was soon drawn inland to the blackwater rivers and swamps—Merchants Millpond and the Waccamaw and White Oak Rivers. The concentration of wildlife in these rivers and swamps is amazing. Magazine assignments sent me in pursuit of red wolves in Alligator River National Wildlife Refuge and red-cockaded woodpeckers in the Green Swamp. My love of sports took me farther afield—fishing for false albacore off Cape Lookout, windsurfing on Bogue Sound, and sea kayaking at Ocracoke and Bear Islands. Research for this guidebook exposed me to the cultural highlights of the coast—outdoor dramas, museums, historic sites, and restaurants.

Over time, I've seen the coast undergo some dramatic changes, not always for the better. Development has overtaken the wild northern reaches of the Outer Banks. Pollution has sickened some of the rivers and bays. Hurricanes and pine beetles have ravaged some of the most beautiful forests. Yet nature has a way of being resilient, and man's interference is often a plus. Seedlings are sprouting amidst the stumps of storm-damaged pines. Historic downtown districts are being renovated.

So much is changing that even veterans of the coast could use a guide to keep up. My hope is that this book will expose readers not just to the well-known sites covered in other books, but also to some of the lesser-known gems, particularly natural areas, that dot the coastal region. For every place I have been, there is another yet to explore. And that will keep me visiting the coast for years to come.

Acknowledgments

Many people had a hand in shaping this guidebook. I would especially like to thank Phillip Manning for his sizable contribution to the chapter on the natural history of the coast and David Thurber for his companionship in my exploration of the swamps and rivers. Thanks also to the following for reviewing sections of the book: Quinn Capps of the Outer Banks Visitors Bureau; Barbara Blonder and John Taggart of the North Carolina Estuarine Research Reserve; Rob Bolling of Cape Hatteras National Seashore; Jeff Horton and Merrill Lynch of The Nature Conservancy; Don Pendergraft of the Museum of the Albemarle; Bill Lloyd of Croatan National Forest; Margie Brooks of the Historic Albemarle Tour; Karen Duggan of Cape Lookout National Seashore; Michelle Chappelle of Pocosin Lakes National Wildlife Refuge; Penny Leary-Smith of the Dismal Swamp Canal Visitor/Welcome Center; Bonnie Strawser and John Wallace of Alligator River National Wildlife Refuge; Vanessa Truman of Merchants Millpond State Park; and Sid Shearin of Pettigrew State Park.

How to Use This Book

The Natural Traveler Along North Carolina's Coast is specifically oriented to the tourist who has an interest in nature, but it also includes all the popular sites found in traditional guidebooks. Those who love to canoe, kayak, bird-watch, and hike will enjoy the detailed information about the parks, wildlife refuges, rivers, and swamps of the coastal region. The guide also includes information about beaches, lighthouses, historic sites, and museums, as well as a sampling of restaurants and lodgings.

The book is divided into four chapters: an introductory chapter on the natural history of the coast, followed by chapters on three relatively distinct geographic regions—the Outer Banks, the sound country, and the southern coast. While there is no official definition of how far inland the coast extends, sites are included up to the end of the tidal reaches of coastal rivers, and in some cases beyond. Note that the Outer Banks parallel the sound country and that the two are separated in places by a distance of only a few miles. These two regions have been placed in different chapters for organizational purposes. However, you may find yourself visiting sites in both regions on the same day.

For each of the geographic regions, sites are listed from north to south. Important sub-sites, such as historic homes within larger historic districts, are featured in bold. For each town, you'll find a selection of restaurants and lodgings. These are by no means all-inclusive lists. They highlight those places that offer a particularly distinctive cuisine or setting. Restaurants and lodgings are classified as *inexpensive, moderate,* or *expensive.* For restaurants, *inexpensive* translates to $25 or less per person for a three-course meal, *moderate* to $26 to $50, and *expensive* to more than $50. For lodgings, *inexpensive* translates to $50 or below for one night's stay during peak season, *moderate* to $51 to $100, and *expensive* to more than $100.

Maps are provided for each of the major areas discussed. For more detailed road maps, you may want to consult DeLorme's *North Carolina Atlas*. Boaters traveling the coast will want to pick up the *North Carolina Coastal Boating Guide*, available free of charge at most tourism offices or through ncwaterways.com. Canoeists and kayakers should look for the *North Carolina Coastal Plain Paddle Trails Guide*, also available free at most tourism offices. For individual state parks, national parks, and wildlife refuges, trail maps are usually available at park headquarters.

Words to the wise: Climate and weather at the coast can change dramatically from season to season and even from day to day. A calm, easily swimmable ocean one day can be aswirl with treacherous riptides or heavy breaking waves the next. Rivers, too, change significantly with the weather. Rains can send a river over its banks and into the trees, making the channel difficult to follow. Conversely, drought can lower the water level and turn what should be a half-day paddle into an all-day drag. Take the time to assess the environmental conditions before you take any excursion into the water or woods.

As a general rule, waters off the North Carolina coast reach comfortable swimming temperatures by June and remain so through October. Waters warm sooner and stay warm longer on the southern coast than on the Outer Banks. This is also the preferred time to canoe or kayak in coastal waters. Unless you are a seasoned kayaker with a "bombproof roll," avoid paddling in coastal waters when they are too cold for comfortable swimming. Should you capsize, cold water can drain your strength before you can get back in your boat. Always travel with a group, and wear the appropriate lifesaving equipment.

Sun and heat can be oppressive on the coast during the summer. It's best to stay indoors during the middle of the day and to always wear sunscreen when you go outdoors. Avoid dense woods and swamps during summer. They are muggy and buggy. Mosquitoes are a particular problem in areas such as Pea Island National Wildlife Refuge and Portsmouth Island. Here, bug repellant is not enough to keep the mosquitoes at bay. You need to wear a long-sleeved shirt, long pants, and a hat with bug netting to avoid being bitten.

Sharks are also present on the North Carolina coast. Several fatal attacks have taken place over the last few years. Avoid swimming late in the day, and always swim with a friend.

Taking these precautions into account, you should enjoy your visit to the North Carolina coast.

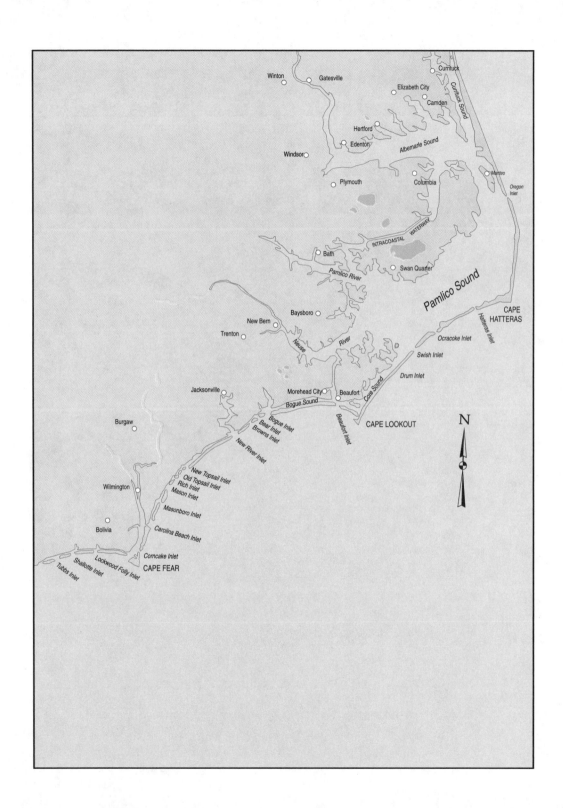

The Natural History of the North Carolina Coast

A classic North Carolina beach—broad, clean, and uncrowded

Geologic History

On March 12, 1969, astronaut Rusty Schweickart aimed a camera out the window of the *Apollo 9* spacecraft and snapped a picture of North Carolina's coast. Reproduced in magazines and posters worldwide, that picture revealed an image of astounding beauty. The thin, white line of the Outer Banks hung like a necklace around the pale blue waters of Currituck, Albemarle, and Pamlico Sounds. The mainland appeared as a checkerboard of brown and green squares—the huge agricultural fields, pine plantations, and natural woodlands and swamps of the coastal plain.

North Carolina's coastline is distinctive, unlike any other on the eastern seaboard, and those who understand something of its natural history will find a visit to the coast that much more interesting. Tourists do not share the vantage point of the astronauts, but even down on hands and knees, there are wondrous things to be seen.

The varied natural areas of the North Carolina coast all have one thing in common: they were once underwater. As recently as 60 million years ago, the sea covered much of eastern North Carolina, reaching as far as 150 miles inland from the present coast, all the way to the fall line, where the rolling hills of the Piedmont begin and the first rapids occur on the rivers. The coastal plain, the part of North Carolina that was buried under ancient seas, is characterized by flat topography with a gradual upward slope from seashore to fall line.

During the Ice Ages of the Pleistocene Epoch, which began 2 million years ago, sea levels fell dramatically as glaciers locked up increasing amounts of the planet's water. At the Pleistocene's lowest sea levels, the coastline was 20 to 50 miles *east* of today's beaches. During interglacial periods, the seas rose far higher than current levels, leaving a series of six gentle terraces on the coastal plain that mark the old coastlines.

When the last Ice Age ended about 17,000 years ago, the ocean started to rise again, and today's coast began to form. As the waters rose, rivers and ocean currents deposited sand on the dune ridges of ancient beaches. Slowly, some of these sand bars grew large enough to emerge from the sea and become what we now call barrier islands. Pushed by storm overwashes, tides, and predominantly easterly winds, these sandy islands began to migrate westward, a process that continues today. North Carolina's Hatteras Island is moving toward the mainland at a rate of almost five feet per year, a fact that recently prompted the National Park Service to move the famous Cape Hatteras Lighthouse 2,900 feet inland.

Where no rivers flowed, few sand bars formed, and the breakers of the rising waters crashed directly onto the mainland. In other areas, rivers and creeks cut channels behind the mainland shores, leaving remnant islands. Because remnant islands were once part of the mainland, they are more stable than the sandy, fickle barrier islands.

Agents of Change

The North Carolina coast is constantly changing. Some changes are dramatic, literally happening overnight as a result of hurricanes or powerful storms.

Hurricanes regularly visit the North Carolina coast and have greatly altered its appearance over the centuries. An example of this is the opening and closing of inlets along the Outer Banks. Inlets are generally cut through the Banks in the wake of hurricanes. As a hurricane approaches the shore, seawater may be pushed over the Banks and into the sounds behind. Winds blowing counterclockwise to the storm then push the water back toward the ocean, and may move enough sand to form an inlet. Both Oregon and Hatteras Inlets were created by a single powerful hurricane that swept up the coast in 1846.

Winter storms known as nor'easters, so named for the direction from which the winds blow, are another common occurrence along the coast and may re-shape the land as much as hurricanes. N.C. 12, the main road running the length of the Outer Banks, is frequently overwashed by nor'easters and has been re-routed farther inland several times.

The impact of hurricanes and nor'easters is especially obvious on barrier is-lands. Almost 40 percent of the landward movement of barrier islands is due to storm overwashes (seawater washing over the land). The rest is a result of tides and strong easterly winds that blow sand from the dunes, causing them to mi-grate westward.

Storms also close inlets. Today, only three inlets penetrate the Outer Banks between Cape Lookout and the Virginia border, but 24 are known to have ex-isted at one time or another. The influence of storms has been and will continue to be felt everywhere along this coast. It is worth remembering that the beach people are enjoying today could have been an inlet a few decades ago, and it might be a sand dune a few years from now.

Hurricanes and nor'easters dramatically alter the coast, but more subtle changes are occurring all the time. Sand bars form and disappear; some beaches accrete while others erode; channels and inlets come and go. These changes are caused by the movement of sand, propelled by currents, tides, and waves.

The Gulf Stream, warmed by equatorial waters, sweeps north along the North Carolina coast, coming as close to shore as 15 miles at Cape Hatteras. Gyres from the Gulf Stream peel away from the main current, curl south, and bathe the beaches with warm water. The water temperature at Cape Hatteras in August averages 80 degrees Fahrenheit, while ocean temperatures at a compa-rable latitude in California are 12 degrees cooler. These gyres also create the south-flowing longshore currents that move sand down the coast, contributing to the waxing and waning of beaches and leaving a sandy ocean floor appreciated by swimmers.

Flood tides move sand from the ocean through inlets, forming sand bars called flood-tide deltas behind the barrier islands. As these deltas grow, they contribute to the landward movement of sand that is characteristic of barrier islands. Sometimes, smaller ebb-tide deltas form on the seaward side of inlets. An ebb-tide delta can create a hazard for boats navigating an inlet and may eventually close it.

Waves do much of the nitty-gritty work of moving sand to and removing it from the beaches along the North Carolina coast. Short, steep waves called collapsing breakers add sand to steeply sloped beaches. Other breakers remove sand from the shore. As the surface of a wave moves toward the beach, the backwash sweeps along the bottom, sucking the beach's sand back into the ocean.

The Present Coast

Today's North Carolina coast is a medley of barrier islands, mainland beaches, and remnant islands. Long, thin barrier islands dominate from the Virginia border to Cape Fear. Because the islands in the northern part of that ribbon of sand lie far out to sea, 40 miles or so from the mainland, they are called the Outer Banks. Between them and the mainland lie great estuaries—Currituck, Albemarle, and Pamlico Sounds—where freshwater rivers meet the salty sea.

Unlike the Outer Banks, where unprotected land is being developed rapidly, the land to the west of these sounds is some of the wildest country in North Carolina. Much of it is covered by pocosins—thick, impenetrable tangles of brush and small trees. Black bears (*Ursus americanus*), bobcats (*Lynx rufus*) and red wolves (*Canis rufus*) roam freely in the sound country. Three of North Carolina's largest national wildlife refuges—Alligator River, Pocosin Lakes, and Mattamuskeet—offer these animals protection.

At Cape Lookout, the coastline turns sharply west. Here, smaller barrier islands hug the mainland, forming two great crescents. Behind many of these islands are marshes threaded with tidal creeks and backed by shallow bays. Bear Island, the home of Hammocks Beach State Park, is one of few such islands that has never been developed.

Each of the coastal regions supports many different natural communities. The following is an introduction to the coast's most important habitats.

Open Water

On any summer day along the North Carolina coast, you can see swimmers 200 feet or more from shore wading in waist-deep water. Get that far from a California beach and you'll be over your head. The water is shallow here because the gradual slope of the coastal plain extends far out to sea—50 miles or more to the edge of the continental shelf. The gentle, shallow water is one reason why North Carolina beaches are so popular.

Many species of fish ply these waters. The big three for surf fishermen are summer flounder (*Paralichthys dentatus*), bluefish (*Pomatomus saltatrix*), and red drum (*Sciaenops ocellatus*). These fish reach large sizes in the warm coastal waters. A big summer flounder, called a "doormat" because of its flat body, can weigh up to 20 pounds. "Chopper" blues get their name from their habit of chopping schools of baitfish into bits of flesh. The world-record bluefish, a 31-pound eating machine, was caught in North Carolina. The current world-record red drum—a 94-pound whopper—was also caught in the state.

Good surf fishing is available on many beaches along the North Carolina coast, especially in the fall, when big, ravenous bluefish pass by on their way south. At times, favorite fishing spots such as Cape Point at Cape Hatteras are lined with fishermen wielding nine- or 10-foot-long surf rods. On a good day, you can see their catch of blues lying on the beach, because the fishermen don't want to take time out from the action to put them on ice.

The Edge of the Sea

To most people, the North Carolina coastline conjures up images of waves splashing onto white-sand beaches. Of course, the coastline isn't really a line; it's two of them, marking the extent of the highest and lowest tides. The area between the two lines is called the intertidal or littoral zone. On the landward side of the intertidal zone lie the dunes, a rim of sand sometimes anchored by grass that protects the land from the rampages of the sea. The dunes have their own natural community, which is quite different from that found in the intertidal zone.

⌒⌒The Beaches

People love to visit beaches, but it is hard to imagine a less hospitable natural environment for an animal—a sandy, sun-baked plain at low tide; a turbulent, shallow saltwater lagoon at high tide. Beaches are littered with the remains of living creatures—cockleshells, the egg cases of skates, cannonball jellyfish, and the carapaces of crabs. On windy days, spindrift blows across these beaches like tumbleweeds across a desert. Like other harsh environments—the arctic tundra, for example—beaches do not support prolific biodiversity. There are more species in a square yard of rain forest than in a square mile of beach. But what beaches lack in biodiversity, they make up for in sheer numbers.

Scoop up seawater in a bucket and you will collect—suspended in the water, invisible to the eye—millions of unicellular photosynthetic algae called diatoms. Viewed through a microscope, diatoms are beautiful organisms. Their bodies are encased in two-part, glassy shells marked by intricate designs and colors.

Diatoms are a food source that, in one way or another, supports almost every living creature in the sea. Zooplankton, the animal component of the free-floating mixture of tiny plants and animals called plankton, feed on diatoms. At the other end of the scale, Northern right whales (*Eubalaena glacialis*), which migrate past these shores, feed on plankton. In just two steps, this simple food chain goes from the microscopic to the gigantic.

The tiny coquinas (*Donax variabilis*) that live beneath the sand of the intertidal zone of the beach also eat diatoms. Coquinas are bivalves, animals with two shells that resemble ordinary clams but are less than an inch long. Like diatoms, their shells are decorated with concentric whorls or rays of orange and purple, brown and white. Coquinas lie in the slurry of sand and water just beneath the surface of the beach, and a receding wave or a child digging in the sand will occasionally uncover hundreds of them. In this harsh environment, coquinas settle in the sand, raise siphons almost as long as their shells, and suck in bits of food, including any unlucky diatoms that the surf washes by them.

Sharing the sandy intertidal zone with coquinas are mole crabs (*Emerita talpoida*), sometimes called sand fleas. Mole crabs are larger than coquinas. They are pale gray and have egg-shaped carapaces. Like coquinas, they are usually found in huge numbers. Mole crabs, a favorite bait for fishermen, can be gathered from the beach by hand or by straining sand through half-inch-mesh hardware cloth.

Mole crabs are especially favored by those who fish for sheepshead (*Archosargus probatocephalus*), the most delicate nibblers and best bait-stealers in the Atlantic Ocean. Sheepshead don't appear delicate; they are robust-looking, oval-shaped fish with black vertical bands. The North Carolina-record sheepshead weighed over 18 pounds. They have very large, very sharp front teeth, which they use to graze on sluggish crabs and shellfish such as barnacles and mussels. They can use their razorlike teeth to pick a sand flea off a hook without the fisherman feeling the slightest jerk. Veteran sheepshead fishermen say that the best way to catch one is to set the hook just before the fish bites!

Excellent beaches line the entire North Carolina coast. To see beachfront in its most natural state, visit Cape Hatteras National Seashore, Cape Lookout National Seashore, or Bear Island in Hammocks Beach State Park.

∾ Sand Flats

Near the northern tip of Portsmouth Island in Cape Lookout National Seashore, a break in the dune line allows the ocean to flood a sand flat covering almost five square miles. The flat is white, splotched with browns and greens, and at low tide, it looks more like desert than seashore. But its barren appearance is misleading. The tracks of birds and raccoons cover the flat, and the many holes and mounds in the sand hint at a vigorous natural community beneath the surface.

As with the beaches, the food web of the sand flats starts with algae, the single-cell organisms that color the flats. Unlike the beaches, though, these algal mats support complex communities of protozoans, crustaceans, and worms. The most numerous visible occupants are the armies of fiddler crabs that scuttle across the sand. They move sideways, each holding an outsized pincer in the air like a tiny fighter ready for combat. Louis Bosc, who observed these crabs on the Carolina shore in 1802, must have had that image in mind when he named them *Uca pugilator*.

Herons, egrets, sandpipers, plovers, terns, and gulls all feed on the sand flats. The piping plover (*Charadrius melodus*), listed by the federal government as a threatened species, depends almost entirely on the flats for its food. The plover runs around the flats seemingly at random, then pauses and pecks when it spots a worm, insect, or small crab.

Besides the one on Portsmouth Island, sand flats can be observed at the Rachel Carson Estuarine Research Reserve near Beaufort and at the eastern end of Bear Island in Hammocks Beach State Park.

Dunes

Dunes rise behind almost every beach along the North Carolina coast, except where they have been washed out by storms. Depending upon where they are located relative to the shore, dunes can support varied flora. The primary dunes—the ones closest to the sea—are usually anchored by sea oats (*Uniola paniculata*) or, north of Cape Hatteras, American beach grass (*Ammophila breviligulata*). These grasses are crucial to the dune system; their roots stabilize the dunes, and their leaves trap wind-blown sand, which allows the dunes to grow.

Behind the primary dunes are swales, the low areas between dunes that are often covered in beach grass and salt meadow cordgrass (*Spartina patens*), and lines of secondary and tertiary dunes. Because these landward dunes are partially protected from the ocean and its salty spray by the primary dunes, hardy shrubs—cottonbush (*Baccharis halimifolia*), wax myrtle (*Myrica cerifera*), and yaupon (*Ilex vomitoria*)—grow on their leeward side.

Animals use the dunes, too. Female loggerhead turtles drag themselves across the beach in the dead of a midsummer night to lay their eggs just above the berm at the front of the dune line. The eggs attract raccoons and foxes looking for a protein-rich meal. Yellow-rumped warblers (*Dendroica coronata*) also frequent the dunes to feed on wax myrtle berries.

But all dunes are not alike. The top of Jockey's Ridge, the tallest natural sand dune in the eastern United States, is all wind and white sand. Not a scrap of vegetation mars the smooth surfaces of the dune. Even here, though, there is life. Ants and other insects prowl the dune, and conical pits in the sand reveal the presence of ant lion larvae, or doodlebugs, members of the family Myrmeleontidae. Adult ant lions resemble damselflies. They are innocuous-looking nectar feeders with knobby antennae and oversized, transparent wings. The larvae, however, are fierce predators with big, wicked jaws. They dig pits in the sand, and when an ant enters one, it slides down the steep side. Buried in the sand

Sea Oats

Along the North Carolina coast, visitors frequently see signs prohibiting the picking of sea oats. The reason for the ban is a good one. As windblown sand collects around the base of sea oats, the plants send out runners, called rhizomes, which put out new shoots. The network of roots and rhizomes beneath the sand holds the dune in place and protects the land behind the dune from overwash.

Where livestock once ran free, as on Shackleford Banks before it became part of Cape Lookout National Seashore, cows and horses grazed on sea oats. The unstable dunes blew over the island, killing much of its maritime forest. Today, when the restless sand in such places shifts, it sometimes exposes a "dead forest" of black trunks, the remains of once-healthy trees.

at the bottom is the ant lion, which then dispatches its prey.

Dune systems can be found on almost every beach along the North Carolina coast, but signs are often posted to warn people to stay off them to prevent them from eroding. This is typically the case for dune systems in front of developed areas. Some of the best places to climb on dunes are Jockey's Ridge State Park and Hammocks Beach State Park.

Tidal Marshes

Wetlands are complex ecological systems referred to by a variety of terms that describe different characteristics. Marshes are wetlands without trees; swamps are wetlands with trees. Tidal marshes are periodically flooded by salt water, brackish water, or fresh water.

The easiest way to visualize these different marshes is to take a cruise up an imaginary coastal river. From the open ocean, you proceed through an inlet flanked by two barrier islands into an estuary. Immediately behind the islands is a saltwater marsh, of which there are two types. Low marsh is flooded twice a day at high tide by salt water. As its name implies, the high marsh lies at a slightly higher elevation. Thus, it escapes the twice-daily inundations of salt water and is flooded only during spring tides and storms. Upriver, fresh and salt water mix, and the salinity of the water gradually drops from the 30 parts per thousand found in the ocean to about half that. However, high tides still back up water and flood the adjacent flatlands, which creates another kind of wetland—the brackish water marsh. Farther upriver, the salinity drops to less than 0.5 part per thousand, but high tides still cause the river to rise, flooding the adjacent wetlands with fresh water. This is a tidal freshwater marsh.

Each of these four coastal wetlands—low saltwater marsh, high saltwater marsh, brackish water marsh, and freshwater marsh—supports different flora and fauna, although there is overlap at the borders.

∽Low Saltwater Marshes

The causeway to Sunset Beach, the southernmost beach in North Carolina, passes through an expanse of low marsh, characterized by waist-high grass that is green in summer but brown in late fall and winter. Low tide exposes the black, muddy flats that anchor the grass, but at high tide, a foot or two of water covers the flats.

Low marshes are dominated by a single plant species, smooth cordgrass (*Spartina alterniflora*). A coarse grass that sometimes reaches a height of eight feet, it is supremely well adapted to living in salt water. Almost all plants and trees are composed of cells with low concentrations of salt in an aqueous solution. The walls of these cells act as semipermeable membranes. When two solutions of different concentrations are separated by such a membrane, osmosis occurs. Osmosis causes water to flow from the diluted solution to the concentrated one, as nature—moving as always toward equilibrium—tries to equalize the concentration of salt on the two sides of the membrane. Thus, when most plants are exposed to salt water, which has a higher concentration of salt than the plants' cells, osmosis sucks water out of the cells and eventually kills the plants. Cordgrass cells, however, contain water with a higher concentration of salt than salt water. So, when cordgrass is exposed to ocean water, it extracts fresh water from the salty solution, rather than losing water as other plants do. That is why cordgrass thrives even though the tides flood it twice a day with salt water.

Cordgrass dominates the low marsh, but it is not the only organism that lives there. Diatoms, the single-celled algae that coquinas eat on the beach, also flourish in the low marsh. And a menagerie of crabs, bugs, snails, oysters, clams, and worms feeds on either the diatoms or on detritus from decomposing cordgrass. Even so, biodiversity is low, since only a few organisms are sufficiently specialized to survive in this harsh environment. The dearth of interspecies competition appears to help those specialists, though, because the productivity of low salt marsh is astoundingly high. An acre of salt marsh produces almost 10 tons of organic matter in a year. A fertilized wheat field yields less than two tons. The reason for the marsh's prodigious growth is the continuous supply of nutrients, furnished twice a day by the tides. The marsh extracts those nutrients from the regularly replenished seawater and from the soil that washes downriver into the estuary.

An aerial view of virtually any low saltwater marsh shows tidal streams winding through the cordgrass. These streams act as nurseries for fish, crabs, shrimp, and other organisms that feed on the detritus (or feed on something else that feeds on the detritus) produced in these marshes. A cast net thrown into one of

Low saltwater marshes are dominated by a single species—smooth cordgrass.

these streams can corral enough baitfish to last a fisherman for a day or enough shrimp to serve for lunch.

Low marshes flourish along all parts of the North Carolina coast. Good sites include the North Carolina Aquarium at Fort Fisher and the Cedar Point Tideland Trail near Cape Carteret, both of which have trails that pass through or over low marshes.

High Saltwater Marshes

The high marsh lies landward of the low marsh. Along the North Carolina coast, high marshes are usually dominated by either salt meadow cordgrass (*Spartina patens*) or black needlerush (*Juncus roemerianus*).

S. patens is more common along the northern part of the coast than elsewhere. It is shorter—only one to three feet tall—and finer than smooth cordgrass and often lies down in mats called "cowlicks." In colonial New England, settlers grazed their cows on salt meadow cordgrass, which is how the plant got *meadow* as its middle name.

Unlike the two *Spartina* species, black needlerush is not a grass but a rush. It is a dark plant, standing as tall as six feet. Its long, slender leaves are tubular and sharp pointed. A walk through needlerush is a prickly torture to be avoided.

A good example of a salt meadow cordgrass marsh is behind Bear Island at Hammocks Beach State Park. Black needlerush can be seen all along the sound side of the Outer Banks.

Brackish Water Marshes

Brackish water marshes lie upstream from saltwater marshes and border those parts of tidal rivers where salt and fresh water mix. Brackish marshes are more diverse ecosystems than their downstream cousins, but their seaward edges grade into the vegetation typical of high saltwater marshes. Black needlerush, salt meadow cordgrass, and a smattering of smooth cordgrass often grow at this seaward edge.

As the influence of fresh water increases, new species begin to appear. Switch grass (*Panicum virgatum*), lance-leaved arrowhead (*Sagittaria lancifolia*), rose mallow (*Hibiscus moscheutos*), Olney's three-square (*Scirpus americanus*), and dozens of other species flourish in brackish marshes. Shrubs such as wax myrtle and yaupon can be seen on the landward edges of the marshes, and the showy white flowers of the marsh spider lily (*Hymenocallis crassifolia*) appear in late spring.

Brackish water marshes can be observed on most tidal rivers along the North Carolina coast. Currituck Sound also offers an example of this habitat.

The Carolina Water Snake

Kayakers cruising the shallows of the North Carolina sounds may catch sight of a heavy-bodied water snake hiding among the black needlerush or sunning on a log. This is most likely a Carolina water snake (*Nerodia sipedon williamengelsi*), a subspecies of the Northern water snake. The Carolina water snake is adapted to brackish water, where it hunts fish and frogs. It is distinguished from the Northern water snake by broader bands spaced more closely together than the Northern's.

The Carolina water snake is often mistaken for the venomous water moccasin. Named after University of North Carolina zoology professor William Engels, who first identified it as a subspecies, *williamengelsi* is found on the Outer Banks from Oregon Inlet south to the North River near Morehead City.

Freshwater Marshes

Freshwater marshes occur upstream of brackish marshes and are the most biologically diverse of all tidal marshes. The *Spartina*s and needlerush that dominate saltier marshes are completely absent, but many species of reeds, rushes, and sedges flourish here, as do grasses such as wild rice (*Zizania aquatica*) and Walter millet (*Echinochloa walteri*).

The vegetation of freshwater marshes varies from river to river, but representatives of one genus, the cattail (*Typha* spp.), are almost always present. Cattails are widespread and can tolerate a hint of salt, which is why they thrive in coastal regions. They can become pests in some places, crowding out other species. In some Florida marshes, biologists routinely apply topical herbicides to cattails to control their growth, usually in vain. But cattails have some supporters. Euell Gibbons, the enthusiastic advocate of eating wild foods, called cattails "the Supermarket of the Swamp" and suggested ways of cooking "delicious" meals from their leaves and roots. Few people eat cattails along the North Carolina coast, but some do make baskets and hats from their tough, fibrous leaves.

The diverse vegetation of these marshes attracts a variety of animals. Bullfrogs (*Rana catesbeiana*) boom their hoarse *jug-o'rums* across the shallow water, while stately great egrets (*Casmerodius albus*) stand motionless, searching for minnows. Yellow-belly slider turtles (*Chrysemys scripta*) lie head to tail on half-submerged logs. In winter, the Northern harrier (*Circus cyaneus*), or marsh hawk, skims over the cattails. When it spies something edible, it hovers for a moment, then pounces talons first. With its meal—often an unlucky mouse or frog—secured, the marsh hawk usually retires to a stump to consume its prey.

Freshwater marshes are found along all of the coastal rivers in North Carolina. Good examples include the shorelines of the White Oak, Cape Fear, and Lockwood Folly Rivers.

∞ Swamps

Southern swamps have a mythic component to them. In early American literature, they were often described as places of misery, places to be feared, places where a man could hide and never be found. John Lawson, one of the earliest explorers of the Carolinas, encountered such a swamp in 1700. He described how his party was forced to "strip stark-naked" and how it faced "much a-do to save ourselves from drowning in this Fatigue [but] with much a-do got Thro."

The early explorers' fear of swamps was not totally unfounded. Alligators, black bears, and water moccasins lurk in Southern swamps, as did cougars and wolves before those fearful explorers wiped them out. Today, we know these predators aren't nearly as dangerous as folklore made them out to be. Nevertheless, many people still approach Southern swamps with trepidation, probably because they look so spooky. In early morning, mists hang over the swamps.

The tannin-stained water lies black and still. Often, the silence is broken by mysterious splashes. As the mist lifts, great trees with strange, buttressed trunks appear. Gray tendrils of beardlike moss drip from their branches. Surrounding the trees like families of gnomes are clusters of cone-shaped knobs.

Two kinds of cypresses are found in North Carolina swamps—the bald cypress (*Taxodium distichum*) and the pond cypress (*Taxodium ascendens*). Some botanists consider the pond cypress to be a separate species, while others classify it as a subspecies (var. *nutans*) of the bald cypress. The two trees are almost identical in appearance and occupy the same habitat, so many naturalists think of them as one species and leave the nomenclatural dispute to specialists.

The bald cypress is an oddball tree. First, it is not a member of the cypress family but is instead classified with the redwoods. It has needles but is deciduous, hence the name *bald* cypress. Finally, it has knees, the mysterious knobs that usually surround these trees.

In the 1950s, botanists believed that the function of cypress knees was to absorb oxygen from the air and circulate it to the submerged roots of the trees. But in the 1960s, a researcher at Duke University showed that no oxygen passed between knees and roots. Botanists then speculated that the purpose of the knees was to stabilize the trees in the soft pond muck where cypresses usually grow. But cypresses growing on dry ground also send up knees. Today, most scientists admit that they really don't know what purpose the knees serve.

The gray tendrils dangling from the cypresses are Spanish moss (*Tillandsia usneoides*), a misnomer if there ever was one. The plant is not Spanish, nor is it a moss. In fact, Spanish moss is a bromeliad, or air plant, and it is as American as apple pie.

Sharing the swamp with the bald cypress is a host of other trees. These include swamp tupelo (*Nyssa biflora*), which like the bald cypress has a bell-shaped trunk, red maple (*Acer rubrum*), and an assortment of ashes, willows, and bays.

The vegetation and isolation of these swamps attract an equally wide variety of wildlife. Raccoons (*Procyon lotor*) are plentiful, and American alligators (*Alligator mississippiensis*) can be found along the southern part of the coast. But the most conspicuous wildlife are the birds. Great blue herons (*Ardea herodias*) nest in the upper branches, and green herons (*Butorides striatus*) stand among the cypress knees, waiting to strike at passing frogs or crayfish. The most spectacular bird in these swamps is the pileated woodpecker (*Dryocopus pileatus*), a crow-sized creature with a red topknot. The pileated woodpecker looks like Woody Woodpecker and has a similar manic attitude. Using its sturdy two-inch bill, it can tear apart a rotting tree in a few seconds of mad hammering as it searches for grubs and beetles.

Merchants Millpond State Park is a good example of a cypress swamp, as is the aptly named Cypress Cathedral in the Lower Roanoke River bottom lands.

⚮Carolina Bays

Travelers flying over the North Carolina coast will notice many oval depressions and lakes scattered across the landscape. These are Carolina bays, so named because about 90 percent of them occur in North and South Carolina. They range in size from mere dimples to thousands of acres. Though scientists have investigated every aspect of these bays, their origins remain a mystery.

All of the bays were once lakes, but vegetation has filled in most of them, leaving nearly impassable peat bogs rimmed by vegetation typical of a cypress swamp. Carolina bays have several things in common: their oval shape, their nearly unvarying northwest-to-southeast orientation, and their sand rims raised above the level of the surrounding area.

Since no known geological activity can account for the presence of the bays, early investigators felt free to speculate on their origins, putting forth proposals ranging from the presence of artesian wells to the dissolving of the bays' underlying clay soil by the acidic peat fill.

In 1933, armed with aerial photographs, scientists came up with the theory that the bays are remnants of a meteor shower. If one assumes a certain angle of impact, meteorite strikes could account for the bays' elliptical shapes and for the uniform alignment of their axes. However, no meteorite fragments have ever been found in or near a Carolina bay.

In 1945, zoologist Chapman Grant, writing in *Scientific Monthly*, proposed a stranger-than-science-fiction theory about the origin of Carolina bays. He suggested that the bays were the spawning beds of huge schools of now-extinct fish that migrated annually, like salmon or shad, from the ocean into fresh water to spawn. In this case, Grant's theory went, the fresh water came from a great upwelling of artesian springs along this portion of the Atlantic coast. Once the schools reached the fresh water of the springs, each fish, driven by the ancient urge to procreate, fanned out its own small spawning bed. The millions of tails swaying in unison cleared the sand from large areas, exposing hard ocean floor.

Carolina bays are oval-shaped lakes and depressions of unknown origins.
PHOTOGRAPH © JODY DUGGINS

Then the ocean receded, and, voilà, thousands of hard-floored, sand-rimmed Carolina bays were left, pocking the now-dry coastal plain.

Grant's theory was almost immediately discredited (how did the spawning beds survive the pounding surf of the receding ocean?), but new ones have come along to take its place. The most recent involves an exploding comet whose fragments generated shock waves that blasted out the Carolina bays. So far, at least 20 theories have been proposed to account for the origin of these bays, but none has been sufficiently persuasive to convince a majority of geologists.

The largest and most visible of the Carolina bays is Lake Waccamaw at Lake Waccamaw State Park. Others can be found in Croatan National Forest.

Pocosins

When seeing a pocosin for the first time, many people describe it as "scraggly." Shoulder-high shrubs thick with briars and cane cover the black soil, a monotony interrupted only by a scattering of undersized trees. So thick is the brush that pocosins appear impassable on foot, but a few explorers have tried. The 19th-century surveyor Ebenezer Emmons said one could traverse a pocosin only "at the expense of a man's coat, pantaloons and shirt."

Pocosins are unique to the Southeast, and they are especially common in North Carolina. They developed after streams cut through the sandy soil of the coastal plain. When the streams were dammed—perhaps by beavers—freshwater marshes appeared. Over the years, the dead vegetation of the marshes accumulated and peat formed. Bald cypresses and other trees and shrubs invaded the wetlands, and more peat accumulated when they died. Eventually, domes of peat that grew thicker at the rate of about a foot every thousand years covered the old stream channels. The plants that grew there became stunted because their roots could not reach the mineral soil beneath the deepening layer of peat. The result of this process was a pocosin, which is an Algonquian word meaning "swamp on a hill."

Early settlers avoided the boggy soil of the pocosins, but when modern ditching and draining equipment became available in the 1960s, thousands of acres of pocosins were drained and planted in corn and soybeans. During the Arab oil embargo of the early 1970s, several large corporations bought vast amounts of pocosin land with the intention of mining the peat for use as fuel. Within a few years, the declining price of oil and pressure from conservationists dealt twin blows to peat mining, but not before considerable damage was done to the environment. Evidence of that can be seen at Alligator River and Pocosin Lakes National Wildlife Refuges, which have open areas that support only a scant covering of weeds. All these areas were stripped of their original vegetative cover to get at the peat. Today, only about a third of the original 2.2 million acres of pocosins in North Carolina still exist in a natural state.

Naturalists call pocosins "shrub swamps" because of their vegetation. Fetterbush (*Lyonia lucida*), honeycup (*Zenobia pulverulenta*), and titi (*Cyrilla racemiflora*) dominate most pocosins. Laced through the brush are many species of briars, especially *Smilax* spp., which can shred one's pantaloons and shirt, just as they did in the 19th century. A few scattered and stunted pond pines (*Pinus serotina*) and red bays (*Persea palustris*) also manage to eke out a living in the peaty soil.

Fire is a normal occurrence in a pocosin. Carnivorous flowers such as the pitcher plant (*Sarracenia purpurea*) and the sundew (*Drosera intermedia*) often pop up after a blaze. These plants do well in the nutrient-poor soil, because they supplement their diet with flies and other insects. Nonetheless, they are often outcompeted by the fast-growing fetterbush and titi.

Because they are nearly impossible for humans to penetrate, those pocosins that escaped draining have proved to be havens for wildlife. Many reptiles and mammals call them home. Canebrake rattlesnakes (*Crotalus horridus*) hide in the brush, and Carolina anoles (*Anolis carolinensis*) are common. Cotton mice (*Peromyscus gossypinus*), marsh rabbits (*Sylvilagus palustris*), gray squirrels (*Sciurus carolinensis*), and white-tailed deer (*Odocoileus virginianus*) are also plentiful in these wetlands.

Good examples of pocosin habitats can be found in Croatan National Forest and at Alligator River and Pocosin Lakes National Wildlife Refuges.

Forests

Seen from either the air or the ground, much of eastern North Carolina is covered in trees. That's good news in many respects, though very little of this is old-growth forest. Virtually all the timber in this region has been cut-over at one time or another, and much of the land is now owned by timber companies that have replaced the natural mix of hardwoods and pines with uniform stands of planted pines. These pine plantations lack the biodiversity of a wild forest, but as the timber companies like to point out, they support more wildlife than a subdivision or a parking lot. The few old-growth forests that have survived are wonders to behold.

Maritime Forests

Like people, trees that live close to the sea have to hunker down. Storms, wind, and salt spray dictate their growth, sending branches out in low, horizontal patterns that often stream away from the prevailing winds. To step inside one of these sea-edge forests, away from the sun and the crash of the surf, is to enter a magical world.

The trees at the seaward edges of maritime forests are likely to be red cedars (*Juniperus virginiana*). Those were the trees spotted first by the earliest explorers of the Outer Banks. Captain Arthur Barlowe, who explored this coast for Sir Walter Raleigh in 1584, said they were "the highest and reddest Cedars of the world." That statement was probably meant to sell potential colonists on

Live oak trees are the signature species of the maritime forest.

the idea of emigrating to America, because most cedars in maritime forests have been pruned by the wind into stunted and misshapen forms.

Deeper in the forests are the trees that have become symbols of the Old South—the magnolia (*Magnolia grandiflora*), the dogwood (*Cornus florida*), and the live oak (*Quercus virginiana*). The live oak is often the dominant tree in maritime forests. It tolerates salt spray, and its dense, tough wood supports huge horizontal limbs that enable it to reach an enormous size without growing tall, thus avoiding most of the high winds and salt water that blow in off the ocean. Like the cypresses of the swamps, live oaks seem to attract Spanish moss, and their prostrate limbs are often draped with it. Lichens seem to prefer these oaks, too. Their muted hues of gray, green, and red make the trees, which can live for 200 years, appear even more ancient.

On the southern part of the coast, most notably on Bald Head Island, the cabbage palmetto (*Sabal palmetto*) lends a tropical air to maritime forests. The palmetto can grow to 90 feet, though it is usually a more modest 30 to 50 feet tall. It often occurs in the understory, growing beneath the loblolly pines (*Pinus taeda*) that are also part of these forests. The palmetto's trunk is unlike that of any other tree in North Carolina. It is not covered with bark, nor does it have a growing cambium layer. (The crisscrossed thatching on some palmettos is not bark, but the remains of dead fronds.) It is composed instead of a mass of tough parallel fibers that give it great strength and resilience. In colonial days, palmetto logs were used to line coastal forts because of their ability to stand up to bullets and shells without splintering or breaking.

Because maritime forests lie so close to desirable oceanfront property, they are disappearing from the North Carolina coast. Fortunately, some outstanding remnant forests have been protected. Buxton Woods, adjacent to Cape Hatteras National Seashore, encompasses about 3,000 acres of maritime forest. Nags Head Woods and Bald Head Island also support good examples of maritime forests.

∽Longleaf Pine Savannas

Imagine a broad plain carpeted with yellow grass, flecked with colorful wild-flowers, and intermittently shaded by towering pines. Small woodpeckers with black-and-white ladder backs and white cheek pouches flit from pine to pine, pecking at the bark for insects. In the grass beneath the trees sits a shy, nonde-script sparrow, visible only when it flutters into a bush to sing its song, a clear whistle followed by a trill. The understory is wiregrass (*Aristida stricta*), the trees

The longleaf pine savanna is characterized by widely-spaced trees and an open understory.
PHOTOGRAPH © JODY DUGGINS

are longleaf pines (*Pinus palustris*), and the birds are the federally endangered red-cockaded woodpecker (*Picoides borealis*) and the rare Bachman's sparrow (*Aimophila aestivalis*).

Two hundred years ago, longleaf pine savannas dominated much of the coastal plain of the Southeastern United States. William Bartram wrote in 1791, "We next entered a vast forest of the most stately Pine trees that can be imagined, planted by nature at a moderate distance, on a level grassy plain, enamelled with a variety of flowering shrubs."

Today, over 98 percent of the longleaf pine savannas are gone. Through the colonial era and beyond, settlers bled the longleaf pines for their resin to make turpentine and tar. When the resin was spent, the trees were logged. And thanks to the white man's insistence on fire suppression, the forests did not regenerate themselves after logging. Longleaf pine seedlings need full sun to grow, and the wiregrass understory requires periodic burning to reseed itself. In pre-colonial times, naturally occurring fires and those intentionally lit by Indians served the dual purposes of keeping competing hardwoods out and allowing wiregrass to reseed. But when European settlers and their descendants began suppressing fire, hardwoods began to shade out the young pines. As a result, mixed pine and hardwood forests with no wiregrass came to predominate where longleaf pine savannas once stood.

Today's foresters understand the problem and are conducting controlled burns in areas such as Brunswick County's Green Swamp in an attempt to re-create longleaf pine savannas. Wiregrass flowers in the summer or fall, but only if it has been defoliated by fire or grazing in the previous nine months. The most vigorous flowering occurs after a late-spring or early-summer fire. However, most foresters prefer to burn in winter, when fires are easier to control.

Good examples of mature longleaf pine forests can be found in The Nature Conservancy's Green Swamp Preserve, the Holly Shelter Game Land, and the Millis Road savanna in Croatan National Forest.

Bottom Lands

Upstream of the marshes, where the tides no longer influence water levels, dense forests border the rivers of the North Carolina coastal plain. Paddling a canoe down one of these rivers will take you into a world of dark pines and mixed hardwoods. The tallest trees in these forests are usually loblolly pines.

Loblollies raised in commercial pine plantations are usually harvested after 20 to 30 years, never reaching their full height. Left to grow on their own, loblollies in an old-growth bottom-land forest often tower over a hundred feet. Mixed in with the pines is an assortment of oaks—laurel (*Quercus laurifolia*), overcup (*Q. lyrata*), willow (*Q. phellos*), and water (*Q. nigra*). Sweet gums (*Liquidambar styraciflua*) and red maples are also present.

One of the more common summer visitors to the bottom lands is the prothonotary warbler (*Protonotaria citrea*), a small golden bird that brightens the dark forests. Year-round residents include the highly venomous cottonmouth (*Agkistrodon piscivorus*) and the Eastern hognose snake (*Heterodon platyrhinos*), which gapes like a cottonmouth when provoked, then rolls over on its back and plays dead.

The most outstanding example of a bottom-land forest is that lining the Lower Roanoke River.

Human History

Native Americans

As early as 12,000 years ago, roving bands of Paleo-Indians hunted mastodons and ground sloths along the North Carolina coast, leaving behind their signature Clovis spear points. Their descendants were primarily fishermen and farmers, and thanks to Sir Walter Raleigh, we have a reasonably accurate picture of the way they lived. Raleigh never made it to the North Carolina coast, but in 1585, he organized the first English attempt to colonize America. He chose an artist, John White, to draw what the expedition found and Thomas Harriot to record those findings. Harriot included some of White's drawings in his 1590 publication, *A briefe and true report of the new found land of Virginia*, copies of which can be seen in museums and visitor centers along the North Carolina coast.

The colonists landed on Roanoke Island, just west of what is now Nags Head. White drew an Indian village composed of long houses and enclosed by a stockade, an architectural style typical of the Algonquian culture. He showed corn growing in the fields, fish being roasted on wooden racks, dugout canoes being excavated, and women boiling food in huge earthen vats. The overall impression was one of a sophisticated society, a society that Europeans would soon overwhelm.

Aside from arrowheads and shards of pottery, few of the implements created by this Native American culture have ever been found. One exception is the dugout canoe. In 1982, some 30 dugout canoes between 3,000 and 4,000 years old were discovered under the waters of Lake Phelps in Pettigrew State Park. The naturally acidic water of this lake, lethal to wood-eating microbes, allowed the wooden canoes to survive through the eons largely intact. Several of these canoes are on display at the park.

The European Invasion

The men of Sir Walter Raleigh's 1585 expedition built a fort on Roanoke Island, but their relations with the Native Americans deteriorated. After a year, the settlers retreated to England. In 1587, White led a new expedition to Roanoke with 150 men, women, and children to establish a permanent English colony in America. White sailed back to England for supplies. When he returned three years later, the settlers had abandoned the fort, leaving behind only the letters CRO carved into a tree and the word CROATOAN, possibly a reference to the Indian town of Croatan on nearby Hatteras Island, carved into a post of the palisade. Although historians have long speculated about the fate of the Lost Colony, no one actually knows what happened to the settlers. No bones were ever found.

Only after the English founded Jamestown in 1607 in what is now Virginia did the first permanent settlers reach North Carolina. They trickled down from the north and settled along the coast.

The impact of European settlements on Native Americans was sudden and severe. Smallpox, influenza, typhus, and measles were epidemic in Europe and had conferred a limited immunity to the settlers, many of whom had been exposed to the diseases. Native Americans, however, had no immunity. To the Indians, every settler was a Typhoid Mary—except that the diseases they brought with them were not limited to typhus.

Thomas Harriot noticed it first. After visiting several Indian villages, he wrote,

"The people began to die very fast." He never suspected that he was the cause of those deaths. The settlers also brought rum with them, which turned out to be almost as harmful to the Indians as disease. John Lawson, the explorer who became surveyor general of North Carolina, wrote about the effects of disease and alcohol on the natives in his 1709 book, *A New Voyage to Carolina*: "The Small-Pox and Rum have made such a Destruction amongst them, that on good grounds, I do believe, there is not the sixth Savage living within two hundred Miles of all our Settlements, as there were fifty years ago." In half a century, Europeans had wiped out, by Lawson's estimate, 83 percent of the Native Americans along much of the Carolina coast without lifting a warlike finger.

Of course, there were wars, too. Though most of the coastal Indians were peaceful, the Tuscaroras presented a serious threat to the colonists. In 1711, they sought revenge on the settlers who were uprooting them. That year, John Lawson was captured by the Tuscaroras while taking a canoe trip up the Neuse River. After three trials for unspecified crimes, Lawson was put to death. Unfortunately, his death didn't satisfy the Tuscaroras. They attacked the settlements near New Bern, killing 130 settlers and starting a war that threatened the existence of the English foothold in North Carolina. Only when help arrived from South Carolina was the rebellion put down. The fierce fighting so decimated the Tuscaroras that they never again posed a threat to settlers. Only a few tribes survived the coming of Europeans. Their descendants—the Waccamaws, the Lumbees, and a few Tuscaroras—still live along the North Carolina coast.

The destruction of Native American cultures was not the only by-product of the European invasion; the newcomers also altered the environment. In addition to disease and rum, they brought steel axes and livestock. The axes were used to tap pines for their resin and to clear land for farms and pastures, resulting in the almost complete destruction of the longleaf pine ecosystem.

For nearly four centuries after the first white settlement, the North Carolina coast developed slowly. Cities and towns arose on the mainland, usually at river mouths that provided natural ports. Many of these port cities thrived during the 18th century but went into decline with the advent of railroads and the development of deepwater ports elsewhere along the coast. Little development occurred along the Outer Banks, which were suitable for neither agriculture nor ports. Resort towns arose in Nags Head and Wrightsville Beach, but as late as the 1950s, these attracted primarily local people.

In the last few decades, however, the coast has experienced enormous development, drawing both permanent residents and vacationers from all over the world.

Most of the oceanfront property not preserved as state or national parks or as land conservancies has been developed. The last area to fall was the stretch of the Outer Banks north of Kitty Hawk. In 1970, only a dirt road connected Kitty Hawk with the tiny villages of Duck and Corolla. The road was passable only at low tide, and the few homes on it were scattered along the sound side of the island. Today, million-dollar beachfront houses line the pavement between the two towns.

The State of the Coast

The number of people living on the coast continues to grow rapidly, outstripping the overall population growth of the rest of the state. In the last decade of the 20th century, the coastal counties in North Carolina grew at *twice* the rate of the state as a whole. The sleepy villages of the 1950s are gone, transformed into modern residential developments and tourist shops. Only the names, such as Whalebone and Duck, hint at their past. Some people still fish or farm along this coast, but the big money is in tourism and development.

All this development comes at a price. Water quality has declined in creeks and estuaries up and down the coast. At any one time, approximately 350,000 acres of salt and brackish water in North Carolina are closed to shell-fishing due to pollution. That amounts to about 20 percent of our coastal waters. Moreover, many of the wetlands that once slowed and purified storm-water runoff have been replaced by houses, parking lots, and highways, which sluice unwanted microbes directly into the water. Consequently, even more areas have to be temporarily closed to shell-fishing after heavy rains.

Upstream runoff also troubles the coast. Nutrients from urban, agricultural, and livestock sources can cause algae blooms that use up the oxygen in the water, creating "dead zones" in which marine creatures cannot survive. Some algae, such as *Pfiesteria piscicida*, which was discovered in the Neuse River in 1991, appear to produce toxins that kill fish. In the open ocean, toxic algae can cause a similar deadly phenomenon called a "red tide."

Most of these problems are not new (a red tide was described in the Bible), nor are they confined to the North Carolina coast. But Donald Anderson, a senior scientist at Woods Hole Oceanographic Institute in Massachusetts, says that the problem of toxic algae blooms "has expanded significantly in the last few decades." The North Carolina coast is no exception to this trend.

In addition to hastening the decline in water quality, the burgeoning population has displaced shorebird colonies and disrupted sea-turtle nesting along the coast. The congestion has also created traffic problems, as anyone who has tried to travel to or from the Outer Banks on a holiday weekend knows. So far, the traffic is only a minor inconvenience, but if a hurricane were to hit the coast on one of those weekends, inconvenience could turn into nightmare. In some places, only a few roads connect the mainland to the coast, and evacuation would be painfully slow. North Carolina has a disaster plan in place, but only time will tell how effective it is.

Hope for the Future

Fortunately, the North Carolina coast has many friends, as it has had them throughout the years. By 1900, plume hunters had slaughtered most water birds on the coast. Only six least tern nests and no laughing gull nests were found that year in North Carolina. A plume hunter summed up the prevailing attitude of the time: "The good Lord put us here and the Good Book says, 'man shall have dominion over all creatures.' They're ourn to use."

Into this charged atmosphere stepped T. Gilbert Pearson, a bird enthusiast who was asked to organize the first Audubon Society in North Carolina. He lobbied legislators, spoke at meetings, and wrote newspaper articles. On March 6, 1903, the North Carolina legislature passed the Audubon Bill, which offered some protection to nongame birds. Thanks to the new law, water birds started to recover. Pearson left the state in 1905 and later became president of the National Audubon Society, but the trend he started endures to this day. The National Audubon Society manages a coastal refuge in North Carolina that continues to protect shorebirds.

Many others have contributed to the conservation effort started by Pearson. Long before water pollution became the problem it is today, federal and state governments—urged on by the National Audubon Society, The Nature Conservancy, and other environmental organizations—were acquiring land for parks, national seashores, national forests, and wildlife preserves. Some large landholders donated their properties to the state. Consequently, a substantial amount of land along the coast is protected. Together, Cape Hatteras National Seashore, Cape Lookout National Seashore, and Pea Island National Wildlife Refuge preserve nearly 120 miles of seashore on the Outer Banks.

Without the vigilance of early conservationists, these protected areas and others like them would probably have been developed. Instead of mitigating pollution, as they do now, these areas would be contributing to it. The foresight of those men and women made the North Carolina coast what it is now—troubled in a few highly developed areas but nearly pristine in others.

Today, one major nonprofit organization acts as the watchdog of the North Carolina coast. The North Carolina Coastal Federation led the fight to get the state to establish natural buffers along coastal rivers, thus minimizing runoff and improving water quality in the rivers and estuaries. The federation has lobbied for better protection of wetlands, an important ingredient in the recipe for improving water quality.

The growing popularity of the North Carolina coast attests to the success of these organizations and others past and present. Red wolves and black bears roam the pocosins. Brown pelicans sail overhead, and white ibises nest by the thousands. People can fish, swim, and boat on millions of acres of water. And most of the nearly 350 miles of white-sand beaches are clean and uncrowded. Yes, there are problems on the coast, but there is much to be enjoyed. The following chapters suggest where to find the best that the North Carolina coast has to offer.

The Outer Banks

Wild horses still roam the Currituck Banks.

The Outer Banks—the very name conjures up a feeling of excitement, the anticipation of being at sea and on land at the same time. In fact, North Carolina's Outer Banks are unique among the world's landforms. Barrier islands extend along the eastern seaboard from Maine to Texas, but none are situated as far from the mainland as the Outer Banks, and few have a shape that differs from the coast they parallel. At some points, the Outer Banks lie 40 miles offshore, and nothing is visible to either side but open water. Less than half a mile wide in places, they look as if they could be washed over by a powerful storm, as indeed they have been on many occasions.

Tourists began visiting the Outer Banks as far back as 1830, when the first hotel was constructed at Nags Head and vacationers arrived via steamship from the mainland. But even into the latter half of the 20th century, vast reaches of the Banks were known only to local residents and a select group of sportsmen willing to travel great distances to stay in rustic surroundings and pursue the area's legendary fish and fowl. Now, all of that has changed. Millions of people from all over the world visit the Banks each year. Motels and beach houses line much of the waterfront, and the roads can be clogged with traffic.

Despite all of this development—and in some cases because of it—many of the best facets of the Outer Banks have been preserved. Abandoned hunting lodges and lifesaving stations have been restored and opened to the public. Natural areas have been set aside, and trail systems have been added. An all-but-forgotten cultural heritage is being showcased in museums and galleries.

If you're accessing the Outer Banks by road, be sure to stop at one of the two excellent visitor centers operated by the **Outer Banks Visitors Bureau** (800-446-6262; www.outerbanks.org). The Aycock Brown Welcome Center is located in Kitty Hawk at Milepost 1.5 on the south side of U.S. 158 just across the Wright Memorial Bridge. The Outer Banks Welcome Center is located on Roanoke Island on the south side of U.S. 64 Bypass. Both of these centers maintain listings of all hotels, motels, bed-and-breakfasts, and campgrounds from Duck to Hatteras Island. They also offer brochures on area attractions and guide services. Staff will assist you in making reservations.

Currituck Banks

Approaching the Outer Banks on U.S. 158, you will see a vast body of water stretching to the north of the Wright Memorial Bridge. This is Currituck Sound, and it runs all the way to the Virginia state line. The portion of the Outer Banks that parallels this sound to the east is known as Currituck Banks. A mere 6,000 feet across at its widest, Currituck Banks dwindles to as little as 1,000 feet in some places. This was the last portion of the Outer Banks to be developed, and it still contains a number of unique natural areas.

Through the mid-20th century, Currituck Banks was legendary for its duck hunting. Private hunt clubs, most of whose members were wealthy Northerners, offered a sporting life one can only imagine today. Author Lawrence S. Earley wrote in the July 1993 issue of *Wildlife in North Carolina* magazine, "The northerners who were founders and members of these clubs possessed wealth beyond the reckoning of local landowners, and so, like medieval baronies, each club accumulated thousands of acres of island, marsh, dune, and beach. Clubs enlisted the services of hunting guides, skiff makers, decoy makers, and marsh guards from the local citizenry. . . . In this patrician atmosphere, the sportsmen enjoyed prodigal shooting unrestricted by seasons or limits."

The hunt clubs thrived into the 1940s, and in some cases the 1950s and

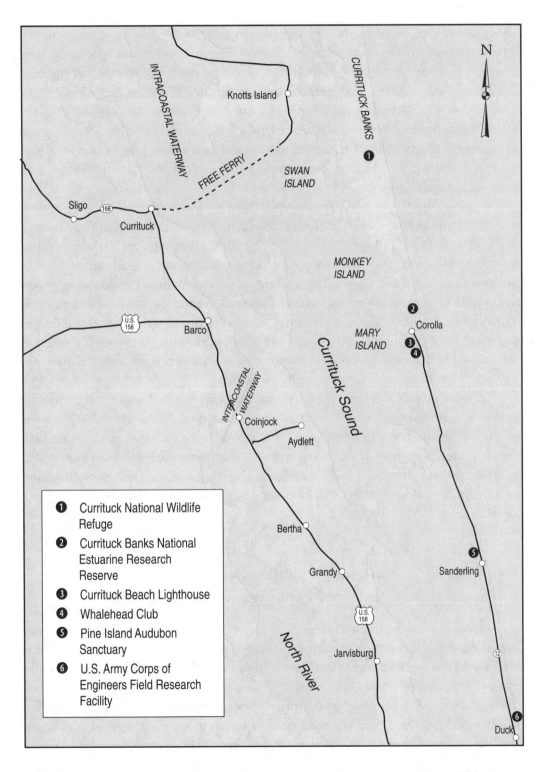

Map legend:

1. Currituck National Wildlife Refuge
2. Currituck Banks National Estuarine Research Reserve
3. Currituck Beach Lighthouse
4. Whalehead Club
5. Pine Island Audubon Sanctuary
6. U.S. Army Corps of Engineers Field Research Facility

1960s. After that, they seemed to lose their vigor. Real-estate developers began to take interest in the land for its vacation-home potential, and when the state acquired and paved the private road to Corolla in 1984, the floodgates opened. Land prices skyrocketed, and subdivisions sprang up left and right. From 1990 to 2000, more second homes were built in Currituck County than any other place in the country except the Hawaiian island of Kauai. Today, the oceanfront in towns like Corolla is lined with nine-bedroom mansions. Clubs entice members with golf courses and heated indoor pools, rather than oil-lamp-lit lodges and cold duck blinds.

During the 1980s, waterfowl populations plummeted in Currituck Sound. The North Carolina Wildlife Resources Commission counted approximately 300,000 waterfowl in the sound in 1976. By 1992, that number had dropped to around 12,000. Various reasons were cited for this decline, including an increase in development on the Outer Banks, construction of artificial impoundments on the mainland, and increased salinity in Currituck Sound due to a lack of rainfall. The increased salinity killed underwater plants the ducks fed on. It also killed or drove off largemouth bass (*Micropterus salmoides*), which had previously thrived in the sound. Where fishermen could once count on catching a hundred bass per day, mere handfuls were being caught in the early 1990s.

The sound has now returned to what is largely a freshwater state. Aquatic grasses are recovering, which is attracting more ducks and geese back to the sound. Largemouth bass populations remain low, but another popular game fish, the striped bass or rockfish (*Morone saxatilis*) is thriving, thanks to creel and size limits set by the state of North Carolina. These and other species of flora and fauna can be found in the expansive waters, wetlands, and wilds of Currituck Banks.

Currituck National Wildlife Refuge/ Currituck Banks National Estuarine Research Reserve_____

Just north of the town of Corolla, N.C. 12, the main road along the Outer Banks, dead-ends in a line of drifting sand and sea oats. The land north of here is a semiwild "outback," a patchwork of public and private holdings that includes some 500 scattered homes, along with rolling dunes and thickets. Half a dozen tracts of land have been set aside for wildlife preservation. Currituck National Wildlife Refuge owns five separate parcels totaling approximately 4,100 acres, and the North Carolina National Estuarine Research Reserve owns a 335-acre tract. These lands are open to the public. They encompass all the natural habitats of the Outer Banks, including beaches, dunes, tidal flats, shrub thickets, maritime forests, and freshwater and brackish marshes.

The most accessible tract is the North Carolina National Estuarine Research Reserve, located on the west side of N.C. 12 just before the road turns onto the beach. A sign identifies the reserve and a small parking area. A short (0.33-mile) handicapped-accessible boardwalk leads from there to the sound. This trail provides a superb view of the transitional vegetation zones common to the sound-side marshes of the Outer Banks and offers a shady respite from the noise and glare of the beach. Starting on high ground, the boardwalk passes through a maritime forest of twisted live oak and loblolly pine with an understory of high bush blueberry (*Vaccinium arboreum*). White-tailed deer, red foxes, and a variety of songbirds frequent these woods. As the elevation drops and the ground becomes wetter, red maple trees begin to dominate, and the high bush blueberry is replaced by marsh fern (*Thelypteris palustris*). Just beyond an information kiosk describing the ecology of the reserve, the forest gives way to a shrub thicket dominated by wax myrtle. Currituck Sound comes into view and the boardwalk ends at a platform surrounded by a classic array of tidal marsh plants—salt meadow cordgrass and black needlerush.

Scanning the water, you may see patches of duckweed (*Spirodela*) floating on the surface. Duckweed is considered an oligohaline (salt-intolerant) species, which indicates that the sound is primarily fresh water. However, the balance is always changing. Fresh water arrives via rivers and rain, while salt water is pushed into the sound via inlets. At present, the nearest inlet is well to the south of Currituck Sound; however, a major storm could open up a new inlet across the Banks, as has happened several times in the past.

Beyond the reserve, the paved road ends. To reach the scattered tracts of Currituck National Wildlife Refuge, you can either paddle a kayak along the sound side or drive up the beach. (Walking is difficult, as there are no public parking areas.) Driving on the beach is a longstanding tradition on the Outer Banks and can be fun for those who know how to do it properly and have a four-wheel-drive vehicle. However, the number of vehicles on the beach has exploded in recent years, and the scene in peak season can be nothing short of mayhem, with vehicles getting stuck and tempers flaring. A better option is to arrange for a guided all-terrain vehicle (ATV) or four-wheel-drive tour with one of several local outfitters, including **Corolla Outback Adventures** (252-453-4484), **Corolla Adventure Tours** (252-453-6899), and **Back Country Outfitters and Guides** (252-453-0877). These guide services specialize in showing customers key historical and natural sites and the most popular animal on Currituck Banks, the Spanish mustangs.

Written records dating back to the 1700s mention horses roaming wild on the northern reaches of the Outer Banks, and they continue to do so to this day. Legend has it that these horses are descendants of Spanish barbs, a small, sturdy breed originating on the Barbary Coast of northern Africa. Local residents theorize that the horses were intentionally left or shipwrecked by Spanish explorers in the early 1500s or by English explorers at a later date. Scientific research, including DNA testing, supports the claims of Spanish origins. Other people say the present herd is a mix of all manner of horses turned loose over the years. In either case, the horses are a popular tourist attraction.

Until the late 1990s, the mustangs were free to roam up and down the Banks and were considered very much a part of the local color. However, they became a hazard to the growing tourist traffic and are now confined to the 15,000 acres north of Corolla by a four-foot-high sound-to-sea fence. The horses are easily photographed but should not be approached at close range, as they can deliver a fatal blow with one swift kick.

Other sites commonly visited on the guided tours include a former lifesaving station (now a private residence) built in 1879; Luark's Hill, the second-largest sand dune on the Outer Banks (after Jockey's Ridge); and Wash Woods, a graveyard of old tree stumps visible in the surf at low tide. Wash Woods is all that remains of an 800-year-old forest that once grew on the sound side of the Banks, was buried by shifting sand, and has reappeared on the ocean side. Here is clear evidence that natural forces are pushing the Banks steadily westward.

The oceanfront sites above are most easily visited by ATV or four-wheel-drive tours, but to get away from the crowds and see wildlife up close, the best way to travel is by kayak. The same outfitters that provide motorized tours typically offer kayak trips that take visitors to their own private reserves, as well as to the sound-side wetlands of Currituck National Wildlife Refuge. Kayakers see all manner of wading birds, including blue and green herons and great and snowy egrets. Ospreys can be seen nesting in abandoned duck blinds. And various snakes ply the waters, including cottonmouths and Carolina water snakes (*Nerodia sipedon williamengelsi*), a subspecies of Northern water snakes.

The refuge lands are prime bird-watching territory. Hundreds of species ranging from giant tundra swans (*Olor columbianus*) to tiny marsh wrens (*Cistothorus palustris*) pass through this area at different times of year. John Fussell, author of *A Birder's Guide to North Carolina*, says that Currituck Banks in spring is the best place on the North Carolina coast to see a variety of warblers and other land birds. Consult his guide for the best times to see particular species.

ᴐ Corolla Village

Corolla (pronounced ka-RAH-la) is the northernmost incorporated town on the Outer Banks, lying at the end of N.C. 12. For nearly a century, Corolla was a sleepy village whose handful of residents worked for the now-defunct lifesaving station or as hunting and fishing guides. The lone road to Corolla from Sanderling was unpaved and went through private land, which prevented tourists from reaching the town. But when the road was made part of the state highway system in the mid-1980s, real-estate developers proceeded to buy up land and erect vacation houses and support services. Today, Corolla is a bustling summertime resort complete with shopping centers, condominiums, and luxury rental homes. Developments such as Corolla Light Village provide indoor and outdoor swimming pools and tennis courts, along with access to the sound and oceanfront beaches. The Currituck Club even features a Rees Jones-designed 18-hole golf course.

Amidst this modern development are some beautiful historic landmarks. **Corolla Historic Village**, located on the west side of N.C. 12, encompasses more than a dozen historic buildings within walking distance of each other. Most prominent among these is the **Currituck Beach Lighthouse**. Bordered by a white picket fence and shaded by old hardwoods and pines, the lighthouse compound is a world unto itself. Two residences built for the former lighthouse keepers and their families share the grounds, along with cisterns to collect rainwater and a two-hole privy. All have been beautifully restored by the nonprofit Outer Banks Conservationists, Inc. The smaller keeper's quarters serves as a lighthouse museum and gift shop.

Built in 1875, the Currituck Beach Lighthouse is one of seven constructed along the Outer Banks by the United States Bureau of Lighthouses. Each tower has its own unique exterior design, and each light flashes at a distinctive time interval in order to be identified by ships at sea. Currituck is distinguished by its unpainted red-brick exterior and a light (now automated) that flashes every 20 seconds. With 214 steps rising 158 feet, it is no easy climb, but the view from the top is well worth the effort. The narrowness of Currituck Banks is readily apparent from up there. So, too, is the density of development along the oceanfront. The need to preserve what open land remains along Currituck Banks is clearly evident. The Currituck Beach Lighthouse (252-453-4939) is open daily from late March until Thanksgiving, weather permitting; it is closed during thunderstorms. The hours are 10 A.M. to 5 P.M. An entrance fee is charged.

The Currituck Beach Lighthouse

Within short walking distance of the lighthouse stand a number of other historic buildings, including several cottages, shops, a one-room schoolhouse, and the **Corolla Chapel**. Built in 1885, the chapel offers weekly interdenominational services year-round. Locals are fond of saying, "You haven't been to Corolla until you've been to the chapel." Indeed, services here have become quite popular, so you should arrive early to avoid standing out on the lawn. Call the chapel at 252-452-4224 for service times.

Directly south of the lighthouse stands the magnificent **Whalehead Club**. Built in 1925 by railroad executive Edward Collings Knight, Jr., for his wife, Marie Louise, the Whalehead Club is the grandest of all the remaining hunt clubs on the Outer Banks. Marie Louise Knight was reportedly denied membership in the traditionally all-male hunt clubs of the area. So she and her husband sought their revenge by building the most opulent club on the Outer Banks, complete with 20 bedrooms, 15 baths, Tiffany light fixtures, and cork floors. Over the years, the club served as headquarters for the United States Coast Guard, Corolla Academy, and various developers, but it eventually fell into disrepair. Thanks to the efforts of Currituck County and a dedicated group of volunteers called the Whalehead Preservation Trust, the club has been renovated and opened to the public. For information on times and entrance fees, call 252-453-9040 or visit www.whaleheadclub.com.

The newly-restored Whalehead Club, a relic from the glory days of duck hunting on the Currituck Banks

Restaurants in Corolla

Corolla has a wide variety of restaurants, most of them located in either Monteray Plaza or Timbuck II Shopping Village on N.C. 12.

Grouper's Grille & Wine Bar
Timbuck II Shopping Village, N.C. 12, Corolla; 252-453-4077
Moderate to expensive

People come to Grouper's for the high-quality beef, free-range chicken, fresh seafood, and vegetarian entrées made with unusual spices and sauces. The environment is upscale, though casual dress is accepted. Reservations are recommended.

Horseshoe Café
Corolla Light Village Shops, N.C. 12, Corolla; 252-453-8463
Moderate

This café offers seafood, steaks, and chicken with a Southwestern flavor, as well as homemade desserts.

JK's
Timbuck II Shopping Village, N.C. 12, Corolla; 252-453-4336
Moderate

High-quality seafood, steaks, veal, lamb, ribs, and chicken cooked over a mesquite grill are the specialties here.

North Banks Restaurant and Raw Bar
Timbuck II Shopping Village, N.C. 12, Corolla; 252-453-3344
Moderate

This small, informal restaurant specializes in fresh seafood. Steamed oysters, clams, mussels, shrimp, and snow crab are available in season. Guinness is on tap.

Route 12 Steak & Seafood Co.
Timbuck II Shopping Village, N.C. 12, Corolla; 252-453-4644
Moderate

Local seafood, steaks, barbecued chicken, and ribs are served in a roadhouse atmosphere here. This restaurant is great for families.

Steamer's Shellfish To Go
Timbuck II Shopping Village, N.C. 12, Corolla; 252-453-3305
Inexpensive

> Steamer's is a great alternative to expensive restaurant service. It offers fresh fish and shellfish steamed to go or put in a steamer pot for you to cook at home. Steamer pots are cans layered with seafood, red bliss potatoes, yellow onions, and corn on the cob.

LODGINGS IN THE COROLLA AREA

Lodgings in Corolla are almost exclusively upscale single-family homes and villas. Rentals are by the week during the summer season. Multiday stays are possible in the off-season. Contact the Outer Banks Visitors Bureau (800-446-6262; www.outerbanks.org) for a list of real-estate companies serving the area.

Hampton Inn & Suites Outer Banks
333 Audubon Drive, Corolla; 252-453-6565; www.hamptoninn.com
Expensive

> Located on the ocean nine miles south of Corolla, this deluxe 123-room hotel has a resort-style atmosphere. It features a large courtyard leading to the beach, indoor and outdoor pools, an exercise room, and a game room. The hotel is across the street from the Pine Island Audubon Sanctuary.

The Inn at Corolla Light
1066 Ocean Trail, Corolla; 800-215-0772; www.corolla-inn.com
Expensive

> This 43-room inn is located in Corolla Light Resort Village. With an outdoor pool and deck overlooking the sound, it combines a romantic setting and excellent bird-watching. Kayaks and waverunners are available for rent.

Marsh rabbits are common throughout the Outer Banks.

Pine Island Audubon Sanctuary

Approximately eight miles south of Corolla, you will pass through an undeveloped area, part of which is owned by the National Audubon Society. The Pine Island Audubon Sanctuary encompasses 5,400 acres running from sea to sound, the majority lying west of N.C. 12. As of this writing, there were no parking facilities exclusively for the sanctuary. However, visitors may park at the Pine Island Racquet Club with the permission of the club manager.

From the back of the Pine Island Racquet Club, a trail runs 2.5 miles through a magnificent live oak forest paralleling N.C. 12. You'll have a good chance of seeing deer and foxes here in the morning or evening, and marsh rabbits almost any time of day. Midway along, a side trail leads to an observation platform overlooking the sound.

More than 200 species of birds have been identified in the sanctuary at different times of year. In spring, this is an excellent place to watch for diurnal migrants, as many shift their flight line from the sound to the beach at this point on the Outer Banks. Notable species you're likely to see in the summer include prairie warblers (*Dendroica discolor*), Caspian terns (*Sterna caspia*), and Forster's terns (*Sterna forsteri*). During fall migration, the sanctuary is an excellent place to see raptors, including the once-endangered peregrine falcon (*Falco peregrinus*).

United States Army Corps of Engineers Field Research Facility

Just north of Duck along N.C. 12, an unadorned metal gate leads to a long concrete pier and a cluster of buildings comprising the United States Army Corps of Engineers Field Research Facility. This is the nation's premier facility for studying coastal geology, most specifically the effects of ocean currents on beach erosion. The information gathered here has been vital to scientists' understanding of how the Outer Banks and other coastlines respond to the continual onslaught of longshore currents and waves and has led to wiser policies of coastal development.

Twelve scientists work year-round at the research facility, conducting experiments and monitoring a host of equipment. Among the latter is the CRAB (Coastal Research Amphibious Buggy), a 35-foot-tall tripod mounted on giant rubber wheels that hauls people and instruments into the surf zone.

Duck

South of Corolla, the Banks narrow to less than half a mile in width. In the 1790s, Caffey's Inlet divided the Banks near where the Sanderling Inn Resort stands today. This was but one of five inlets that have opened and closed on Currituck Banks in recorded history. At the town of Duck, the Banks widen and gain elevation. Thanks to its rolling, wooded terrain, Duck has more of the feel of Cape Cod than of the predominantly flat, treeless Outer Banks. The beautiful topography combined with first-rate—albeit expensive—accommodations, restaurants, and art galleries make Duck a prime tourist destination.

Named for the birds that once flocked to its shores in droves, Duck existed for the better part of the 20th century as a tiny fishing and seasonal duck-hunting community. Tourism took over in the 1980s and is now far and away the predominant source of employment. As the majority of buildings have gone up since 1990, the town has a new, upscale feel. Commercial establishments are confined by zoning to N.C. 12, reserving the oceanfront for homes, whose size and opulence boggle the imagination.

Watersports are Duck's main attraction, and various outfitters provide sales, rentals, and instruction. Kayaks, waverunners, sailboats, and more can be rented from such places as **Duck Village Outfitters** (252-261-7222), **Sunset Watersports** (252-261-7100), **North Duck Watersports** (252-261-4200), and **Nor'Banks Sailing Center** (252-261-2900).

Bicycling is also a premier attraction on this part of the Outer Banks. A paved bike path runs parallel to N.C. 12 from Sanderling south to Kitty Hawk. This 11-mile-long trail winds in and out of some of the prettiest wooded areas on the northern Banks. Many bed-and-breakfasts have bikes available for loan, and sports shops have them for rent.

RESTAURANTS IN THE DUCK AREA

Duck has more than a dozen restaurants offering great views and great food. As in Corolla, most of the restaurants are located on N.C. 12, the main road through town. Street numbers are not used to identify addresses.

Blue Point Bar & Grill
The Waterfront Shops, N.C. 12, Duck; 252-261-8090
Expensive

> This waterfront bistro with 1950s décor consistently wins great reviews for its contemporary Southern cuisine. Specialties include crab cakes served with black beans and rice, homemade soups, steaks, and salads. Reservations are recommended.

Duck Deli
N.C. 12, Duck; 252-261-3354
Inexpensive

> A local favorite, Duck Deli specializes in barbecued pork, beef, chicken, and ribs. Breakfasts are also popular here.

Elizabeth's Café & Winery
Scarborough Faire, N.C. 12, Duck; 252-261-6145
Expensive

> Called one of America's best restaurants by the International

Restaurant and Hospitality Rating Bureau, Elizabeth's specializes in country French and California cuisine, accompanied by vintage wines from the restaurant's walk-in wine cellar and homemade pastry desserts. Reservations are recommended.

Fishbones Sunset Grill and Raw Bar
N.C. 12, Duck; 252-261-3901
Moderate

Best known for its sunset views and award-winning soups, this restaurant serves a wide variety of entrées, including yellowfin tuna topped with crabmeat, Caribbean lobster sautéed in coconut milk and curry, filet mignon stuffed with Brie, and jerked pork medallions topped with mango-citrus chutney.

Herron's Deli and Restaurant
N.C. 12, Duck; 252-261-3224
Inexpensive

The casual-dining and takeout options here include Herron's signature she-crab soup, pastas, and a variety of surf-and-turf entrées. This restaurant is good for kids.

The Lifesaving Station Restaurant
1461 N.C. 12, Duck; 252-449-6654
Expensive

Located just north of Duck and part of the Sanderling Inn, this gourmet restaurant combines Outer Banks history with great food. Housed in the restored Caffey's Inlet Life Saving Station, it contains some of the station's original equipment, including oars from a lifeboat, a brass bell, and a brass cannon used to launch rescue ropes. Be sure to try the shrimp, corn, and crab chowder.

Roadside Bar and Grill
N.C. 12, Duck; 252-261-5729
Moderate

This casual eatery, located in a renovated 1932 cottage, has tables both inside and out. Live jazz and blues are featured in the summer. Specialties include shrimp and grits, lamb chops with blueberry compote, and "Roadside Stew," which contains Hatteras clams, mussels, langostinos, and scallops.

Swan Cove
N.C. 12, Duck; 252-255-0500
Moderate

An elegant restaurant with great views of the sound, Swan Cove serves such specialties as bacon-wrapped shrimp, beef tenderloin topped with asparagus and crabmeat, and bouillabaisse over saffron fettuccine.

Lodgings in the Duck Area

The lodgings in Duck consist largely of condominiums and single-family homes, rented by the week. Contact the Outer Banks Visitors Bureau (800-446-6262; www.outerbanks.org) for a list of real-estate companies.

Advice 5 Cents
111 Scarborough Lane, Duck; 800-238-4235 or 252-255-1050
Expensive

This attractive bed-and-breakfast in the heart of Duck offers views of both sea and sound. The four guest rooms and one suite all have private baths and decks. Guests enjoy the swimming pool, the tennis courts, and the private walkway to the beach.

Sanderling Inn Resort
1461 N.C. 12, Duck; 252-261-4111; www.thesanderling.com/
Expensive

A luxurious inn built in the style of the old Nags Head beach homes, the Sanderling Inn stands among the swaying sea oats and pines five miles north of Duck. This is a complete resort featuring private beaches, indoor and outdoor pools, tennis courts, jogging trails, a fitness center, and a full-service spa. The main lobby showcases woodcarvings and bronze sculptures of waterfowl by renowned artist Grainger McKoy. Weekend guests must stay Friday and Saturday nights during summer.

The Kitty Hawk / Kill Devil Hills / Nags Head Area

Travelers arriving on the Outer Banks via U.S. 158 or U.S. 64/264 may be shocked to find not the grass-covered dunes of picture postcard fame, but rather bumper-to-bumper traffic and miles of strip development. Welcome to the Kitty Hawk/Kill Devil Hills/Nags Head commercial district, locally known as French Fry Alley. Formerly small tourist towns separated by open country, Kitty Hawk, Kill Devil Hills, and Nags Head have grown into a single metropolitan area of some 12,000 year-round residents and more than 100,000 summertime visitors. The traffic congestion and strip development are indeed depressing, but you should be aware that there are some beautiful wooded areas and neighborhoods in these towns, not to mention the famous Atlantic beaches.

Kitty Hawk is the northernmost of the three communities. According to *The North Carolina Gazetteer*, the name probably derives from Chickehauk, an Indian name that appeared on early maps of the region. Kitty Hawk began as a fishing and farming community. In 1874, the federal government built one of the seven original Outer Banks lifesaving stations here. The following year, the government opened a weather station, which later provided the Wright brothers with the wind data that led them to choose the Outer Banks as the place for testing their flying machines. In the 1930s, a group of Elizabeth City businessmen built a bridge across Currituck Sound from Point Harbor to Kitty Hawk. This marked the first time that tourists could reach the barrier-island beaches without traveling by boat, and it sparked Kitty Hawk's development as a summertime tourist destination.

Just to the south of Kitty Hawk lies Kill Devil Hills. Legends abound concerning the derivation of this name. One attributes the name to wealthy planter William Byrd of Virginia, who reported in 1728 that the rum consumed in this region was "powerful enough to kill the devil." Like Kitty Hawk, Kill Devil Hills was sparsely populated prior to the completion of the bridges to the mainland. The community was thrust into the national spotlight because of the events of December 17, 1903, when the Wright brothers made their historic flights on the flat land below the dunes at Kill Devil Hills. But it was another half-century before the town was even incorporated.

Nags Head, the southernmost of these communities, also has numerous

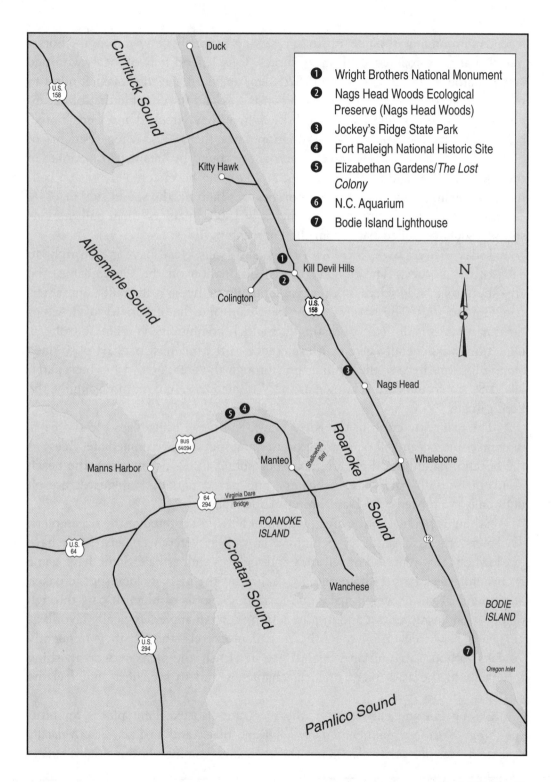

Duck

1 Wright Brothers National Monument
2 Nags Head Woods Ecological Preserve (Nags Head Woods)
3 Jockey's Ridge State Park
4 Fort Raleigh National Historic Site
5 Elizabethan Gardens/*The Lost Colony*
6 N.C. Aquarium
7 Bodie Island Lighthouse

Currituck Sound

U.S. 158

Albemarle Sound

Kitty Hawk

1 Kill Devil Hills
2
Colington
U.S. 158

N

3 Nags Head

5 **4**
BUS 64/294
6
Manteo
Shallowbag Bay
Roanoke
Whalebone

Manns Harbor

64 294 Virginia Dare Bridge

U.S. 64

ROANOKE ISLAND

Croatan Sound

Sound

12

Wanchese

BODIE ISLAND

U.S. 294

7
Oregon Inlet

Pamlico Sound

legends surrounding its name. Historians say it is probably derived from the horses (nags) that once roamed wild on its shores. One legend tells of locals who tied lanterns around horses' necks and drove them up and down the beach at night to trick ships at sea. The motion of the lanterns was said to resemble that of ocean-going vessels, which lured ships to shore, where they wrecked and were looted. Nags Head has been a tourist destination since the 1830s, when residents of Elizabeth City and Norfolk traveled across the sound by steamer to luxuriate in the ocean breezes and tumbling waves. A 200-room hotel complete with a ball-room, a bowling alley, and covered porches was built on the sound side in 1838. Seaside cottages began appearing in the early 1900s, many of them built on logs so they could be rolled back from the encroaching tides.

Today, Kitty Hawk, Kill Devil Hills, and Nags Head have grown right to each other's borders. The primary tourist destination on the Outer Banks, the area supports a wide selection of accommodations, shops, restaurants, and enter-tainment facilities. The flatness of the landscape and the uniformity of develop-ment can make it difficult to distinguish which community you are actually in. Directions are generally given with reference to the milepost markers positioned along U.S. 158 Bypass, the main artery through the area. N.C. 12, which paral-lels U.S. 158 to the east, is known as the Virginia Dare Trail or, more simply, the Beach Road.

The main attraction in the Kitty Hawk/Kill Devil Hills/Nags Head area is, of course, the ocean. All oceanfront houses and motels have immediate access to the beach. In addition, there are numerous public access points along the Beach Road, many with bathhouses, showers, and paved parking. Lifeguards are on duty daily from Memorial Day through Labor Day.

Fishing is popular in the area, with most activity centered at the ocean piers. The piers are great spots for beginning as well as veteran anglers. Most have tackle shops that rent and/or sell rods and reels, as well as bait. Some have game rooms and snack bars. Fish commonly caught off the piers include spot, croaker, and flounder—all of which make good eating. Schools of bluefish pass through on occasion, inspiring fast and furious action. Veteran anglers typically favor big-ger game fish—red drum, sheepshead, and mackerel—though they frequently go days without catching one. Even if you don't fish, the piers are worth visiting to chat with the assortment of local characters and to see, hear, and feel the power of the ocean.

During fall and early winter, the piers are also excellent places for bird-watching. Northern gannets (*Morus bassanus*), black and surf scoters (*Melanitta nigra* and *Melanitta perspicillata*), red-throated and common loons (*Gavia stellata* and *Gavia immer*), double-crested cormorants (*Phalacrocorax auritus*), and red-breasted mergansers (*Mergus serrator*) are commonly seen heading south over open water.

Kitty Hawk Fishing Pier (252-261-2772) is located at Milepost 1 on the Beach Road; **Avalon Fishing Pier** (252-441-7494) at Milepost 6; **Nags Head Fishing Pier** (252-441-5141) at Milepost 12; **Jennette's Pier** (252-441-6116) at Milepost 16.5; and the **Outer Banks Pier and Fishing Center** (252-441-5740) at Milepost 18.5. Most of these piers are open from late March to early December. Only Nags Head Fishing Pier is open year-round.

To see bottle-nosed dolphins (*Tursiops truncatus*), you should head out to sea with one of the local cruise boats operated by companies including **Nags Head Dolphin Watch** (252-449-8999) and **Outer Banks Cruises** (800-629-2789 or 252-480-9151). The captains of many of these charter boats know local dolphins by name and can get them to come right up to the boats.

Surfing, windsurfing, kayaking, waverunning, and sailing are other popular activities in this area. Shops all along U.S. 158 and N.C. 12 rent and sell the necessary equipment to get you on the water in virtually any craft you choose. Some, including **Carolina Outdoors** (252-441-4124), **Kitty Hawk Kayaks** (800-948-0759), **Bodie Island Adventures** (252-441-6822), and **Coastal Kayaks** (252-261-6262), offer guided tours to such destinations as Pea Island National Wildlife Refuge (see page 86), Alligator River National Wildlife Refuge (see page 169), Kitty Hawk Woods, and Cape Hatteras National Seashore (see page 92).

Bottle-nosed dolphin often frolic next to tour boats.

Thanks to the abundance of wrecks to explore off the coast, scuba diving is also a popular sport here. The water off the northern Banks is much colder and requires more equipment than the water at the more southerly sites, but the wrecks tend to be closer to shore. Two Nags Head dive shops offer equipment sales, rentals, and repairs, as well as tank refills, charters, and instruction. These are **Sea Scan Dive Centre** (252-480-3467), located at Milepost 10.5, and **Outer Banks Dive Center** (252-449-8349), located at Milepost 12.5 on N.C. 12 in Nags Head.

The Kitty Hawk/Kill Devil Hills/Nags Head area includes some major land-based tourist destinations. Some are world famous, others little known beyond the immediate locale.

∞ *Wright Brothers National Memorial*

On December 17, 1903, Kill Devil Hills took a step toward worldwide notoriety when Wilbur and Orville Wright flew the first powered airplane above this remote spot on the Outer Banks. The bicycle-shop owners from Dayton, Ohio, chose this location because of its open ground, its winds, and the presence of sloping dunes from which they could launch gliders in preparation for motorized flight.

Wright Brothers National Memorial features a 60-foot-tall granite monument atop Big Kill Devil Hill, the lone survivor of the small group of dunes from which the gliders were launched. Visitors should make the climb to the top of this hill not just to see the monument, but to take in the magnificent view of sea and sound. At the base of the hill, cement markers identify the distances of the four motorized flights of December 17. Next to these markers are replicas of the wooden sheds the Wright brothers used as hangars, as a storage area for tools, and as living space.

The visitor center houses a gift shop, a museum, and a lecture hall with a life-sized replica of the Wright Flyer; the original hangs from the ceiling of the National Air and Space Museum in Washington, D.C. Standing beside the Flyer, a ranger describes the basic principles of flight and tells how the Wright brothers translated them into aircraft design. This fascinating lecture, delivered every hour on the hour, is a high point of a visit to Wright Brothers National Memorial.

Nags Head Woods Ecological Preserve

Driving among the wall-to-wall buildings in Nags Head proper, you may find it hard to imagine that there is anything resembling a forest on this part of the Outer Banks. However, tucked away on the sound side of Nags Head is a remarkable copse of maritime forest known as Nags Head Woods. This is a must-see for visitors with an interest in nature and a great refuge from the glare and noise of the beach.

Nags Head Woods is a mixture of maritime deciduous forest, maritime swamp forest, and several other biological communities. This type of maritime decidu-ous forest, known to exist in only four other places in the world, has been de-clared a globally endangered forest system by The Nature Conservancy.

Nags Head Woods encompasses 1,400 acres, 1,100 of which have been purchased or are protected under easement by The Nature Conservancy, the town of Kill Devil Hills, and the town of Nags Head. The Nature Conservancy main-tains an administrative office and a visitor center in the preserve, from which trails fan out through different sections of the forest.

The diverse ecosystem of Nags Head Woods exists in large part because the forest is shielded from the salt-laden ocean breezes by a ridge of ancient sand dunes. The dunes also absorb and release a large amount of rainwater into the underlying aquifer and freshwater ponds and swamps. These factors, combined with the woods' location at a latitude where Northern and Southern species overlap, has led to an uncommon diversity of flora and fauna.

More than 300 plant species have been identified in the preserve, including several that are considered rare in North Carolina: woolly beach heather (*Hudsonia tomentosa*), water violet (*Hottonia inflata*), Southern twayblade (*Listeria australis*), and mosquito fern (*Azolla caroliniana*). The forest includes many hardwoods believed to be as much as 400 years old, as well as one live oak that is at least 500 years old.

Nags Head Woods has the most diverse population of reptiles and amphibians of any area on the Outer Banks. More than 20 species of snakes, eight species of turtles, and five species of lizards, including the legless eastern glass lizard (*Ophisaurus ventralis*), are found in the forest. Among the amphibians are five species of salamanders and 14 species of frogs and toads. The forest is an important nesting ground for more than 50 species of birds, including green herons, wood ducks (*Aix sponsa*), red-shouldered hawks (*Buteo lineatus*), clapper rails (*Rallus longirostris*), ruby-throated hummingbirds (*Archilochus colubris*), pileated woodpeckers, prothonotary warblers, and summer tanagers (*Piranga rubra*). Mam-

Brackish marsh with salt meadow cordgrass on the sound side of Nags Head Woods

mals found in the forest include river otters, gray foxes, white-tailed deer, raccoons, and opossums.

Six trails ranging from 0.25 mile to 2.5 miles in length will take you through a variety of the preserve's habitats. These trails can be combined to provide a four- to five-hour hiking experience. Trail guides are available at the visitor center.

The Nature Conservancy's Nags Head Woods office prides itself on its educational programs and field trips, including kayak trips on the sound side of the preserve. Regular guided trips are offered three days a week in June, July, and August. Children's nature camps are scheduled each summer. Special programs such as the Wild Women Weekend and EcoCamp for Grownups are offered throughout the year.

DIRECTIONS
From U.S. 158 in Kill Devil Hills, turn west near Milepost 9.5 on to Ocean Acres Drive. Follow the drive through a residential area approximately one mile to the Nags Head Woods Visitor Center.

ACTIVITIES
Hiking, kayaking, bird-watching, field trips, educational programs

FACILITIES
The Nature Conservancy maintains a small visitor center with a gift shop and restroom facilities.

DATES
The visitor center and trails are open from 10 A.M. to 3 P.M. Monday through Friday from October to April and from 10 A.M. to 3 P.M. Monday through Saturday from May to September.

FEES
There is a suggested fee to enter the preserve.

CLOSEST TOWN
Kill Devil Hills is one mile away.

FOR MORE INFORMATION
Nags Head Woods Ecological Preserve, 701 West Ocean Acres Drive, Kill Devil Hills, N.C. 27948 (252-441-2525)

Fishing on the Outer Banks

There are many ways to fish the Outer Banks, each requiring a different investment of time, money, and physical endurance. Offshore fishing for tuna, marlin, dolphin, mackerel, and wahoo is typically done by charter boat. Charters last all day and cost between $700 and $1,200 per group. Bottom fishing for sea bass, triggerfish, grouper, and snapper is done from a head boat. Head boats charge around $30 per person and provide all the necessary equipment. Half-day trips are the norm. Pier fishing is the cheapest and easiest way to fish. A basic spinning rod equipped with hook and sinker is all that is needed. Fish you are likely to catch from a pier include croaker, spot, and sea mullet. Surf casting from the beach is done during fall and winter, when red drum, bluefish, sea trout, and striped bass cruise the shoreline. Surf fishing requires a good pair of waders and a stout 10- to 13-foot rod.

Best Times and Locations for Catching Fish

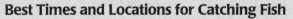

Months	Sound	Surf	Inshore	Offshore
January February March	Stripers	Stripers	Stripers	Bluefin Tuna
April May June	Flounder Speckled Trout Redfish	Flounder Speckled Trout Redfish Big Bluefish Stripers	Cobia Bluefish Stripers Spanish Mackerel Amberjack	Dolphin Billfish Wahoo Yellowfin Tuna
July August September	Flounder Speckled Trout Small Bluefish	Flounder Speckled Trout Small Bluefish Spanish Mackerel Pompano	Cobia Bluefish Spanish Mackerel Amberjack False Albacore	Dolphin Billfish Wahoo Yellowfin Tuna
October November December	Redfish Speckled Trout Stripers	Redfish Big Bluefish Speckled Trout Stripers False Albacore	False Albacore Stripers Big Bluefish King Mackerel	King Mackerel Bluefin Tuna

Hang gliders soar and children run at Jockey's Ridge State Park.

Jockey's Ridge State Park

If there is one natural attraction on the Outer Banks that is likely to impress all ages and interest groups, it is Jockey's Ridge. The state park here incorporates eight massive sand dunes spread over 420 acres on the sound side of U.S. 158. The tallest of the dunes, at 78 feet, is Jockey's Ridge. It was once as high as 110 feet but is shrinking, possibly due to the million or more visitors who climb it each year.

Geologists have attempted to date the dunes by conducting carbon-14 dating of vegetation buried in the layers of sand. Their best estimate is that these dunes began forming around 700 A.D., stabilized, and grew again in stages until the mid-1800s. Aerial photography shows that the dune system is changing, the peaks growing smaller and the area in between growing larger. Driven by predominantly onshore winds, the dunes are gradually migrating to the south-southwest.

Historians believe Jockey's Ridge got its name from early residents' practice of capturing wild horses and racing them on the flat surface at the base of the dune. Today, most visitors head straight to the top, where they can catch magnificent views of the sea and sound, run or roll down the sandy slopes, and watch or engage in the park's most famous sport, hang gliding.

Thanks to year-round winds, an open flying area, and a soft landing zone,

Jockey's Ridge is the premier hang-gliding spot on the East Coast. On any given day, you may see veteran fliers who can stay aloft indefinitely and raw beginners who crash and burn after 25-yard flights. Jockey's Ridge is the site of the nation's oldest continuous hang-gliding competition, held each May. Hang-glider rentals and lessons are available from **Kitty Hawk Kites** (800-334-4777 or 252-334-4777), which maintains an outpost at the state park.

For those who don't want to go airborne, kite flying is also popular at the park. Kitty Hawk Kites' Nags Head store (252-449-2210) claims to have the East Coast's largest collection of kites.

Another highlight of the park is the Tracks in the Sand nature trail, which runs in a 1.5-mile loop from the visitor center. Tracks in the Sand winds along the base of the dunes beside wooded areas that bear footprint evidence of a surprising variety of wildlife—white-tailed deer, gray foxes, opossums, raccoons, and assorted reptiles such as hognose snakes and six-lined racerunners (*Cnemidophorus sexlineatus*). Numbered signposts point out vegetation that survives in sandy soil, including the bayberry bush (*Myrica pensylvanica*) and the black cherry tree (*Prunus serotina*), both of whose berries are important food sources for birds.

The Jockey's Ridge State Park Visitor Center, located on Carolista Drive off

The Six-Lined Racerunner

The six-lined racerunner (Cnemidophorus sexlineatus) is the only member of the racerunner family found in North Carolina. This slender lizard is recognized by its six or seven light stripes separated by dark greenish brown bands. It is common in the coastal plain and on the Outer Banks, where it prefers open, sandy habitats. It can tolerate temperatures up to a hundred degrees and is thus most active during the daylight hours.

The racerunner is the fastest lizard in North Carolina, reaching burst speeds of approximately nine kilometers per hour. When threatened, it runs on its hind feet, tail erect, arms tucked to its sides. Herpetologists say it is virtually impossible to catch by hand.

Racerunners are best seen by sitting quietly in areas they are known to inhabit, such as the grassy fringes of Jockey's Ridge. The lizards emerge from their sandy burrows in the morning and move from one patch of vegetation to another, looking for insects to eat.

U.S. 158, features an excellent museum that describes the effects of wind on sand and highlights various plants and animals in the park. Natural-history programs, including stargazing and bird-watching, are conducted from the center throughout the summer. Handicapped visitors can take a 360-foot boardwalk from the visitor center to a platform overlooking Jockey's Ridge. A short nature trail to a sound-side overlook is located at the end of Soundside Road.

DIRECTIONS
The entrance to Jockey's Ridge State Park is located at Milepost 12 on U.S. 158 in Nags Head.

ACTIVITIES
Hiking, hang gliding, kite flying

FACILITIES
Visitor center with a museum, restrooms, and a snack bar

DATES
The park is open 8 A.M. to 6 P.M. from November to February; 8 A.M. to 7 P.M. during March and October; 8 A.M. to 8 P.M. during April, May, and September; and 8 A.M. to 9 P.M. from June through August.

FEES
Admission is free

CLOSEST TOWN
Nags Head

FOR MORE INFORMATION
Jockey's Ridge State Park, P.O. Box 592, Nags Head, N.C. 27959 (252-441-7132; www.jockeysridgestatepark.com)

RESTAURANTS IN THE
KITTY HAWK/KILL DEVIL HILLS/NAGS HEAD AREA

The more than 75 restaurants in the Kitty Hawk/Kill Devil Hills/Nags Head area serve every type of food. The main emphasis is on fresh seafood brought in daily from the neighboring sound and ocean. Here are a few of the most popular establishments.

Carolina Blue Restaurant
The Marketplace, U.S. 158, Southern Shores; 252-255-1543
*Moderate*_____

One of the best-kept secrets on the Outer Banks, Carolina Blue has a superb chef who commands a loyal following. Specialties include shrimp and grits with red-eye gravy; roasted duck with apples, prunes, and onions; and salmon with horseradish. Reservations are recommended.

Argyles Restaurant
Milepost 2.5, U.S. 158, Kitty Hawk; 252-261-7325
*Moderate*_____

This fine-dining establishment features candlelight dinners with live piano music in the background. The traditional French kitchen prepares a variety of fresh foods, including breads and desserts. More than 400 wines are in stock. Children are allowed. Reservations are recommended.

Art's Place
Milepost 2.5, N.C. 12, Kitty Hawk; 252-261-3233
*Inexpensive*_____

A favorite among locals for more than 20 years, this tiny eatery serves basic all-American fare at reasonable prices. It is open for breakfast, lunch, and dinner.

John's Drive-In
Milepost 5, N.C. 12, Kitty Hawk; 252-261-2916
*Inexpensive*_____

An Outer Banks institution, John's is the ideal place for a casual beach lunch. Seafood sandwiches and crinkle-cut fries are served in takeout bags. The milk shakes here are legendary. Seating is on picnic tables across from the ocean.

Ocean Boulevard
Milepost 2, N.C. 12, Kitty Hawk; 252-261-2546
*Expensive*_____

Occupying the former Virginia Dare Hardware Store, Ocean Boulevard is an upscale eatery in a beautifully decorated setting. Specialties include macadamia-encrusted mahi-mahi served with rum-baked beans and passion fruit butter sauce. Reservations are recommended.

Colington Café
1029 Colington Road, Kill Devil Hills; 252-480-1123
Moderate

Located in a restored Victorian home beneath shady live oaks, the Colington Café offers a respite from the brightness and crowds of the beach. Specialties include she-crab bisque and pasta and seafood with cream sauces. The café serves dinner only. Reservations are recommended.

Etheridge Seafood Restaurant
Milepost 9.5, U.S. 158, Kill Devil Hills; 252-441-2645
Inexpensive to moderate

Etheridge's features seafood right off the boats from the family-run seafood operation in Wanchese. Specialties include seafood egg rolls, crab cakes, and entrées such as blackened Cajun crawfish.

JK's
Milepost 9, U.S. 158, Kill Devil Hills; 252-441-9555
Moderate

Serving the same excellent fare as its Corolla restaurant, JK's specializes in mesquite-grilled ribs, chicken, steak, and seafood. It is also known for its excellent wine list.

Owens' Restaurant
Milepost 16.5, N.C. 12, Nags Head; 252-441-7309
Moderate to expensive

The Owens family has operated this Beach Road restaurant since 1946. Modeled after the old Nags Head Life Saving Station, the restaurant is decorated with memorabilia of the Outer Banks and the Owens family. Dinner features homemade soups and entrées such as bouillabaisse, crab cakes, and smoked scallops over penne pasta. The restaurant serves dinner only.

Penguin Isle Soundside Grille
Milepost 16, U.S. 158, Nags Head; 252-441-2637
Expensive

An elegant restaurant with a great view of Roanoke Sound, the Penguin Isle Soundside Grill serves a variety of local seafood, handmade pasta, steaks, chicken, and duck in creative pairings. *Wine Spectator* magazine named this restaurant's wine list "one of the best in the world." Reservations are recommended.

Sam & Omie's
Milepost 16.5, N.C. 12, Nags Head; 252-441-7366
Moderate

On any given summer morning, lines form outside this humble Beach Road shack to take part in an Outer Banks tradition—breakfast at Sam & Omie's. Named after a local father-and-son fishing team, Sam & Omie's has been serving solid, if unglamorous, meals since 1937. It offers three meals a day.

Tale of the Whale
Manteo-Nags Head Causeway, Nags Head; 252-441-7332
Moderate

Owned and operated by the same family for more than 20 years, this restaurant offers spectacular views of Roanoke Sound. It specializes in fresh local seafood.

LODGINGS IN THE
KITTY HAWK/KILL DEVIL HILLS/NAGS HEAD AREA

There are some 50 motels and bed-and-breakfasts in the Kitty Hawk/Kill Devil Hills/Nags Head area, along with a wide selection of rental houses and apartments.

Bald View Bed and Breakfast
3807 Elijah Baum Drive, Kitty Hawk; 252-255-2829
Expensive

This four-bedroom bed-and-breakfast offers views of the sound and paths leading through 11 acres of maritime forest. It is a quiet getaway well suited for adults.

3 Seasons Bed and Breakfast

Milepost 2, U.S. 158, Kitty Hawk; 800-847-3373 or 252-261-4791; www.threeseasonsouterbanks.com

Expensive

This five-bedroom inn sits on a hill with views of the ocean. Golfers will appreciate its proximity to the Seascape Golf Course. Tennis courts and a swimming pool are on the premises. Children under 18 are not allowed.

Cypress House Bed and Breakfast

500 North Virginia Dare Trail, Kill Devil Hills; 800-554-2764 or 252-441-6127; www.cypresshouseinn.com

Expensive

This six-bedroom bed-and-breakfast is located in a renovated hunting and fishing lodge featuring cypress-paneled walls and ceilings. It is only 500 yards from the beach. Children 14 and older are allowed.

Days Inn Oceanfront Wilbur & Orville Wright

Milepost 8.5, N.C. 12, Kill Devil Hills; 800-329-7466 or 252-441-7211; www.outer-banks.com/days/oceanfront

Moderate to expensive

This 1940s-era oceanfront motel has a nostalgic feel and modern amenities. The 52 rooms have been renovated with modern furniture, cable TV, etc. The amenities include an outdoor pool, a volleyball court, a barbecue pit for cookouts, and a boardwalk to the beach.

Quality Inn John Yancey

Milepost 10, N.C. 12, Kill Devil Hills; 800-367-5941 or 252-441-7141; www.johnyancey-nagshead.com

Expensive

This family-style hotel offers a heated outdoor pool and access to a wide, lifeguarded beach. Children 12 and under stay free.

Ramada Inn at Nags Head Beach
Milepost 9.5, N.C. 12, Kill Devil Hills; 800-635-1824 or 252-441-2151;
www.ramadainnnagshead.com.
*Expensive*_____

This five-story oceanfront motel with 172 rooms is ideal for tour groups and conferences. Among the amenities is an oceanfront indoor-outdoor swimming pool. Peppercorn's restaurant serves breakfast and dinner year-round and lunch on the deck during summer.

Tanya's Ocean House Motel
Milepost 9.5, N.C. 12, Kill Devil Hills; 252-441-2900;
www.oceanhousemotel.com
*Moderate*_____

Each of the 47 rooms at this seaside motel was individually decorated by original owner Tanya Young. Children under 18 stay free. Guests enjoy use of the outdoor pool.

Comfort Inn South
Milepost 17, N.C. 12, Nags Head; 800-334-3302 or 252-441-6315;
www.choicehotels.com
*Expensive*_____

The tallest building on the Outer Banks, this seven-story oceanfront hotel has 105 rooms, many with great ocean views. A good family hotel, it offers an oceanfront pool and deck and easy access to Jennette's Pier.

First Colony Inn
Milepost 16, U.S. 158, Nags Head; 800-368-9390 or 252-441-2343;
www.firstcolonyinn.com
*Expensive*_____

Built in 1932 with overhanging roofs and wide porches, the First Colony Inn is the last of the old Nags Head-style hotels on the Outer Banks. It is listed on the National Register of Historic Places. The rooms are decorated with antique English furniture. Among the amenities are a swimming pool and a sun deck in the back. Out front, a boardwalk leads to an oceanfront gazebo.

Nags Head Inn
Milepost 14, N.C. 12, Nags Head; 800-327-8881 or 252-441-0454;
www.nagsheadinn.com
Expensive

This five-story oceanfront hotel with a wide beach and a heated indoor-outdoor swimming pool is ideal for families.

Owens' Motel
Milepost 16, N.C. 12, Nags Head; 252-441-6361
Moderate

A family-owned and -operated motel, Owens' was one of the first on the beach. Located adjacent to the family's famous restaurant, it offers easy access to the ocean and to Jennette's Pier.

Roanoke Island

Lying just west of Nags Head between Croatan and Roanoke Sounds, Roanoke Island is technically not part of the Outer Banks, but it is close enough to merit inclusion in this chapter. With its forested terrain and small-town atmosphere, Roanoke Island offers a wonderful respite from the glare and bustle of the Outer Banks. Its streets are lined with flowering crape myrtle (*Lagerstroemia indica*), and a paved bike path parallels U.S. 64/264 the length of the island. There are no beaches here, so activity tends to center around the shops, art galleries, and historic sites celebrating the island's unique role in European settlement of the New World.

During the reign of Queen Elizabeth (1558-1603), the English sought to establish a permanent settlement on the American coastline, both as a means of laying claim to the mainland and as a base from which to launch raids on Spanish galleons transporting gold and other merchandise from Mexico. Through a series of voyages beginning in 1584 and financed by Sir Walter Raleigh, the English determined that Roanoke Island, then accessible by an inlet through the Outer Banks, would make a suitable site.

Following a failed settlement attempt in 1585 by colonists under Governor Ralph Lane, naturalist John White led a group of 110 men, women, and children to Roanoke Island in July 1587. Their intention was to sail on to Chesapeake Bay, but the ship's pilot said the summer was too advanced to go any farther. The colonists unloaded at Roanoke Island and set about repairing the cottages and military quarters left by Lane's party.

From the start, things did not go well. Vital supplies the colonists were supposed to pick up in Haiti were left behind. Relations with the local Indians were dicey, as Lane's soldiers had previously attacked and killed Wingina, chief of the Roanoke tribe. Some Indians were willing to help the settlers plant crops, fish, and hunt for food. Others, seeking revenge for the killing of their chief, fomented plans to drive the settlers off.

With the colonists in need of food, supplies, and manpower, White sailed back to England in the fall of 1587. He arrived to find his country immersed in a war with Spain and Queen Elizabeth unwilling to provide the ships or manpower needed for a return voyage. When White was finally able to return in 1590, he found the people gone and the settlement in shambles. No trace of them has ever been found, giving rise to the name and legend of the Lost Colony.

Today, this first attempt at a settlement in the New World is celebrated through a collection of museums, historical sites, gardens, and an outdoor drama, all located on Roanoke Island.

FOR MORE INFORMATION

Outer Banks Visitors Bureau, 1 Visitor Center Circle, Manteo, N.C. 27954 (800-446-6262 or 252-473-2138; www.outerbanks.org)

Fort Raleigh National Historic Site

Fort Raleigh National Historic Site encompasses 150 wooded acres on the northern tip of Roanoke Island. It contains the remnants of what was originally thought to be the fort built by Governor Lane in 1585. Archeologists now believe this fort is of a later design and that the settlements may well have been elsewhere on the island. That said, Fort Raleigh is still worth a visit to gain a sense of what life on Roanoke Island was like for the first English settlers.

The Lindsay Warren Visitor Center at Fort Raleigh contains artifacts extracted from what is believed to have been a metal shop set up by the 1585 expedition. It also offers displays demonstrating European and Indian life on the island and showcases copies of John White's watercolors of local Algonquian Indians and indigenous flora and fauna. The center houses an entire room extracted from a 16th-century Elizabethan manor and transported to the United

States by William Randolph Hearst in 1926. Park rangers use this room as a backdrop to explain to visitors what life in Elizabethan England was like and why a group of ordinary citizens was willing to leave everything behind to come to the New World. A complementary film re-creates the main events surrounding the attempted settlement of Roanoke Island.

DIRECTIONS
From the intersection of U.S. 158 and U.S. 64/264 at Whalebone Junction on the Outer Banks, drive west on U.S. 64/264 for approximately nine miles across the sound, through the town of Manteo, and to the north end of Roanoke Island. The entrance to Fort Raleigh is on the north (right-hand) side of the road. From the mainland, proceed east from the merger of U.S. 64 and U.S. 264 for approximately eight miles to the Fort Raleigh National Historic Site entrance.

ACTIVITIES
Touring historic site and museum

FACILITIES
Museum, bookstore

DATES
Fort Raleigh is open from 9 A.M. to 5 P.M. every day except Christmas.

FEES
None

CLOSEST TOWN
The historic site is approximately two miles from downtown Manteo.

FOR MORE INFORMATION
Fort Raleigh National Historic Site, Route 1, Box 675, Manteo, N.C. 27954 (252-473-5772; www.gov/fora)

⟡Elizabethan Gardens

Adjacent to Fort Raleigh National Historic Site are the Elizabethan Gardens, formal gardens created by The Garden Clubs of North Carolina, Inc., to commemorate the Lost Colony. The gardens contain more than a thousand varieties of trees, shrubs, and flowers. Circular paths lead through a shady canopy of native loblolly pines, live oaks, and water oaks to individual gardens featuring different collections of native and exotic plants. The gardens are colorful year-round as different plants and shrubs bloom and fade. Azaleas blossom in mid-April, camellias from November through March, hydrangeas in June and July, and chrysanthemums in the fall.

DIRECTIONS
From the intersection of U.S. 158 and U.S. 64/264 at Whalebone Junction on the Outer Banks, drive approximately nine miles west on U.S. 64/264 across the sound, through the town of Manteo, and to the north end of Roanoke Island. The entrance to the Elizabethan Gardens is on the north (right-hand) side of the road. From the mainland, proceed approximately eight miles east from the merger of U.S. 64 and U.S. 264 to the entrance.

ACTIVITIES
Touring gardens

FACILITIES
Restrooms, gift shop

DATES
The Elizabethan Gardens are open every day except Christmas and New Year's. The hours are 9 A.M. to 7 P.M. from March through November and 10 A.M. to 4 P.M. during December, January, and February.

FEES
A fee is charged.

CLOSEST TOWN
The gardens are approximately two miles from downtown Manteo.

FOR MORE INFORMATION
Elizabethan Gardens, 1411 U.S. 64/264, Manteo, N.C. 27954 (252-473-3234; www.elizabethangardens.org)

The Lost Colony *Play*

The most moving rendition of the plight of the English settlers—and a must-see for visitors to the Outer Banks—is the dramatic production of *The Lost Colony* at the Waterside Theater, located adjacent to Fort Raleigh National Historic Site. Written in 1937 by Pulitzer Prize-winning playwright Paul Green and produced by the Roanoke Island Historical Association, *The Lost Colony* is the longest-running outdoor drama in America. The play is performed nightly except Saturday from June 7 through August 27. It features elaborate staging and music and a cast of a hundred performers in full costume dress. The story takes the audience from Queen Elizabeth's sumptuous London court, where Sir Walter Raleigh pleads for money to finance his expedition, to the wilds of Roanoke Island, where Indians in loincloths dance around a fire. The colonists' joy at arriving in the New World and then their growing fear as food runs low and the Indians close in are convincingly played out against the backdrop of dark woods and nighttime sky above Roanoke Sound.

DIRECTIONS

From the intersection of U.S. 158 and U.S. 64/264 at Whalebone Junction on the Outer Banks, drive approximately nine miles west on US 64/264 across the sound, through the town of Manteo, and to the north end of Roanoke Island. The entrance to the theater is on the north (right-hand) side of the road. From the mainland, proceed approximately eight miles east from the merger of U.S. 64 and U.S. 264 to the entrance.

ACTIVITIES

Viewing outdoor drama

FACILITIES

Outdoor theater, restrooms, gift shop

DATES

The Lost Colony is performed at 8:30 every night except Saturday from June 7 through August 27.

FEES

An admission fee is charged. Advance reservations are highly recommended, as many shows sell out.

CLOSEST TOWN

The theater is approximately two miles from downtown Manteo.

FOR MORE INFORMATION

The Lost Colony, 1409 U.S. 64/264, Roanoke Island, N.C. 27954 (800-488-5012 or 252-473-3414; www.thelostcolony.org)

The North Carolina Aquarium on Roanoke Island

In the spring of 2000, the state of North Carolina completed renovations of its aquarium on Roanoke Island, one of three state-owned aquariums on the coast. Each of these aquariums has its own theme; at Roanoke Island, it's "The Waters of the Outer Banks." Visitors progress through each of the aquatic environments of the Banks, including freshwater wetlands, estuaries, the surf zone, and the deep ocean. Each room has educational displays and tanks bearing live reptiles, crustaceans, and fish common to that zone. Most impressive is the Coastal Freshwater Gallery, a giant atrium with cypress-shaded ponds housing alligators, turtles, and otters. Close Encounters features a hands-on exhibit where children can touch live crabs and rays under the supervision of aquarium staff. The Graveyard of the Atlantic, a 285,000-gallon aquarium, houses handsome specimens of cobias, groupers, crevalle jacks, and sharks swimming around a one-third scale model of the USS *Monitor*, the Civil War ironclad that lies off Cape Hatteras.

DIRECTIONS
From Manteo, drive two miles north on U.S. 64/264. Turn left on Airport Road and drive one mile past the airport to the aquarium.

FACILITIES
Museum, picnic area, restrooms

DATES
The aquarium is open 9 A.M. to 7 P.M. every day except Christmas and Thanksgiving.

FEES
An admission fee is charged.

CLOSEST TOWN
Manteo is three miles away.

FOR MORE INFORMATION
North Carolina Aquarium on Roanoke Island, P.O. Box 967, Manteo, N.C. 27954 (252-473-3494; www.ncaquariums.com)

Located at the northern end of Roanoke Island, the town of Manteo is a major tourist destination. The county seat of Dare County, Manteo contains a number of historic government buildings. It also has a wealth of restaurants, lodgings, gift shops, and galleries.

The **Manteo waterfront** is always buzzing with activity. Various guide services and outfitters stand ready to take you into the back channels of Shallowbag Bay and out into the sound to see the local flora and fauna. **Outer Banks Cruises** (252-473-1475) conducts two-hour dolphin watches and half-day fishing/ sightseeing trips on its 53-foot motorized launch. Daytime and sunset sailing cruises are offered aboard the *Downeast Rover* (252-473-4866), a reproduction of a 19th-century sailing schooner. **Outer Banks Outdoors** (252-473-2357) rents sailing vessels by the hour or day. Guided kayak trips are offered by **Carolina Outdoors** (252-473-2357). **Waterworks Boat Tours** (252-441-6822) in the nearby town of Wanchese offers offshore dolphin- and whale-watching tours and the area's only airboat tour of remote wetlands and islands.

Through the centuries, Manteo has been a center of wooden boat building. That activity is kept alive at the **North Carolina Maritime Museum on Roanoke Island** (252-475-1750), located in the George Washington Creef Boathouse on Fernando Street. The museum contains a number of vintage craft, including an 1883 shad boat, an excellent example of North Carolina's most unique indigenous watercraft. The boathouse is also a working museum. Staff members engage in the construction and restoration of historic boat designs on the premises. The museum is open from 10 A.M. to 6 P.M. Tuesday through Saturday.

ROANOKE ISLAND FESTIVAL PARK

For a full appreciation of the history of Roanoke Island from the first English settlement through the early 1900s, a visit to Roanoke Island Festival Park in Manteo is a must. The park, completed in 1998, features an exhibit hall, a theater, an art gallery, a museum store, an outdoor performance pavilion, the Outer Banks History Center, and a life-sized reproduction of the ship that carried the 1585 military expedition to Roanoke Island.

Lying at anchor across from the Manteo waterfront, the *Elizabeth II* is the centerpiece of Festival Park. This three-masted bark, built on-site in 1983, is authentic in almost every detail, down to the 7,000 wooden fastening pegs. You can access the boat from the park via a gangway, atop which the crew, dressed in period clothing, will greet you in English accents. The crew describes every aspect of life aboard the ship. You cannot help but come away impressed that 50-odd people could survive a month at sea in such a craft.

In the marshy woods near the ship, you can walk through the **Settlement Site**, an encampment designed to replicate the one that the first military expedition set up to defend the island. As with the *Elizabeth II*, the site features actors in full costume. They demonstrate such activities as carpentry, cooking, and weapon-making.

Also in Festival Park is the **Roanoke Island Adventure Museum**, which catalogs key events in the island's history through the early 1900s. Along with being the home of the first attempted English settlement in the New World, Roanoke Island was the site of a large colony of freed slaves during the Civil War. At that time, the Outer Banks were a key military target and a staging ground from which raids could be launched against ships along the coast. After Union forces invaded and occupied Roanoke Island in 1862, black slaves from the various Confederate forts along the Outer Banks and from the nearby mainland flocked to the Union camp, where they were allowed to live in freedom. In 1863, the federal government declared an official freedmen's colony on Roanoke Island and granted the former slaves ownership of the lands that locals had abandoned. As many as 3,500 African-Americans lived in the freedmen's colony, where they built their own houses, school, store, church, and hospital. But once the war was over, the government returned all lands to the original owners, and the colony was abandoned.

The Roanoke Island Adventure Museum also tells the story of Native Americans in the area. In its spacious auditorium, a 45-minute film, *The Legend of Two Path*, portrays the dilemma that local Indians must have faced when whites arrived on the island. The film focuses on the divergent attitudes of two Indians, Wanchese and Manteo, who were brought to England by the first military expedition, then returned to Roanoke Island to act as mediators between their people and the white settlers.

Those interested in conducting in-depth research on the Outer Banks will want to visit the **Outer Banks History Center** (252-473-2655), located within Festival Park. The center contains a reading room and a library housing more than 25,000 books; 4,500 official documents of the United States Coast Guard and the United States Life Saving Service; 30,000 photographs; a thousand periodicals; 700 maps; and hundreds of audio and video recordings. Open from 9 A.M. to 5 P.M.

Monday through Friday and from 10 A.M. to 3 P.M. on Saturday, this is an excellent place to spend a rainy day.

From the end of June to the middle of August, visitors can experience top-quality drama, modern dance, ballet, and music as part of Roanoke Island Festival Park's Summer Scenes arts festival. The festival features the work of faculty, students, and alumni of the North Carolina School of the Arts in the park's waterfront pavilion, film theater, and art gallery. The outdoor evening performances overlooking the sound are a treat for all ages.

DIRECTIONS
From the intersection of U.S. 158 and U.S. 64/264 at Whalebone Junction on the Outer Banks, take U.S. 64/264 west to Roanoke Island. In the town of Manteo, turn right on Sir Walter Raleigh Street and follow the signs to the Manteo waterfront and Roanoke Island Festival Park.

ACTIVITIES
Viewing outdoor performances, films, and historical reenactments

FACILITIES
Museum, theater, library, outdoor pavilion, art gallery

DATES
Roanoke Island Festival Park is open year-round. Hours vary according to the season.

FEES
There is an admission fee that covers all activities within the park.
For more information: Roanoke Island Festival Park, 1 Festival Park, Manteo, N.C. 27954 (252-475-1500 or 252-475-1506; www.roanokeisland.com)

The Elizabeth II, *a reproduction of the ship that carried the first colonists to Roanoke Island, lies at anchor in Shallowbag Bay.*

Restaurants on Roanoke Island

The majority of Roanoke Island's typically excellent restaurants are located in the town of Manteo. A few are in the fishing community of Wanchese, and one is in Pirate's Cove, a private development and marina on the eastern side of the island. Restaurants on U.S. 64/264 do not have street numbers posted.

Big Al's Soda Fountain and Grill
U.S. 64/264, Manteo; 252-473-5570
Inexpensive

Taking "The past is back, have some fun" as its motto, Big Al's features traditional American food in a 1950s atmosphere. Fresh fried seafood shares the menu with burgers and fries. Make sure you leave room for an ice-cream sundae.

Clara's Seafood Grill and Steam Bar
The Waterfront Shops, Queen Elizabeth Street, Manteo; 252-473-1727
Expensive

A fine restaurant with an excellent view of Shallowbag Bay and the *Elizabeth II*, Clara's prides itself on seafood specialties such as she-crab soup, tuna kabobs, and a mixed grill of shrimp, crab cakes, and tuna.

Darrell's Restaurant
N.C. 64/264, Manteo; 252-473-5366
Moderate

A family-style restaurant specializing in fried and broiled seafood served with French fries, coleslaw, and hush puppies, Darrell's also serves steamed and raw clams, oysters, and scallops.

1587
The Tranquil House Inn, 405 Queen Elizabeth Street, Manteo; 252-473-1587.
Expensive

Named for the year that the Lost Colony was established on Roanoke Island, 1587 is an upscale restaurant located in The Tranquil House Inn overlooking Shallowbag Bay. Gourmet seafood, beef, and duck dishes are prepared with herbs grown in the inn's own garden. This restaurant has received rave reviews from travel writers and food critics around the country. Reservations are recommended.

Full Moon Café
The Waterfront Shops, Queen Elizabeth Street, Manteo; 252-473-6666
Moderate

Located next door to Clara's and sharing a waterfront view, Full Moon features nouveau Southern cuisine at reasonable prices. Its specialties include shrimp and crab quesadillas and Low Country shrimp and grits. The Half Moon Junction is the restaurant's ice-cream and coffee bar.

The Green Dolphin Restaurant and Pub
201 Sir Walter Raleigh Street, Manteo; 252-473-5911
Inexpensive

A Manteo tradition, the Green Dolphin is a down-home eatery with a strong local following. The walls are lined with nautical memorabilia, and the food is good and cheap. The bar is hopping on Friday nights, when live entertainment—usually acoustic guitar music—is offered.

The Weeping Radish Brewery & Bavarian Restaurant
U.S. 64/264, Manteo; 252-473-1157
Moderate

Owner Uli Bennewitz brings the cuisine of his native Germany to Roanoke Island in this Bavarian-style restaurant. Entrées include veal, sauerbraten, and a variety of sausages. Three microbrews and several seasonal beers are brewed and served here. Thanks to its outdoor playground and neighboring toy store, candy store, and Gingerbread House and Bakery, this is a great place to take the kids.

Fisherman's Wharf
N.C. 345, Wanchese; 252-473-5205
Moderate

Located in the fishing community of Wanchese, Fisherman's Wharf gives diners a view of trawlers bringing their catch right to the docks. Seafood doesn't come any fresher than this.

Queen Anne's Revenge
1064 Old Wharf Road, Wanchese; 252-473-5466
Moderate

Named after one of Blackbeard's pirate ships, Queen Anne's Revenge lies off the beaten path in a wooded neighborhood of Wanchese. Specialties include bouillabaisse, filet mignon, and fried shrimp, plus homemade pasta and desserts.

Hurricane Mo's Restaurant and Raw Bar
Pirate's Cove, 1 Sailfish Drive, Manteo-Nags Head Causeway, Manteo; 252-473-2266
Moderate

With game fish mounted on the wall and expansive views of Roanoke Sound and the local charter fleet, Hurricane Mo's captures the excitement of game fishing for which the Outer Banks are known. Mo's offers such specialties as Cajun-fried mahi-mahi étouffée and a mixed grill of filet mignon, tuna, and marinated shrimp kabob.

Lodgings on Roanoke Island

Roanoke Island is home to a handful of motels, but the true character of this historic island is found in the bed-and-breakfasts located mostly in the town of Manteo. Most motels on U.S. 64/264 do not have street addresses.

Dare Haven Motel
U.S. 64/264, Manteo; 252-473-2322; www.manteomotels.com
Inexpensive

Another reasonably priced option for families and fishermen, this one-level motel features 26 rooms with cable TV. A craft shop on the premises offers work by local artisans.

Duke of Dare Motor Lodge
U.S. 64/264, Manteo; 252-473-2175
Inexpensive

This 57-room motel is ideal for families and fishermen on a budget. All rooms have queen-sized beds and cable TV. Guests enjoy the outdoor swimming pool.

The Elizabethan Inn

814 U.S. 64/264, Manteo; 800-346-2466 or 252-473-2101; www.elizabethaninn.com

Expensive

With a distinctive Tudor architecture reflecting the area's historic ties to England, The Elizabethan Inn stands out in many ways. The inn includes 80 rooms, efficiencies, and apartments in three separate buildings. It has conference facilities, a staffed fitness center, heated indoor and outdoor pools, racquetball courts, a gift shop, and a restaurant. Since there's so much to do inside, this is a good place to be when the weather turns bad.

Island Motel & Guest House

U.S. 64/264, Manteo; 252-473-2434

Moderate

This 14-room motel in the heart of Manteo offers daily, weekly, and monthly rates. Bicycles, fishing poles, and other sports equipment are available for guests. Dogs are allowed for a nominal fee.

Roanoke Island Inn

305 Fernando Street, Manteo; 877-473-5511 or 252-473-5511; www.roanokeislandinn.com

Expensive

Built for owner John Wilson's great-great-grandmother in the 1860s, this historic inn was renovated in 1982 and enlarged in 1990. The interior is decorated with turn-of-the-20th-century antiques and Oriental rugs. Each of the eight rooms is individually decorated. The inn is within easy walking distance of the Manteo waterfront.

Scarborough House Inn

323 Fernando Street, Manteo; 252-473-3849; www.bbonline.com/nc/scarborough

Moderate

Owned and operated by Phil and Sally Scarborough, this modern bed-and-breakfast has five bedrooms, each with a kitchenette. The inn is decorated with antiques inside and a beautiful flower and water garden outside. Bicycles are available for use by guests.

Scarborough Inn
524 U.S. 64/264, Manteo; 252-473-3979; www.scarborough-inn.com
Moderate

Not to be confused with the Scarborough House Inn, the older Scarborough Inn offers six rooms in two buildings. Each room has its own exterior entrance and is tastefully furnished with antiques and Scarborough family heirlooms. Bicycles are available for guests.

The Tranquil House Inn
405 Queen Elizabeth Street, Manteo; 800-458-7069 or 252-473-1404; www.tranquilinn.com
Expensive

This 25-room inn on Manteo's waterfront was built in the style of old Outer Banks hotels, noted for their pitched roofs, cedar shake siding, and expansive porches. The inn fronts the shops of Queen Elizabeth Street on one side and Shallowbag Bay on the other. All rooms are individually decorated. Bicycles are available free to guests.

The White Doe Inn
319 Sir Walter Raleigh Street, Manteo; 800-473-6091 or 252-473-9851; www.whitedoeinn.com
Expensive

This much-photographed Queen Anne-style Victorian house was converted to a bed-and-breakfast in 1994 by retired National Park Service rangers Bob and Bebe Woody. The inn has seven guest rooms, one guest suite, a wraparound porch, and beautifully land-scaped gardens.

Bodie Island

Until the early 1800s, an inlet separated the land south of Whalebone Junction from the northern Banks. That inlet has since closed. However, the land south of Whalebone Junction and north of Oregon Inlet is still referred to as Bodie (pronounced BAH-di) Island.

Bodie Island is the northern terminus of Cape Hatteras National Seashore (see page 92), which extends 75 miles from Whalebone Junction to Ocracoke Inlet. Upon entering the seashore on N.C. 12, you'll note how the intense development of Nags Head disappears, replaced by green thickets, sun-dappled ponds, and miles of untrammeled beaches.

Approximately 5.3 miles south of Whalebone Junction, a sign points the way to the parking area and bathhouse at **Coquina Beach**, part of the national seashore. Coquina Beach is named for the tiny butterfly-shaped coquina clams that burrow into the sand. This is an excellent place to swim and surf away from the crowds of Nags Head. The bathhouse provides changing rooms, showers, and restrooms.

From the parking lot, a boardwalk leads to the beach and the remains of an old schooner, the ***Laura A. Barnes***. Since the 1500s, when European explorers first arrived on these shores, more than a thousand ships have wrecked along North Carolina's Outer Banks. What is left of these wrecks lies submerged off the coast or is buried beneath the shifting sands. The massive timbers of the *Laura A. Barnes*, protruding from a dune on Coquina Beach, are as much as you will see of a shipwreck onshore. In her prime, the *Laura A. Barnes* was a 120-foot-long, four-masted schooner, one of the last coastal schooners built in the United States. Sailing south from New York in 1921, the ship encountered a nor'easter and was driven aground on the beach just north of here; all members of the crew survived. The ship was moved to its present site by the National Park Service in 1973 for safekeeping, although the elements continue to take their toll.

Tall dunes and untrammeled beaches parallel N.C. 12 for much of the length of Bodie Island. At the south end of the island, just before the Herbert C. Bonner Bridge, a road cuts west to the **Oregon Inlet Fishing Center** (800-272-5199 or 252-441-6301). This National Park Service-owned marina is home to an impressive array of private charter fishing boats. It is an excellent place to sign on for a day-long fishing trip to the Gulf Stream. Most boats carry parties of six anglers and supply all the necessary bait and tackle. Even if you don't plan to fish, this is an exciting place to come at the end of the day, when the boats return and unload their catches. The world-record blue marlin, a 1,142-pound monster, was caught out of this inlet in 1974. It is displayed in a glass case near the marina.

Just behind the fishing center stands the **Oregon Inlet Coast Guard Station** (252-441-1685). This 10,000-square-foot building houses a state-of-the-art maintenance shop and communications center. You can tour the facility and see one or more of the three Coast Guard boats docked here.

On the opposite (east) side of N.C. 12 from the fishing center, an entry road leads to the National Park Service's **Oregon Inlet Campground**

(252-473-2111). This campground has 120 sites set among the dunes. Water, cold showers, flush toilets, picnic tables, and charcoal grills are available. The campground is open from Easter weekend through September on a first-come, first-served basis. A fee is charged.

At the south end of Bodie Island, sand flats fan outward toward a narrow strip of swirling water—**Oregon Inlet**, the only break through the Outer Banks on the 140-mile stretch from Cape Henry, Virginia, to Cape Hatteras. As such, it is a vital link to the ocean for commercial and recreational fishermen in the northern coastal region. However, its constantly shifting channel and sandy shoals make for treacherous passage during rough weather. Without constant dredging by the United States Army Corps of Engineers, it would quickly become impassable.

The Herbert C. Bonner Bridge across the inlet offers an excellent vantage point from which to view evidence of the powerful forces of nature. When the bridge was built in 1964, the Bodie Island terminus stood at the very edge of the inlet. Now, the bridge runs for nearly 0.75 mile before reaching the inlet, which serves as evidence that Bodie Island is extending southward. This is the result of longshore currents, which in this part of the Outer Banks run parallel to the shore from north to south, carrying beach sand with them. By contrast, the northern tip of Pea Island, located just south of the inlet, is eroding as longshore currents draw sand southward. Only the construction of a sand-retaining structure has kept the northern end of Pea Island from eroding further and collapsing the bridge. Whether this structure will become a permanent part of the landscape has not yet been determined.

On both the sound and ocean sides of the inlet, broad sand deltas are visible at low tide. These deltas are the result of a different set of forces. During incoming (flood) and outgoing (ebb) tides, rapid currents course through the inlet, eroding sand from the sides and bottom of the channel. As they reach the sound and ocean, respectively, the currents slow down, and the sand is deposited. Left to nature, the resultant shoals would eventually close the inlet altogether.

Since the 1970s, the United States Army Corps of Engineers has been fighting to keep Oregon Inlet open by dredging sand from its mouth and depositing it in the ocean. It is a costly and only marginally effective tactic, since new shoals constantly appear and make passage through the inlet a hazard. Backed by commercial fishing interests and state and local politicians, the corps has proposed to supplant its constant dredging with a pair of stone-and-steel jetties that would stretch nearly a mile into the ocean and block the buildup of sand. Critics say that in the process of blocking the longshore movement of sand, the jetties would

Constant dredging is needed to keep Oregon Inlet from filling with sand.
PHOTOGRAPH © JODY DUGGINS

also deprive the Banks to the south of sand, which would cause erosion at Pea Island and portions of Cape Hatteras National Seashore. Scientists also say the jetties would prohibit fish larvae that drift along the shore from being able to pass through the inlet into the estuarine nursery in the sound. To date, the latter arguments have held sway in Washington, preventing the jetties from being funded.

> **FOR MORE INFORMATION**
> Bodie Island Visitor Center (252-441-5711); Cape Hatteras National Seashore, 1401 National Park Road, Manteo, N.C. 27954

Bodie Island Lighthouse and Visitor Center

Across N.C. 12 from Coquina Beach on the sound side of the island is the Bodie Island Lighthouse. Set amidst a wide, grassy prairie, the 150-foot-tall, black-and-white-ringed lighthouse is among the most beautiful in North Carolina. When constructed in 1872, the lighthouse stood right next to Oregon Inlet. Now, the inlet is nearly two miles away, evidence that the island is migrating south. Although the lighthouse looks to be in good shape, the tower has fallen into disrepair. The iron in the spiral staircase, the canopy, the lantern room, and the gallery deck is corroding, window frames are rotting, and blocks and tiles at the

The Bodie Island Lighthouse and Visitor Center

base are crumbling. Visitors are allowed into the base during the summer but cannot climb the tower. Park officials hope to reopen the tower in the future if and when sufficient funds (estimated at $1.7 million) are appropriated for its repair.

Fortunately, the keeper's quarters next to the lighthouse have been renovated and now serve as the Bodie Island Visitor Center for Cape Hatteras National Seashore. Displays in the visitor center detail the lighthouse's construction and explain how a Fresnel lens bends light from a single thousand-watt bulb and redirects it on a horizontal plane across miles of ocean. Other displays explain the role of lighthouses in America, describe the life of lighthouse keepers, and show examples of the many different kinds of lighthouses built in this country.

Directly behind the lighthouse is a large pond. This is one of the best spots in the state to see long-billed dowitchers (*Limnodromus scolopaceus*). It is also a good place to see black-necked stilts (*Himantopus mexicanus*), American avocets (*Recurvirostra americana*), and, in September and October, Hudsonian godwits (*Limosa haemastica*). Two observation decks overlook the pond.

DIRECTIONS

From the intersection of N.C. 12 and U.S. 64/264 at Whalebone Junction, follow N.C. 12 south for six miles. The driveway for the lighthouse is on the west side of the road.

ACTIVITIES

Picnicking, summer programs

∽Bodie Island Dike Trail

At the south end of the parking area for the Bodie Island Lighthouse, you can access the Bodie Island Dike Trail. This six-mile loop trail runs along an earthen dike that offers views of freshwater marshes to the east and saltwater marshes to the west. You should first stop at the visitor center and pick up a trail guide, which describes the history of the area and the flora and fauna you are likely to see at the numbered stations.

During the early 1900s, the natural marshes beside the lighthouse were dammed up by the Bodie Island Gun Club to produce a freshwater pond ideal for duck hunting. Earthen dikes were built to contain the water within the marshes, and floodgates were installed to control water level.

Along the trail, you will pass a stand of loblolly pines. Some of the pines on Bodie Island are native, but most were planted by either the gun club or the National Park Service to protect the land and the ponds from storm overwash. Between 1938 and 1961, the National Park Service planted more than 75,000 pine seedlings as part of an erosion-control project. The pine grove is a good place to spot migrating land birds after autumn cold fronts, as it is the first tree-covered area they come to as they fly south along the Outer Banks.

After approximately three miles, the trail reaches a wooden dam across Long Creek. Constructed by the gun club, this dam effectively blocked the tidal flow into and out of the adjacent marshes. In most coastal creeks, tides move salty water to and from upstream freshwater marshes. The constant mixing and recycling of nutrients help make wetlands highly productive and diverse habitats. By installing a dam, the gun club blocked this mixture and created a sharp ecological divide. Note how the marsh on the north side supports freshwater plants such as cattails, while only salt-tolerant needlerush grows on the south side.

From this point, the trail continues north along a power line and beside the paved lighthouse road back to the lighthouse parking area. Many hikers choose to retrace their steps from here back to the start of the trail.

Note: The trail can be hot and muggy during summer, and insect repellent is a must.

Hatteras Island

Lying between Bodie Island to the north and Ocracoke Island to the south is Hatteras Island, which is 50 miles long but rarely more than 0.5 mile wide. The terrain is flat and treeless except at the "elbow" at Cape Hatteras, where the island widens enough to support a substantial maritime forest.

Since two-thirds of its shoreline is oriented east-west and one-third is oriented north-south, Hatteras captures wind and waves from every direction. This makes the island extremely popular with surfers and windsurfers, who come here from around the world to practice their sports. It also means the island bears the brunt of the storms that regularly batter the Outer Banks. Hatteras Island is subject to frequent overwashes during nor'easters and hurricanes. N.C. 12, the only road on and off the island, is often flooded and has had to be relocated several times after storms buckled the pavement. Artificially constructed dunes, visible in numerous locations along the ocean side of the highway, are the only thing preventing the island from being flooded more regularly—and perhaps from being split by a new inlet.

The majority of Hatteras Island is located within either Cape Hatteras National Seashore or Pea Island National Wildlife Refuge and is thus undeveloped. However, there are seven small towns on the island, each offering a variety of services and accommodations.

FOR MORE INFORMATION
Outer Banks Chamber of Commerce, P.O. Box 1757, Kill Devil Hills, N.C. 27948 (252-441-8144; outerbankschamber.com)

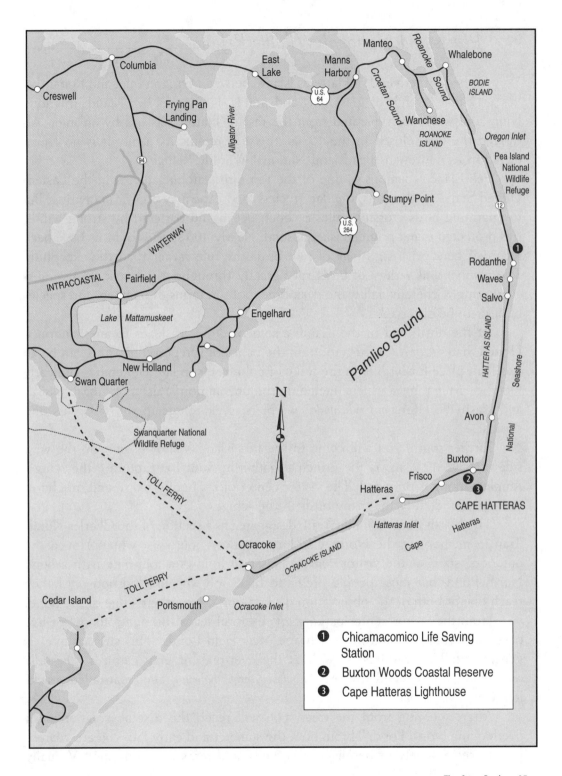

Creswell

Columbia

East Lake

Manns Harbor

Manteo

Roanoke Sound

Whalebone

BODIE ISLAND

Frying Pan Landing

Alligator River

U.S. 64

Croatan Sound

Wanchese

ROANOKE ISLAND

Oregon Inlet

Pea Island National Wildlife Refuge

94

Stumpy Point

U.S. 264

12

❶

Rodanthe

Waves

Salvo

INTRACOASTAL

WATERWAY

Fairfield

Lake Mattamuskeet

Engelhard

Pamlico Sound

HATTERAS ISLAND

Seashore

New Holland

Swan Quarter

N

Swanquarter National Wildlife Refuge

Avon

National

Buxton

Frisco

❷

❸

TOLL FERRY

Hatteras

CAPE HATTERAS

Hatteras Inlet

Hatteras

Ocracoke

OCRACOKE ISLAND

Cape

Cedar Island

TOLL FERRY

Portsmouth

Ocracoke Inlet

❶	Chicamacomico Life Saving Station
❷	Buxton Woods Coastal Reserve
❸	Cape Hatteras Lighthouse

Pea Island National Wildlife Refuge

At the northern end of Hatteras Island, between Oregon Inlet and Rodanthe, lies a 12-mile stretch of grass flats and ponds. Known as Pea Island, this low-lying land was once separated from the rest of Hatteras Island by an inlet. Although the inlet closed in the 1930s, the area retains its name. It is now protected in its entirety as Pea Island National Wildlife Refuge.

Pea Island is famous as one of the top bird-watching places in the Eastern United States. To humans, the flat, treeless landscape may appear uninviting. But to migrating birds crossing miles of open ocean and battered by strong winds, this protected island of green is a godsend. Nearly 400 species of birds have been recorded here, with sightings of rare birds the rule rather than the exception. The number and variety of birds vary greatly throughout the year, so timing is everything. Generally, fall is the peak time, both in terms of numbers and species of birds to be observed.

At the north end of the island, a spur off N.C. 12 leads to an abandoned United States Coast Guard station on the banks of Oregon Inlet. This can be an excellent place for birding in the wake of cold fronts in late September and early October. Migrating warblers, including the uncommon Wilson's (*Wilsonia pusilla*) and Nashville (*Vermivora ruficapilla*) warblers, seek refuge in the tall grass and shrubs.

Farther south, you will come to the Pea Island Visitor Center on the west side of N.C. 12. This is the principal gathering spot for exploring the refuge. Ample parking is provided. The visitor center offers books, maps, and brochures to help you identify the many birds in the refuge.

The **North Pond Wildlife Trail**, designated as a section of the **Charles Kuralt Trail** in memory of the North Carolina broadcast journalist who so loved the outdoors, starts at the visitor center. This trail follows a four-mile path around North Pond, but most people prefer to hike only the first portion until they reach one or both of the observation decks along the southern edge of the pond.

From the visitor center parking lot, the trail leads through a tunnel of live oaks onto a dike separating North and New Field Ponds. This strip of trees is generally full of warblers, as well as the ever-present gray catbirds (*Dumetella carolinensis*), rufous-sided towhees (*Pipilo erythrophthalmus*), and boat-tailed grackles (*Quiscaluis major*).

After emerging from the trees, you will reach the first observation deck overlooking North Pond. Throughout the summer and early fall, you are guaranteed to see a variety of herons, egrets, gulls, and terns from this spot. Virtually every species of dabbling duck known in the state can be seen in the pond in fall and winter, as can a few exotics such as Eurasian widgeons (*Anas penelope*). This is also a good place to see shorebirds, including Hudsonian gotwits, common gallinules (*Gallinula chloropus*), soras (*Porzana carolina*), king rails (*Rallus elegans*), and clapper rails (*Rallus longirostrus*).

On the south side of the dike is a marshy area known as New Fields. White ibises (*Eudocimus albus*), glossy ibises (*Plegadis falcinellus*), black-necked stilts, and American avocets frequent this wetland throughout the summer. Grain is planted here each year; in late autumn and early winter, this is a good place to see grazing geese, most notably snow geese (*Chen caerulescens*) in both their light and dark color phases.

Note: The mosquitoes at Pea Island National Wildlife Refuge are legendary for their numbers and ferocity. They are ever-present from March through November and seem undeterred by bug repellent. To avoid being bitten, wear a long-sleeved shirt and pants and a hat with bug netting.

DIRECTIONS
From the intersection of U.S. 64/264 and N.C. 12 at Whalebone Junction, drive south on N.C. 12 approximately 15 miles to the Pea Island Visitor Center.

ACTIVITIES
Bird-watching, hiking

FACILITIES
The Pea Island Visitor Center, staffed year-round, contains restrooms, wildlife exhibits, and a bookstore. Free nature-trail maps are available. There are two observation decks on the trail.

DATES
The refuge is open year-round. The visitor center is open from 9 A.M. to 4 P.M. daily in summer and from 9 A.M. to 4 P.M. Thursday through Sunday in winter.

FEES
None

CLOSEST TOWN
Nags Head is 15 miles north.

FOR MORE INFORMATION
Pea Island National Wildlife Refuge, P.O. Box 1969, Manteo, N.C. 27954 (252-473-1131; http://peaisland.fws.gov)

The Snow Goose

Snow geese flock to the Pea Island National Wildlife Refuge in late fall.
PHOTOGRAPH © JODY DUGGINS

Beginning in late November, the waters of Currituck Sound and the fields of the northern coastal plain become flecked with the brilliant white forms of snow geese (*Chen caerulescens*). Farmers fret to see flocks of these geese descend on their fields of winter wheat, but to bird lovers, the arrival of snow geese is a real treat. The birds fly 2,000 miles from their nesting grounds north of the Arctic Circle to winter in New Jersey's Delaware Bay, Virginia's Back Bay, and North Carolina's sound country. Snow geese are especially prevalent at Pea Island National Wildlife Refuge, where they feed on fields of planted grain. Snow geese appear in two color phases—pure white and dark gray. During the latter incarnation, the bird is referred to as a "blue goose." While at rest on the water, snow geese emit a constant, gentle cooing that is one of the memorable sounds of nature.

Chicamacomico Life Saving Station

Situated among the beach houses in the town of Rodanthe is the Chicamacomico Life Saving Station. This was one of 29 lifesaving stations built along the North Carolina coast by the now-defunct United States Life Saving Service.

Before the advent of helicopters and diesel-powered Coast Guard cutters, ships that ran aground on the Outer Banks had to depend on the bravery and ingenuity of members of the Life Saving Service for rescue. Lifesaving stations were established every seven miles along the most treacherous parts of the beach. Each one was typically manned by a station master, six crew or "surfmen," and a cook. Using little more than rowboats and ropes, they saved hundreds of people from drowning at sea. The story of these men and some of their truly heroic rescues is told in several places along the Banks, but nowhere so dramatically as at Chicamacomico.

The Chicamacomico complex includes seven buildings dating from 1874 to 1911, each beautifully restored by volunteer labor organized by the Chicamacomico Historical Association. At 2 P.M. each Thursday from mid-June through Labor Day, eight uniformed surfmen demonstrate a beach-to-ship rescue drill. The free demonstration is extremely popular, so make sure you arrive early for ease of parking and viewing.

DIRECTIONS

From the intersection of N.C. 12 and U.S. 64/264 at Whalebone Junction, follow N.C. 12 south for approximately 24 miles. The station is located on the east side of N.C. 12.

ACTIVITIES

Historical building tours, summertime reenactments

FACILITIES

Museum, restrooms

DATES

The station is open from 11 A.M. to 5 P.M. Tuesday, Thursday, and Saturday during the summer. Hours may be extended if volunteers are available. Costumed reenactments are held every Thursday in summer from 2 P.M. to 5 P.M.

FEES

None

CLOSEST TOWN

Rodanthe

FOR MORE INFORMATION

Chicamacomico Historical Association, P.O. Box 140, Rodanthe, N.C. 27968 (252-987-1552; www.chicamacomico.org)

 Avon

The town of Avon, formerly called and still referred to by locals as Kinnakeet, is the home of Hatteras Island's largest commercial complex, including the only large chain grocery store and movie theater. The **Avon Golf and Fishing Pier**

Windsurfers gather from all over the world to play in the Canadian Hole.

(252-995-5480) is considered a hot spot for red drum. The world-record drum, weighing in at 94 pounds, two ounces, was caught a few hundred yards from the pier in 1984. Each year, Avon hosts the World Championship Red Drum Tournament.

Just south of Avon is **Canadian Hole**, one of the best windsurfing spots in the nation. Named for the Canadian windsurfers who first recognized its attributes, this bay is perfectly situated to catch the winds coming across Pamlico Sound. It is shallow enough that windsurfers can generally stand if they fall off their boards. On windy days, windsurfers can be seen ripping across the sound on their brightly colored sailboards, leaping off waves, and making the occasional spectacular wipeout. Windsurfing equipment, kayaks, surfboards, body boards, and more can be rented from **Hatteras Wind n' Surf** (888-WNDSURF or 252-995-4525). The store offers kite-surfing, windsurfing, and kayaking lessons for all levels of experience.

FOR MORE INFORMATION
Outer Banks Chamber of Commerce, P.O. Box 1757, Kill Devil Hills, N.C. 27948 (252-441-8144; outerbankschamber.com)

Buxton Woods Coastal Reserve

The town of Buxton lies south of Avon at the point where the Outer Banks angle sharply to the west. This is the widest and most developed part of Hatteras

Island. Excavations done over the years indicate that Native Americans had a major village here—perhaps the village of Croatan, to which the Lost Colony settlers indicated they fled after abandoning Roanoke Island.

Buxton contains the largest stand of maritime forest in North Carolina. Roughly half of this 3,000-acre forest is in private ownership, with numerous houses built among the live oaks and loblolly pines. The other half is protected by the North Carolina Division of Coastal Management as part of Buxton Woods Coastal Reserve and by the National Park Service as part of Cape Hatteras National Seashore.

The Division of Coastal Management provides a 0.33-mile loop trail through its 950-acre section of the woods. The trail is located at the end of Old Doctors Road on the south side of N.C. 12 in Buxton. You can park at the beginning or, if you have a four-wheel-drive vehicle, at the end of the road. The trail loops through the forest, traversing old dune ridges and interdune swales. Midway along, it offers a view of a large freshwater marsh known as Jennette's Sedge. This is the largest freshwater marsh in any of the maritime forests on the Outer Banks. It is unique in that the fresh water sits like a lens atop the heavier salt water that underlies the Banks from sea to sound.

DIRECTIONS
From N.C. 12 in Buxton, look for the signs for Buxton Woods Coastal Reserve. Turn south on to Old Doctors Road. Park alongside the road.

ACTIVITIES
Hiking

FACILITIES
None

DATES
Open year-round

FEES
None

CLOSEST TOWN
Buxton

FOR MORE INFORMATION
North Carolina National Estuarine Research Reserve, P.O. Box 549, Kitty Hawk, N.C. 27949 (252-261-8891; www.ncnerr.org)

Cape Hatteras National Seashore

Back in the 1930s, nationally renowned artist and entrepreneur Frank Stick had a vision. A resident of Roanoke Island, Stick dreamed of creating a national seashore along the Outer Banks from the Virginia border to Cape Lookout. He teamed up with Washington Baum, a Dare County commissioner, to promote his vision to local property owners and state and federal officials as a way to both improve the depressed local economy and preserve a beautiful section of shoreline forever. Congress agreed and in 1937 authorized the creation of Cape Hatteras National Seashore. Stick was put in charge of the Cape Hatteras National Seashore Commission. Land was purchased, and hundreds of men set to work building protective sand dunes and anchoring them with fences, grass, trees, and shrubs.

Upon the arrival of World War II and the discovery of oil deposits off the Outer Banks, the purchase of land came to an abrupt halt. The project might have ended there, but Frank's son, David Stick, would not let the dream die. In 1952, he secured the backing of the Old Dominion Foundation and the Avalon Foundation, which agreed to provide $600,000 for land acquisition if the state would match the amount. The state concurred and set to work purchasing additional property. In 1953, land acquisition was largely completed, and the federal government officially took ownership of the property. Cape Hatteras National Seashore, the nation's first national seashore, was a reality.

Today, Cape Hatteras National Seashore extends approximately 75 miles from Whalebone Junction to Ocracoke Inlet, encompassing 30,319 acres. Except where interrupted by municipalities, the shoreline is undeveloped. These remote stretches of beach and dunes are ideal for beachcombing, sunbathing, and swimming. Camping is offered at four National Park Service campgrounds and nearby private campgrounds. The former include **Oregon Inlet Campground** on Bodie Island, **Cape Point and Frisco Campgrounds** on Hatteras Island, and **Ocracoke Campground** on Ocracoke Island. Each of these has cold showers, dump stations, drinking water, charcoal grills, and flush toilets. Ocracoke campsites can be reserved for June, July, and August by calling 800-365-2267. All other campsites are available on a first-come, first-served basis.

DIRECTIONS

From the north, Cape Hatteras National Seashore can be accessed by driving south on N.C. 12 from the intersection with U.S. 64/264 at Whalebone Junction in Nags Head. The seashore begins at this intersection and continues for approximately 75 miles. From the south, the seashore can be accessed by driving north on N.C. 12 from Ocracoke village. The seashore begins immediately outside the village.

ACTIVITIES
Swimming, shelling, bird-watching, hiking, kayaking, surfing, camping

FACILITIES
The National Park Service operates manned visitor centers in the keeper's quarters at both the Cape Hatteras Lighthouse and the Bodie Island Lighthouse. There is an unmanned information station at Whalebone Junction. Bathhouses are located at Coquina Beach and Frisco. Campgrounds are located at Oregon Inlet, Cape Point, Frisco, and Ocracoke. There is a day-use area at Salvo.

DATES
The seashore is open year-round.

FEES
None

FOR MORE INFORMATION
Cape Hatteras National Seashore, Route 1, Box 675, Manteo, N.C. 27954 (252-473-2111; www.nps.gov/caha)

CAPE HATTERAS LIGHTHOUSE/HATTERAS ISLAND VISITOR'S CENTER

Within Cape Hatteras National Seashore on Hatteras Island are several notable destinations. Most famous is the Cape Hatteras Lighthouse, located off N.C. 12 in Buxton. You should first stop at the Hatteras Island Visitor's Center, located in the double keeper's quarters and the principal keeper's quarters next to the lighthouse. The visitor center is the field office for the Hatteras Island District of Cape Hatteras National Seashore. It houses a museum and a bookstore that provide information related to all aspects of the seashore and the lighthouse.

After touring the museum, you can tackle the 268 steps to the top of the lighthouse. At 196 feet, Hatteras is the tallest brick lighthouse in the nation. Its handsome black-and-white-spiral facade has been reproduced in countless models and paintings. The lighthouse achieved world fame in 1999 when, threatened

The Cape Hatteras Lighthouse is the tallest brick lighthouse in the U.S.

The Lighthouse Move

On June 17, 1999, North Carolina held its breath as the 198-foot-tall Cape Hatteras Lighthouse began to roll across the sand toward its new home a half-mile away. To transport the 4,800-ton giant, International Chimney Corporation of Buffalo, New York, first had to build a roadway made of crushed stone and steel mats across the sand. It then removed 800 tons of the lighthouse's granite base and fit hydraulic jacks underneath. The lighthouse was lifted six feet in the air, then pushed by another set of hydraulic jacks over rollers positioned atop a steel track.

Watched by more than 20,000 visitors each day, the lighthouse crept along the track at a barely perceptible speed. Motion sensors placed throughout the lighthouse warned of any tilting or cracking. None was detected. On July 9, the lighthouse was lowered onto its new foundation. The move was accomplished on-budget and three weeks ahead of schedule.

with collapse caused by the encroaching sea, it was painstakingly lifted and moved 2,900 feet inland. Reopened to the public in 2000, the lighthouse deck offers one of the great views on the Outer Banks.

DIRECTIONS
From the intersection of U.S. 64/264 and N.C. 12 in Whalebone Junction, drive south on N.C. 12 approximately 46 miles to Buxton. Look for signs for the lighthouse.

ACTIVITIES
Hiking, picnicking

FACILITIES
Restrooms, museum, bookstore

DATES
The visitor center and lighthouse are open seven days a week from 9 A.M. to 5 P.M.

FEES
A fee is charged for climbing the lighthouse.

CLOSEST TOWN
Buxton

FOR MORE INFORMATION
Cape Hatteras National Seashore, Hatteras Island Visitor's Center, P.O. Box 190, Buxton, N.C. 27920 (252-995-4474)

BUXTON WOODS NATURE TRAIL

While visiting the lighthouse, you should explore the Buxton Woods Nature Trail, also part of Cape Hatteras National Seashore. Located off the service road west of the lighthouse, this 0.75-mile loop trail will take you into the heart of the maritime forest as you traverse old dune ridges covered with live oaks, loblolly pines, and yaupon trees. Most of the oaks were blown down by Hurricane Emily in 1993, so the forest is not what it used to be. However, it will recover in time, and it still supports an impressive diversity of flora and fauna.

The L-shaped dune system within the forest bears evidence of the multidirectional winds at work on Cape Hatteras. The first ridge you will encounter

Hikers set off through a maritime forest on the Buxton Woods Nature Trail.

runs north-south. This ancient dune was created by winds blowing onshore across the north-south-running beach. Farther along, the ridge "turns the corner" and runs east-west. This is a result of blowing sand being redirected by winds coming from the south. The battle of winds and waves is constantly changing the shape and position of Cape Hatteras, eroding the north-south beach westward and extending the east-west beach southward.

Midway along, the trail offers a view of Jennette's Sedge, the large freshwater marsh that can be seen from the trail in Buxton Woods Coastal Reserve. The marsh is unique in that the fresh water sits like a lens atop the heavier salt water that underlies the Banks from sea to sound.

CAPE POINT

Approximately 2.5 miles south of the lighthouse, the Outer Banks make an abrupt turn from a north-south to an east-west orientation. This is Cape Hatteras, known locally as Cape Point, part of Cape Hatteras National Seashore. Here, the Gulf Stream, running north, collides with the Labrador Current, running south. The interaction of waves and seafloor at this point is truly fascinating. Waves may come at angles to one another, combining to make an unusually high crest. One wave's crest may occupy another's trough, each canceling the other out. Or two wave crests may collide from opposite directions—an interaction called a claptois—shooting spray high into the air.

The turbulent mix of winds and waves at Cape Hatteras has created a vast shallows known as Diamond Shoals, which extends for miles out to sea. This is the heart of the so-called Graveyard of the Atlantic, the site of hundreds of shipwrecks. Among them is the USS *Monitor*, the Civil War ironclad sunk in 1862. The *Monitor's* gun turret was recovered in 2002 and put on display at the Mariner's Museum at Newport News, Virginia.

During fall and winter, surf fishermen gather at Cape Point in pursuit of the bluefish, cobia, king mackerel, and red drum that prey on schools of baitfish dazed by the colliding currents. Bird watchers come here in spring and fall, hoping to catch sight of pelagic birds—those that spend most of their lives at sea. No other location in the state has produced as many rare-bird sightings as Cape Point. Among the birds seen here in spring are the South Polar skua (*Catharacta skua*), the long-tailed jaeger (*Stercorarius longicaudus*), the masked booby (*Sula dactylatra*), the white-tailed tropicbird (*Phaethon lepturus*), and Leach's storm petrel (*Oceanodroma leucorhoa*). During summer, Cape Point hosts a colony of nesting terns and skimmers, including the sooty tern (*Sterna fuscata*) and the roseate tern (*Sterna dougallii*), as well as the federally endangered piping plover (*Charadrius melodus*). During the fall migration period, the nesting colony may include the buff-breasted sandpiper (*Tryngites subruficollis*), Baird's sandpiper (*Calidris bairdii*), and the American golden plover (*Pluvialis dominica*).

DIRECTIONS

To reach Cape Point, drive past the lighthouse to the end of the National Park Service road. If you have a four-wheel-drive vehicle, you may enter the beach via Ramp 43 or 44 and drive south approximately 1.25 miles. If you plan to hike, park at the designated parking area and walk along the beach.

∽Frisco

Frisco, originally known as Trent Woods, lies just south of Buxton and includes a number of significant landmarks. The **Cape Hatteras Pier** (252-986-2533), locally known as the Frisco Pier, is a favorite spot for catching king mackerel. Frisco is also home to a rather curious-looking museum that boasts one of the nation's most impressive private collections of Native American artifacts. Owned and operated by Joyce and Carl Bornfriend, the **Frisco Native American Museum** (252-995-4440) is housed in an unadorned mustard-yellow building to the west side of N.C. 12. The narrow, low-ceilinged rooms contain a surprising variety of weapons, clothing items, headdresses, beadwork, pottery, and baskets from tribes all across North America. Frisco is also the site of the **Billy Mitchell**

Airport. From this airstrip in 1921, Brigadier General Billy Mitchell led a group of bombers on a successful mission to sink two decommissioned battleships lying off the coast. Prior to Mitchell's demonstration, American military planners had doubted the value of aircraft as offensive weapons. Mitchell's bombing run changed the course of military history.

FOR MORE INFORMATION
Outer Banks Chamber of Commerce, P.O. Box 1757, Kill Devil Hills, N.C. 27948
(252-441-8144; outerbankschamber.com)

ᴐ Hatteras Village

Hatteras village, the southernmost town on the island, was established after an 1846 storm split the island in two, creating Hatteras Inlet. During the Civil War, the Confederates built several forts in Hatteras in an attempt to protect the vital inlet. Union troops stormed the forts in 1861 and used this area as a base to control the rest of the Outer Banks over the coming years.

With its ready access to the ocean, Hatteras village is a mecca for bluewater anglers. It offers the shortest trip to the Gulf Stream anywhere north of Miami. Dozens of charter boats operate out of the village's sound-side marinas. There are also launching ramps and bait-and-tackle stores catering to anglers who have their own boats. Each year, Hatteras hosts surf-fishing tournaments, mackerel tournaments, and the Offshore Open, a billfish and game-fish tournament offering tens of thousands of dollars in prize money.

Hatteras is a popular departure point for wreck-diving enthusiasts. Full-service dive shops that carry divers out to these wrecks include **Outer Banks Diving and Charters** (252-986-1056) at Teach's Lair Marina in Hatteras village. The fascination surrounding the many shipwrecks off the Outer Banks has prompted local citizens to create a museum dedicated to the subject. Opened in 2003 next to the Hatteras-Ocracoke ferry landing, the **Graveyard of the Atlantic Museum** (252-986-2995) chronicles the history of seafaring along the Carolina coast and describe the unfortunate end that many seamen met.

FOR MORE INFORMATION
Outer Banks Chamber of Commerce, P.O. Box 1757, Kill Devil Hills, N.C. 27948
(252-441-8144; outerbankschamber.com)

Hatteras-Ocracoke Ferry

There are no bridges accessing Hatteras Island from the south. The only way to proceed to Ocracoke Island, or to access Hatteras Island from Ocracoke Island, is by private boat or state-run ferry. The ferries operate daily year-round. They depart approximately every half-hour from both Hatteras and Ocracoke beginning at 5 A.M. and ending at midnight. Five ferries operate during the winter and 10 or more in summer. Each one holds approximately 30 cars. The ferry is free and does not require reservations. Restrooms are provided, but there is no food service. Lasting approximately 40 minutes, the ferry ride will give you a chance to relax and enjoy the sensation of being at sea, albeit on the sound side of Hatteras Inlet. You can get out of your car and stroll around the open decks or sit in the passenger lounge and look out the windows. The ferry ride offers an excellent opportunity for bird-watching. Sea gulls soar overhead, hoping for hand-outs of bread from the passengers.

FOR MORE INFORMATION
North Carolina Ferry Division, 113 Arendell Street, Morehead City, N.C. 28550 (800-293-3779; www.ncferry.org)

RESTAURANTS ON HATTERAS ISLAND

Restaurants on Hatteras Island are located primarily along N.C. 12. They do not post numbered addresses.

Down Under Restaurant & Lounge
N.C. 12, Rodanthe; 252-987-2277
Moderate

A restaurant with great views of the sound, Down Under features Australian cuisine in rooms decorated with authentic Aussie memorabilia. Lunch offerings include Vegemite sandwiches, yellowfin tuna tacos, and imported kangaroo burgers. Dinner specialties include shrimp stuffed with jalapeño peppers and cream cheese and wrapped in bacon.

Blue Parrot Café
N.C. 12, Avon; 252-995-6993
Moderate

Breakfast at the Blue Parrot features blackberry pancakes and eggs Benedict with crabmeat. Lunch and dinner appetizers include she-crab soup and shrimp tempura. Seafood, pasta, chicken, and steaks, including an excellent prime rib, round out the menu.

The Fish House
Scott Boatyard, N.C. 12, Buxton; 252-995-5151
Moderate

Overlooking Buxton Harbor, this unadorned wooden building was at one time a fish-processing house. Fresh seafood is served with hush puppies and vegetables. Specialties include tilefish and crab cakes.

Orange Blossom Café and Bakery
N.C. 12, Buxton; 252-995-4109
Moderate

Started by the owners of Papagayo's Restaurant in Chapel Hill, the Orange Blossom serves some of the best Mexican food on the Outer Banks. It is also known for its excellent vegetarian meals and homemade baked goods.

The Pilot House
N.C. 12, Buxton; 252-995-5664
Moderate

This three-story restaurant sits right at the water's edge, offering a fantastic view of Pamlico Sound and its sunsets. Tall ceilings and clerestory windows give the dining room an open, airy feel. Entrées include fresh seafood, steaks, pasta, and vegetarian dishes. Seafood bisque is a specialty.

Bubba's Bar-B-Q
N.C. 12, Frisco; 252-995-5421
Inexpensive

Visitors to North Carolina should not pass up the chance to sample the state's legendary barbecue. Bubba's specializes in hickory-smoked pork, chicken, beef, ribs, and turkey, seasoned with its locally famous hot sauce. Bubba's is also famous for its homemade desserts, including "Mrs. Bubba's Double Devil Chocolate Cake."

Gingerbread House Bakery
N.C. 12, Frisco; 252-995-5204
Inexpensive

The Gingerbread House is famous for its excellent baked goods. Among the favorites here are biscuits, French toast, and bagels for breakfast and gourmet pizza for dinner.

Austin Creek Grill
N.C. 12, Hatteras Landing; 252-986-1511
Moderate

This upscale restaurant features a magnificent view of the sound and Hatteras Landing Marina. It specializes in contemporary Southern cuisine, especially Carolina seafood.

The Channel Bass
N.C. 12, Hatteras; 252-986-2250
Moderate

Serving a wide variety of seafood right off the boat, this family-owned restaurant is a local institution. Entrées include seafood platters, crab cakes, veal, and char-broiled steaks. Desserts include homemade coconut, Key lime, and chocolate cream pies.

Lodgings on Hatteras Island

Lodgings on Hatteras Island are located primarily along N.C. 12. These motels do not post numbered addresses.

Hatteras Island Resort
N.C. 12, Rodanthe; 800-331-6541 or 252-987-2345
www.hatterasislandresort.com
Moderate

Located across from the Hatteras Island Fishing Pier, this oceanfront motel includes 24 motel-style rooms in the main building and 35 two-, three-, and four-bedroom cottages arranged in clusters. Amenities include an oceanfront swimming pool, a patio, and volleyball and basketball courts.

Avon Motel
N.C. 12, Avon; 800-243-5774 or 252-995-5774
www.avonmotel.com
Moderate

Popular with anglers, windsurfers, and sightseers, the Avon Motel has 45 rooms and efficiencies. It is within six miles of the Cape Hatteras Lighthouse and four miles of Canadian Hole.

Cape Hatteras Motel
N.C. 12, Buxton; 800-995-0711 or 252-995-5611
www.capehatterasmotel.com.
Expensive

This motel is popular with anglers for its closeness to the surf-fishing hot spot of Cape Point and with windsurfers for its closeness to Canadian Hole. The 28 efficiency units rent primarily by the week and sleep up to six people each. An outdoor swimming pool and a spa are among the amenities.

Comfort Inn of Hatteras
N.C. 12, Buxton; 800-432-1441 or 252-995-6100
Expensive

Located in the heart of Buxton, the Comfort Inn has 60 units, each with exterior access. Amenities include an outdoor swimming pool and a three-story watchtower.

Falcon Motel
N.C. 12, Buxton; 800-635-6911 or 252-995-5968
www.falconmotel.com
Moderate

A well-maintained, family-oriented motel, the Falcon features 35 rooms and apartments at bargain prices. Amenities include a fish-cleaning station, an outdoor swimming pool, tennis courts, basketball courts, a shaded picnic area with grills, and a boat ramp giving access to Pamlico Sound. Owners Anne and Doug Meekins are real nature lovers who have installed martin and bluebird houses, an osprey platform, and shrubs and flowers designed to attract a variety of birds.

Lighthouse View Motel
N.C. 12, Buxton; 800-225-7651 or 252-995-5680
www.lighthouseview.com
Expensive

As its name implies, this motel is close to the Cape Hatteras Lighthouse, as well as the services of Buxton. The 73 units include motel rooms, efficiencies, duplexes, villas, and cottages, most with an ocean view. The villas have balconies on both the ocean side and the sound side.

Holiday Inn Express
N.C. 12 at Marina Way, Hatteras; 252-986-1110
www.holidayinn.com
Expensive

The Holiday Inn Express has 40 rooms and 32 suites equipped with microwaves, refrigerators, and cable TV. Guests enjoy the outdoor pool.

Sea Gull Motel
N.C. 12, Hatteras; 252-986-2550
www.seagullhatteras.com
Moderate

This quaint, quiet motel is located at the north end of Hatteras village. It is a short walk from the Sea Gull to either the sound or the beach. Amenities include an outdoor pool, a picnic area with grills, and fish-cleaning tables. Gary's Restaurant is just across the street.

Seaside Inn at Hatteras Bed and Breakfast
N.C. 12, Hatteras; 252-986-2700
www.seasidebb.com.
Expensive

Built in 1928 and refurbished by owners Sharon and Jeff Kennedy, the Seaside Inn is one of the few bed-and-breakfasts on this part of the Outer Banks. The inn has 10 guest rooms, each distinctively laid out and decorated. It is well suited for weddings and parties.

The sound side of Ocracoke Island offers a protected environment for sea kayaking.

Ocracoke Island

Of all the inhabited islands on the Outer Banks, Ocracoke has the most secluded feel, an attribute favored by many vacationers, as well as by the writers and other artists who have made it a permanent home. The only ways to reach Ocracoke are by small plane (there is an airstrip in the town of Ocracoke), ferry, or private boat. Aside from the Hatteras-Ocracoke ferry, there are ferries running from Cedar Island and Swan Quarter on the mainland. From Cedar Island, the ride is a full two hours and 15 minutes. The ride from Swan Quarter lasts two and a half hours. Reservations are highly recommended for both the **Cedar Island** (800-856-0343) and **Swan Quarter** (800-773-1094) **ferries**.

Ocracoke has a rich history going back to the time of its habitation by the Woccocon Indians, for whom the island is believed to have been named. Europeans arrived here in the 1500s and set up a village at the southern end, beside Ocracoke Inlet. This inlet was one of the principal points of entry into North Carolina during the colonial era. Local sailors made a living guiding ships through the treacherous shoals and sand bars. Edward Teach, a.k.a. Blackbeard the Pirate, also knew these waters well, preying on merchant ships from his base, known as Teach's Hole. In 1718, Blackbeard was finally trapped and killed in Oregon Inlet by Lieutenant Robert Maynard of the Royal Navy in a classic naval battle.

Ocracoke remained isolated until the 1930s, when the village harbor, known as Silver Lake, was dredged and cleared. The United States Navy established a

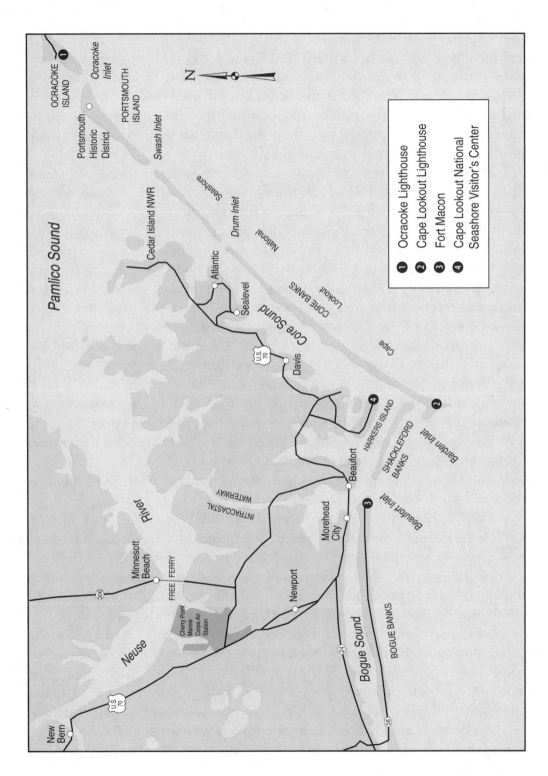

base here in World War II. Then, with the beginning of regular ferry service and the paving of roads on the island, Ocracoke began a transition to a tourist destination. In the 1960s, the United States Army Corps of Engineers built two palisade dunes along the ocean side of the island to prevent storm overwashes. Although overwashes still occur in places, the protection offered by the dunes has encouraged the growth of the thickets and pine-dominated maritime forests that now cover the island.

Today, Ocracoke remains largely undeveloped, mainly because 90 percent of its land is protected by Cape Hatteras National Seashore. Development is confined to Ocracoke village, which clusters around Silver Lake at the southern tip of the island. Even here, most building has been tastefully done and is often hidden behind the old cedar trees planted in front yards.

With no through traffic and relatively few cars on the island, bicycle riding is a favorite pastime on Ocracoke. Riders can easily explore the village in a few hours, stopping in at the craft shops and landmarks tucked on the back streets. Several shops rent bikes, and some lodges provide them free to visitors.

Ocracoke is also a great place to kayak. On the north side of town, the sound is shallow and sheltered. Diamondback turtles (*Malaclemys terrapin*), rays, and jellyfish are frequently seen in the water, while ibises, egrets, and other wading birds stalk the shore. It makes a good day trip to follow the shoreline up to Hatteras Inlet and back, taking time to explore the creeks and coves along the way. **Ride the Wind Surf and Kayak** (252-928-6311) and **Ocracoke Adventures** (252-928-7873) both offer kayak rentals and eco-tours.

Aside from the pristine beaches and sounds, there are several attractions on the island worth visiting.

The National Parks Service's **Ocracoke Island Visitor's Center** (252-928-4531) is on the northwest side of Silver Lake beside the ferry docks. It contains books, maps, and exhibits on the island. Rangers provide a variety of free programs during summer. The center is open 9 A.M. to 5 P.M. daily from March through December. Beside the visitor center are the National Park Service docks, which provide access to Silver Lake for those with their own boats.

Located across the National Park Service public parking lot, the **Ocracoke Island Museum and Preservation Society** (252-928-7375) resides in an old wood-frame house built by the first chief of the Ocracoke Coast Guard Station. The museum contains documentary photographs of local citizens taken in the 1950s, artifacts from the Confederate Fort Ocracoke (now underwater), and an authentic 1930s bedroom and kitchen. The museum also offers a description of Ocracoke's famous dialect, which dates back to Shakespearean English and can still be heard in the speech of some locals. It is open daily in summer and Monday through Saturday in winter. Call for hours.

Also on the west side of Silver Lake, signs point the way down a side road to the **British Cemetery**. This small cemetery holds the graves of four British seamen who died when a German U-boat sank their antisubmarine trawler, the HMS *Bedfordshire*, off Ocracoke. During World War II, Sir Winston Churchill loaned the United States 24 antisubmarine ships to help stave off U-boat attacks. This cemetery and the British flag that flies above it pay tribute to England's generosity.

On the east side of Silver Lake down Lighthouse Road, the **Ocracoke Inlet Lighthouse** peeks its head above the tree line. This is the oldest and shortest of the lighthouses on the Outer Banks. Built in 1823, it stands only 76 feet tall. With its black iron light set slightly askew, the lighthouse is commonly referred to as "cute." It remains in operation but is not open to the public. The keeper's quarters, a two-story white cottage beneath a lovely grove of live oaks, has been restored but is also closed to the public.

Approximately three miles east of Ocracoke village on the north side of N.C. 12 is a parking lot that provides access to the **Hammock Hills Nature Trail**. This 0.75-mile trail offers an excellent view of the different types of vegetation found on the island. It enters a typical Outer Banks thicket dominated by groundsel, wax myrtle, and yaupon holly. Within this thicket is a freshwater creek frequented by wading and diving birds. As with similar bodies of fresh water on the Outer Banks, this creek is actually perched atop salty ground water that extends from the ocean to the sound deep underground. After crossing the creek, the trail veers through a slash pine forest planted in the 1950s. Hardwoods such as live oaks and marsh magnolias, whose saplings can be seen growing in the understory, will eventually succeed this forest. Leaving the pine forest, the trail enters a dune field occupied by such common dune plants as prickly pear cactus, Spanish bayonet, and, at the crest of the dunes, sea oats. Eventually, the trail skirts a sound-side marsh, where the typical gradation from thicket to black needlerush to salt cordgrass can be observed. This is a good place to see wading birds, as well as the fiddler and square-backed crabs that live in the muck. The trail circles back toward the parking lot, traversing an extensive dune field, from which the hammocks that give the trail its name can be observed. Hammocks are forested areas sitting atop slightly higher and sandier ground than is found in the surrounding marsh.

Also on the north side of N.C. 12, approximately seven miles east of the village, are the **Ocracoke Pony Pens**. Legend has it that in 1585, the English flagship *Tiger* ran aground in Ocracoke Inlet while carrying a load of colonists and horses. Sir Richard Grenville ordered the ship unloaded so that it could be refloated, and in the process, a number of horses escaped. The descendants of these horses—or perhaps descendants of horses from Spanish shipwrecks—have survived on Ocracoke for centuries. After the National Park Service took over the management of the seashore, it corralled the herd to prevent overgrazing of the island. About two dozen ponies can be seen inside the mile-long fenced pasture.

Visitors traveling to or from Ocracoke via the Ocracoke-Cedar Island or Ocracoke-Swan Quarter ferries will pass a spoil bank just outside Silver Lake. An artificial island created by the dredging of sand from Ocracoke Inlet, this spoil bank is often crowded with shorebirds, including brown pelicans (*Pelicanus occidentalis*). Brown pelicans are common all along the Outer Banks, but prior to the 1970s, they were considered endangered on the East Coast—victims of the spraying of the pesticide DDT. Only one small colony nested in the state, here on a spoil bank in Ocracoke Inlet. With the termination of DDT spraying and the preservation of nesting sites, brown pelicans have recovered to where they are no longer endangered.

FOR MORE INFORMATION

Greater Hyde County Chamber of Commerce, P.O. Box 178, Swan Quarter, N.C. 27885 (888-493-3826; www.ocracoke-nc.com)

RESTAURANTS ON OCRACOKE ISLAND

All of the restaurants on Ocracoke Island are located in the town of Ocracoke within a few blocks of Silver Lake. Most of the restaurants on N.C. 12 do not post numbered addresses.

The Back Porch
1324 Country Road, Ocracoke; 252-928-6401
Expensive

Housed in a renovated wooden building tucked back in a wooded lot, The Back Porch is an Ocracoke institution. Fresh seafood, fresh vegetables, and homemade sauces, dressings, breads, and desserts are just part of the attraction. You can dine on the screened-in porch or in one of the interior nooks and crannies.

Café Atlantic
N.C. 12, Ocracoke; 252-928-4861
Moderate

Housed in a contemporary two-story building, Café Atlantic serves innovative cuisine in an upscale atmosphere. *Outer Banks Magazine* said it has "the best crab cakes on the entire Outer Banks." Blueberry-pecan pancakes, chicken and broccoli crepes, and "Huevos Rancheros" are featured at brunch.

Captain Ben's
N.C. 12, Ocracoke; 252-928-4741
Moderate

This is where the locals go when they get tired of eating seafood. Ben's prime rib is the main attraction, but his seafood dishes are also excellent, especially the seafood Marsala and the "Pesto Mere Bulles."

Howard's Pub & Raw Bar Restaurant
N.C. 12, Ocracoke; 252-928-4441
Inexpensive to moderate

Howard's is the place to go in Ocracoke for entertainment as well as good food. The wraparound bar, the game room, the large screened-in porch, and the deck provide a setting for everyone. Fresh local fish, oysters, shrimp, crab legs, and clams are featured. Over 200 beers are available. Live music is provided on weekends. Howard's is open every day year-round.

Island Inn Restaurant
25 Lighthouse Road, Ocracoke; 252-928-7821
Moderate

Located in the historic Island Inn, this restaurant specializes in traditional Southern dishes and seafood entrées. All breads, soups, and desserts are homemade. Call to reserve rooms for large parties.

Lodgings on Ocracoke Island

Ocracoke has some of the more handsome inns and lodges on the Outer Banks, most of which are clustered around Silver Lake. Prices tend to be high, and rentals during the summer tend to be by the week. Houses may be rented more cheaply.

Anchorage Inn and Marina
N.C. 12, Ocracoke; 252-928-1101; www.theanchorageinn.com
Expensive

This beautiful five-story inn offers fantastic views of Silver Lake and ready access to a private dock and marina. Amenities include a harbor-side swimming pool and sun deck.

Berkeley Manor Bed and Breakfast
N.C. 12, Ocracoke; 800-832-1223 or 252-928-5911
www.berkeleymanor.com
Expensive

Situated across the street from the ferry landing on a cedar-shaded lawn, this 12-room bed-and-breakfast recalls Ocracoke's bygone days. The manor house was built in 1860 and is paneled in cypress, pine, and cedar.

Blackbeard's Lodge
111 Back Road, Ocracoke; 800-892-5314 or 252-928-3421
www.blackbeardslodge.com
Inexpensive to moderate

Built in 1936, Blackbeard's Lodge is Ocracoke's oldest hotel. It has 37 units that sleep from one to eight people. The lodge is ideal for families and sportsmen on a budget. Units rent by the day or week.

Boyette House
N.C. 12, Ocracoke; 800-928-4261 or 252-928-4261
www.boyettehouse.com
Moderate to expensive

Located a short walk from the restaurants and shops of Ocracoke, the Boyette House features two porch-lined buildings of two stories each. It is ideal for families.

The Castle Bed and Breakfast on Silver Lake
155 Silver Lake Road, Ocracoke; 800-471-8848 or 252-928-3505
www.thecastlebb.com
Expensive

> From the brick walkway lined with lantanas to the cypress tongue-and-groove siding inside, this 10-room bed-and-breakfast exudes beauty and class. Guests have use of the swimming pool and day spa, as well as the lakeside dock.

Island Inn
25 Lighthouse Road, Ocracoke; 252-928-4351
www.ocracokeislandinn.com
Expensive

> This attractive two-story inn sits just one block from the harbor. Built in 1901, the central building is listed on the National Register of Historic Places. The 35 rooms were designed to accommodate a variety of travelers, including families, single adults, and couples. Four villas with full kitchens, Jacuzzis, private decks, and harbor views were added in 1999.

Ocracoke Harbor Inn
144 Silver Lake Road, Ocracoke; 888-456-1998 or 252-928-5731
www.ocracokeharborinn.com
Expensive

> Painted a distinctive pastel green, this three-story inn sits at the north end of Silver Lake. Private decks with Adirondack chairs overlook the harbor. Boat-docking privileges, bike rentals, and outdoor grills are available.

Pirate's Quay
33 Silver Lake Road, Ocracoke; 252-928-3002
Expensive

> A luxurious, four-story combination hotel and condominium with harbor views, Pirate's Quay has six suites, each with a living room, a dining room, a full kitchen, two bedrooms, and one and a half baths.

Pony Island Motel
N.C. 12, Ocracoke; 252-928-4411
www.ponyisland.com
Moderate

An attractive and affordable alternative to the tony inns on Silver Lake, Pony Island offers 50 units for single or double occupancy. Amenities include a swimming pool and a spacious lawn with picnic tables and grills.

Silver Lake Inn & Motel
N.C. 12, Ocracoke; 252-928-5721
www.thesilvelakeinn.com
Moderate to expensive

This four-story, cedar-sided inn features individual porches with hammocks, a perfect perch for viewing the comings and goings on Silver Lake. Both suites and motel-style rooms are available.

How Blackbeard Met His End

On the morning of November 21, 1718, Lieutenant Robert Maynard of the Royal Navy led two sloops into Ocracoke Inlet with the intent of capturing the notorious pirate Blackbeard. From his lair on Ocracoke Island, Blackbeard spotted Maynard and drifted his ship *Adventure* down the channel to meet him. After firing a round of muskets, Blackbeard hoisted sail and headed north. Thinking the pirate was fleeing, Maynard tried to cut him off, but just as Blackbeard planned, Maynard ran aground on a shoal. Blackbeard closed quickly, firing a broadside that killed or wounded a dozen men. But the battle was not over. Gloating in his apparent victory, Blackbeard failed to see that the *Adventure*, too, was drifting onto a shoal. It ran aground just as Maynard freed his sloop. Maynard sailed toward the *Adventure*. During the fierce combat that ensued, the British prevailed. Maynard chopped off Blackbeard's head and hung it from his bowsprit. The golden age of piracy was over.

Cape Lookout National Seashore

South of Ocracoke, the Outer Banks run for 40 miles to Cape Point at Cape Lookout, then angle back to the northwest for another 16 miles. The stretch of islands between Ocracoke and Cape Lookout is known as Core Banks, one of the lowest, thinnest, and most frequently overwashed sections of the Outer Banks. Inlets come and go with the storms, breaking the Banks into separate islands, then joining them back as the inlets fill. This is the longest unmodified section of shoreline in North Carolina. There are no bridges to or improved roads on Core Banks, and there are very few buildings. As Dirk Frankenberg wrote in *The Nature of North Carolina's Southern Coast*, "Core Banks looks today like the Outer Banks must have looked in the late 1920s, before the Civilian Conservation Corps began constructing the palisade dunes that protect most of these banks now."

Vegetation is sparse along Core Banks. There are few trees to provide shade or visual relief. Colors appear almost monochromatic in summer but can be quite vivid in the swing seasons. The *Spartina* grass that dominates the sound-side marshes turns an electric green in spring. In fall, the grasslands take on a bronze hue interspersed with the feathery purple stems of the bunch grass known as purple muhly (*Muhlenbergia capillaris*), the bright yellow blossoms of the marsh golden-aster (*Heterotheca subaxillaris*), and the red-and-yellow daisy-like flower known as beach blanket (*Gaillardia pulchella*).

In 1976, Core Banks was designated as Cape Lookout National Seashore. Any private dwellings have already come under, or will come under, the owner-ship of the National Park Service, and new development is prohibited. Visitors can access the seashore with their own boats or by private ferries from Ocracoke village, Harkers Island, and the towns of Beaufort, Atlantic, and Davis on the mainland. The Atlantic ferry transports vehicles to North Core, the stretch of Core Banks between Portsmouth Island and Drum Inlet. The Davis ferry trans-ports vehicles to South Core, the island south of New Drum Inlet. Only four-wheel-drive vehicles should be taken out to the seashore, as most driving is on soft sand. Typically, anglers who plan to stay for several days are the ones who transport vehicles to the beach. Otherwise, most people take day trips to visit the principal attractions at the opposite ends of Core Banks—Portsmouth village and the Cape Lookout Lighthouse.

Camping is permitted anywhere along Core Banks except within a hundred feet of a structure or within nesting areas marked by the National Park Service. Core Banks is a prime nesting ground for a variety of shorebirds, as well as for giant loggerhead turtles (*Caretta caretta*). On summer nights, female loggerheads weighing up to 400 pounds haul themselves ashore, lumber across the sand to the frontal dunes, and, using their hind flippers, dig out nests in which they deposit anywhere from 80 to 120 eggs. When the eggs are laid, the turtles cover them with sand and head back to the ocean. The beaches are patrolled daily in summer by National Park Service volunteers and staff looking for the telltale "crawls." If they find a nest, the caretakers generally remove the top layer of sand, cover the nest with chicken wire to keep raccoons away, and re-cover it with sand. Nesting grounds may be flagged to keep humans away.

Note: Shackleford Banks, the last island in the chain that makes up Cape Lookout National Seashore, is commonly accessed from Beaufort and is thus covered in the "Southern Coast" chapter.

DIRECTIONS

The central point of access to Cape Lookout National Seashore is the visitor center on Harkers Island. From Beaufort, drive east on U.S. 70 to the crossroads at Otway. Turn right on S.R. 1322 and drive nine miles to the visitor center.

ACTIVITIES

Hiking, fishing, swimming, shelling, camping, picnicking, hunting

FACILITIES

There are restrooms at the visitor centers at Harkers Island, Portsmouth village, and Cape Lookout.

DATES

The visitor center on Harkers Island is open from 8:00 A.M. to 4:30 P.M. daily. It is closed Christmas and New Year's Day.

FEES

Private ferries charge a fee to transport visitors to Core Banks.

FOR MORE INFORMATION

Cape Lookout National Seashore Visitor's Center, 131 Charles Street, Harkers Island, N.C. 28531 (252-728-2250; www.nps.gov/calo)

∽Portsmouth Village

Directly across Ocracoke Inlet lies Portsmouth Island, also known as North Core Banks. In 1753, the North Carolina General Assembly established a port at the north end of the island to service merchant ships transporting goods to and from the mainland. The town that grew up around that port, Portsmouth village, thrived for nearly a century as one of the busiest on the coast.

Due to its shifting shoals and narrow channel, Ocracoke Inlet was not easily navigated by deep-keel merchant ships. These ships would anchor at the mouth of the inlet and transfer their cargo to shallow-draft vessels known as lighters. The lighters would transport the goods to warehouses on Shell Castle Island, just offshore of the village, for later shipment to New Bern or Bath.

Portsmouth residents made good money at lightering, but their fortunes changed in 1846. That year, a hurricane opened up Hatteras and Oregon Inlets to the north, providing better access to the sound. Portsmouth was trapped in an economic eddy, and the population gradually declined. The last remaining residents left in 1971. Five years later, the National Park Service took over the town.

Today, the 250-acre Portsmouth Historic District is listed on the National Register of Historic Places. You can visit the ghost town through private ferry companies operating out of Ocracoke. These include **Portsmouth Island ATV Excursions** (252-928-4484) and **Austin Boat Tours** (252-928-5431). They will take you on a 20-minute ride across the inlet and leave you to wander the town or, if you wish, to take an ATV tour of the island. In Portsmouth, you can tour the old post office/general store, school, church, graveyard, and lifesaving station. National Park Service volunteers are generally in the village during the day and are happy to answer questions. The National Park Service maintains an unmanned visitor center at the Salter/Dixon House in Portsmouth. Restrooms are available here, but water is not. The rule in the national seashore is to bring what you need with you, and to carry it out when you leave.

DIRECTIONS
Access is by private ferry from Ocracoke.

ACTIVITIES
Historic home tour

FACILITIES
Restrooms are available at the Salter/Dixon House.

Cape Lookout Lighthouse

Towering above all else at the south end of Core Banks is the 163-foot-tall Cape Lookout Lighthouse, distinguished by its black and white diamond-shaped markings. Built in 1859, the lighthouse was the first of its style along the Outer Banks. In fact, it served as a model for the lighthouses at Cape Hatteras, Bodie Island, and Corolla. The lighthouse is still owned and operated by the United States Coast Guard and is not open to the public. However, the National Park Service maintains a visitor center with restrooms and displays in the adjacent keeper's quarters.

Although the lighthouse cannot be climbed, this is a lovely place to swim, picnic, and hike and is well worth the trip from the mainland. You can access the lighthouse with your own craft or through private ferries operating out of Beaufort and Harkers Island. For a modest fee, they will drop you off at the dock beside the lighthouse and return a few hours later. The Cape Lookout National Seashore Visitor's Center maintains an up-to-date list of private companies licensed to provide ferry service to and tours of Cape Lookout.

Cape Lookout Village Historic District

A great addition to a trip to the lighthouse is a tour out to Cape Point and to the settlement known as the Cape Lookout Village Historic District. Several private companies offer guided tours, taking passengers in pickup trucks from the dock at the lighthouse to the historic district and/or the point.

The Cape Lookout Village Historic District is a collection of homes built between 1910 and 1950, most of which are occupied only during the summer. When the national seashore was dedicated in 1976, the owners were offered 25-year leases on their properties. As those expire, the National Park Service will manage the buildings on a case-by-case basis. Among the interesting buildings located in the historic district are a lifesaving station built in 1888; a turn-of-the-20th-century keeper's quarters, moved from beside the lighthouse; and a United States Coast Guard station built in 1916 and used until 1983, when the Coast Guard consolidated its operations at Fort Macon. The National Park Service now leases this building to the North Carolina Maritime Museum, which uses it as a research and education area.

DIRECTIONS
See the directions to the Cape Lookout Lighthouse.

ACTIVITIES
Historic home tour

FACILITIES
None

DATES
The historic district is accessible year-round.

FEES
Private guide services charge a fee to transport visitors to Cape Lookout and through the historic district.

CLOSEST TOWN
Harkers Island

FOR MORE INFORMATION
For a list of private companies offering tours, contact the Cape Lookout National Seashore Visitor's Center, 131 Charles Street, Harkers Island, N.C. 28531 (252-728-2250; www.nps.gov/calo).

Cape Point

The southernmost point on Cape Lookout, Cape Point (not to be confused with the Cape Point at Cape Hatteras) is one of the most dramatic spots on the entire Outer Banks. Here, the Banks disappear into the ocean in a distinct, arrowhead-shaped wedge of sand. For hundreds of yards, waves driven by countervailing forces of wind and tide collide over the submerged shoals, sending spray high into the air. These turbulent forces are constantly reshaping Cape Point, sometimes turning it to the east, other times to the west. Researchers who have studied the point using a Global Positioning System say it "wags back and forth like the tail of a dog."

As at Cape Hatteras, Cape Point is a favorite place for surf fishing. Anglers ferry their trucks from the mainland and drive out to the point to stand vigil behind their surf-casting rods, sometimes for days. This is also a good birding spot, especially during migrations and stormy weather. In the warm months, look

Anglers gather at Cape Point for some of the best surf fishing in the country.

for royal (*Sterna maxima*), sandwich (*Sterna sandvicensis*), least (*Sterna albifrons*), and common (*Sterna hirundo*) terns. From late October through April, Northern gannets can be seen feeding just off the point.

From Cape Point, the coastline angles sharply back to the northeast for several miles. The southwest-facing beach is one of the best shelling spots on the Outer Banks. Shells commonly found here include knobbed whelks (*Busycon carica*), Atlantic cockles (*Dinocardium robustum*), king helmets (*Cassis tuberosa*), and calico scallops (*Agropecten gibbus*). Midway along the beach is an old rock jetty that is a favorite fishing spot.

At its northern terminus, the beach forms a hook-shaped point known as Power Squadron Spit or "the Hook." The spit is a popular roosting area for pelicans, cormorants, gulls, and terns. The waters offshore are favorite wintering grounds for common loons.

DIRECTIONS
See the directions to the Cape Lookout Lighthouse.

ACTIVITIES
Hiking, shelling, fishing, swimming, bird-watching

FACILITIES
None

CLOSEST TOWN
Harkers Island

FOR MORE INFORMATION
Cape Lookout National Seashore Visitor's Center, 131 Charles Street, Harkers Island, N.C. 28531 (252-728-2250; www.nps.gov/calo)

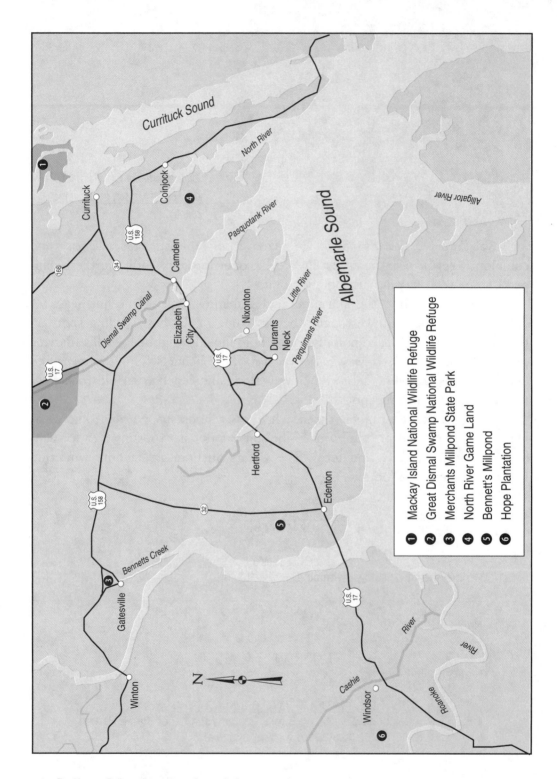

Currituck Sound

North River

Coinjock

④

Currituck

Albemarle Sound

Alligator River

U.S. 158

34

Pasquotank River

Camden

168

Little River

Nixonton

Perquimans River

Dismal Swamp Canal

Elizabeth City

Durants Neck

U.S. 17

U.S. 17

②

Hertford

Edenton

U.S. 158

32

⑤

Bennetts Creek

③

U.S. 17

Gatesville

River

River

N

Cashie

Windsor

Roanoke

Winton

⑥

Mackay Island National Wildlife Refuge
Great Dismal Swamp National Wildlife Refuge
Merchants Millpond State Park
North River Game Land
Bennett's Millpond
Hope Plantation

❶ ❷ ❸ ❹ ❺ ❻

The Sound Country

Osprey nest all along Goose Creek.

Table flat, sparsely populated, full of natural and historical treasures, North Carolina's sound country may be the most underappreciated region of the coast. Because of its flat topography and lack of oceanfront shoreline, the sound country doesn't have the immediate allure of the Outer Banks. But remarkable places are there to be found, down the wooded stream that runs under the bridge or at the end of the tree-lined driveway.

The great Currituck, Albemarle, and Pamlico Sounds shape this land and define its culture. These sounds and the rivers that feed them reach far inland, dividing the coastal plain into a series of long peninsulas. The sound country has no official beginning or end, but for the purposes of this book, it shall be defined as that part of the mainland running from the Virginia line to the southern end of Bogue Sound, extending as far inland as the tidal basins of the Chowan, Pamlico, and Neuse Rivers.

For decades, tourists have bypassed the sound country in their headlong rush to the beaches of the Outer Banks. But with the growing interest in the state's historical sites and natural areas, tourism in the sound country is thriving. Boarded-up main streets have blossomed with restaurants and gift shops. Dilapidated turn-of-the-20th-century homes have been restored and converted into bed-and-breakfasts. Canoe trails have been laid out along the blackwater rivers and swamps.

The promotion of the sound country as a tourist destination is being spurred by a diverse collection of nonprofit and government groups. The Partnership for the Sounds (252-974-1044) promotes environmental education and sustainable economic development through nature-based tourism at five different sites on the Albemarle-Pamlico Peninsula. The **Historic Albemarle Tour** (800-734-1117; www.historicalbemarletour.com) includes 27 historic sites from Northampton County to Ocracoke. The **Albemarle Resource Conservation and Development Council** (252-482-7437), working with the North Carolina Division of Parks and Recreation and the North Carolina Division of Travel and Tourism, has identified sections of 29 streams and rivers totaling more than 1,200 miles for inclusion in the Albemarle Region Canoe and Small Boat Trails System. Square signs bearing the silhouette of a canoe with two canoeists identify access points. Trail guides are available at area tourist sites or can be obtained through the North Carolina Division of Parks and Recreation's **Eastern Region Trails Program** (919-751-2792). Bicycle riders will want to take advantage of roads designated by the North Carolina Department of Transportation (919-715-2341) as part of the **North Carolina Biking Highways System**. Biking highways are chosen based on their relative safety and scenic value. Look for rectangular signs with a silhouette of a bicycle rider against a green oval, or visit www.dot.state.nc.us/transit/bicycles for a complete listing of these routes.

Merchants Millpond State Park

Upon seeing the enormous bald cypress trees rising from the tannin-stained waters, visitors to Merchants Millpond State Park often exclaim, "This looks like a real Southern swamp!" Indeed, this 3,252-acre park, roughly a thousand acres of which comprise the millpond, is a visual delight and one of the most popular natural areas of the sound country.

As its name implies, Merchants Millpond is an impoundment, created by the damming of Bennett's Creek to power a gristmill. However, the dam has been in place so long (since 1811) that the pond has developed into a complex, mature ecosystem. The cypress trees in the swamp are among the largest in the state, reaching as much as eight feet in diameter and 117 feet in height. The state's largest tupelo tree is also located here.

Reptiles and amphibians abound in the millpond. Pond slider turtles lie stacked up on half-submerged logs, and cottonmouth snakes, or water moccasins, sun in the crotches of cypress stumps. Beavers, muskrats, and river otters are common in the wooded upper reaches where Lassiter Swamp flows into the millpond. The upland forest of hardwoods and pines bordering this swamp is home to bobcats, deer, gray foxes, and raccoons.

Merchants Millpond supports a diverse mix of aquatic plants. Mats of white-flowering, fragrant water lily (*Nympheeae oderata*) and yellow-flowering spadderdock (*Nuphar lutea*) stand out against the tannin-colored waters. The pond is also home to a diverse mix of floating plants, including mosquito fern (*Azolla caroliniana*), a dime-sized floating fern with tiny, overlapping leaves, and parrot's feather (*Myriophyllum brasiliense*), whose lime-green foliage trails along the water's surface.

The millpond and swamp are best explored by canoes, available for rent at the park. Two canoe campgrounds—one a family campground with seven sites and the other a group campground with three sites—have been established along the shores of the millpond. Sites at the family campground are available on a first-come, first-served basis, while the group campground is available by reservation. There are nine miles of hiking trails around the swamp. One trail leads to five backpack campsites. A walk-in group camping area and a campsite exclusively for use by

Spanish moss hangs from swamp gum and cypress trees in Merchants Millpond State Park.

fishermen with small boats are also available. Both of these sites contain pit toilets and small wash houses with pay showers.

The best months to visit the millpond are April and May, when reptiles and amphibians are most visible, and October and November, when the red maples and cypresses are in full color. The millpond can be oppressively hot and buggy in summer.

DIRECTIONS
From Gatesville in central Gates County, drive east on U.S. 158 to Easons Crossroads. Turn right on Millpond Road (S.R. 1403) and follow the signs to the park.

ACTIVITIES
Canoeing, hiking, fishing, camping

FACILITIES
Interim nature center, restrooms, boat ramp, picnic area

DATES
The park hours are 8 A.M. to 6 P.M. November through February; 8 A.M. to 7 P.M. during March and October; 8 A.M. to 8 P.M. during April, May, and September; and 8 A.M. to 9 P.M. from June through August.

FEES
There is no fee to enter the park. Fees are charged for renting canoes and camping.

CLOSEST TOWN
Gatesville is six miles away.

FOR MORE INFORMATION
Merchants Millpond State Park, 71 U.S. 158 East, Gatesville, N.C. 27938-9440 (252-357-1191; www.ncsparks.net)

Great Dismal Swamp / Dismal Swamp Canal

Straddling the North Carolina-Virginia state line, the Great Dismal Swamp is the northernmost of a long chain of swamps running along the mid-Atlantic coastal plain. The Dismal is vast—approximately 600 square miles—and by its name alone attracts the attention of adventurous travelers. Unfortunately, there is no public access to the North Carolina portion of the swamp at present. (Access is available in Virginia but is not covered in this book.) And the Dismal, having been logged numerous times, looks more like a typical forest of loblolly pines and red maples than the classic Southern swamp with giant, moss-draped cypresses. However, resource restoration efforts are under way, and you may find the swamp worth exploring, if for no other reason than to appreciate its storied past.

The first written account of the Great Dismal Swamp came courtesy of Colonel William Byrd II, who in 1728 led a surveying party across its width to draw a dividing line between North Carolina and Virginia. The survey crew emerged haggard and worn after several days. "Never has rum, that cordial of life, been found more necessary than in this dirty place," Byrd wrote.

While Byrd despaired of this gloomy wilderness, others saw an opportunity for riches. George Washington, for one, thought the swamp could be drained and converted into agricultural land. He and five other investors purchased 40,000 acres of the swamp in 1763 and started work on a drainage canal. However, the return on his investment was not what he had hoped, and Washington eventually withdrew his interest.

Over the ensuing decades, others succeeded in reaping a profit from the swamp, primarily by harvesting its principal treasure, bald cypresses and Atlantic white cedars (*Chamaecyparis thyoides*), or juniper trees. The wood from these rot-resistant trees was highly prized for use in boat building and in making shingles, siding, and railroad ties. Beginning in the late 1700s and continuing until the mid-1970s, timber companies harvested cypresses and white cedars from the swamp until there were essentially none left. In addition to stripping the native timber, loggers ditched and drained much of the swamp and constructed roadways that blocked the surface flow of water. The drier environment suppressed the regrowth of cypresses and white cedars and allowed loblolly pines, sweet gums, and red maples to flourish in their place.

Preservation of the land began in 1974 when the Union Camp Timber Corporation donated 49,000 acres to The Nature Conservancy. That land was then conveyed to the United States Department of the Interior, which established the **Great Dismal Swamp National Wildlife Refuge**. Other donations and sales followed, enlarging the refuge to its present size of approximately 109,000 acres.

Today, the refuge's managers are seeking to restore the biological diversity that existed prior to human alteration. Water-control structures have been placed in the drainage ditches and are being managed so as to raise the surrounding water table. Cypress and juniper seedlings are being planted, and prescribed burnings are being used to suppress the growth of invasive species. Wildlife habitats are being restored, and hunting is being used to balance populations of animals such as white-tailed deer in accordance with food supplies.

North Carolina has gotten into the picture with the designation of 14,300 acres as **Dismal Swamp State Park**. The park is currently under development. Hiking trails and primitive campsites are in the works. Completion is tentatively scheduled for 2003.

While opportunities for exploring the North Carolina portion of the swamp are limited, the adjacent Dismal Swamp Canal is readily accessible by boat or car. Located on U.S. 17 just south of the Virginia line, the **Dismal Swamp Canal Visitor/Welcome Center** invites travelers to pause and take a look at a remarkable piece of human engineering.

Hand-dug by slaves between 1793 and 1805, the 22-mile-long canal connects the Elizabeth River in Virginia to the Pasquotank River in North Carolina. For nearly a century, it served as a major commercial route for freighters, sternwheel steamboats, barges, and schooners. It was an important highway for the shipment of Confederate goods during the Civil War, though it fell under Union control shortly after the Battle of South Mills in April 1862. By the early 1900s, the development of road and rail systems rendered the canal all but obsolete for commercial traffic. It fell into disrepair and was sold to the federal government in 1929. Since then, the United States Army Corps of Engineers has restored and maintained the canal for use by recreational boaters traveling between Chesapeake Bay and Albemarle Sound.

Visitors to the welcome center can see some impressive boats traveling this narrow waterway and share stories with captains and crew tying up at the dock. On display outdoors is a narrow-gauge Plymouth gasoline locomotive, used from 1943 to 1975 to haul timber out of the Great Dismal Swamp.

DIRECTIONS

The Dismal Swamp Canal Visitor/Welcome Center is located on U.S. 17 three miles south of the North Carolina-Virginia line and 15 miles north of Elizabeth City. The headquarters for the national wildlife refuge are in Suffolk, Virginia.

ACTIVITIES

Boating, fishing, picnicking

FACILITIES
Gift shop, bookstore, 0.25-mile nature trail, picnic tables and grills, 150-foot dock, canoe launch

DATES
The welcome center is open daily from 9 A.M. to 5 P.M. from Memorial Day to the end of October. From November 1 to Memorial Day, it is open from 9 A.M. to 5 P.M. Tuesday through Saturday.

FEES
None

CLOSEST TOWN
Elizabeth City is 15 miles away.

FOR MORE INFORMATION
Dismal Swamp Canal Visitor/Welcome Center, 2356 U.S. 17 North, South Mills, N.C. 27976 (252-771-8333); Great Dismal Swamp National Wildlife Refuge, P.O. Box 349, Suffolk, Va. 23439 (757-986-3705)

Mackay Island National Wildlife Refuge

At the very top of Currituck Sound, a block-headed peninsula protrudes south from the Virginia mainland. The bulk of this peninsula consists of a vast marsh with two islands of high ground—Knotts Island and Mackay Island—located in the east and southwest corners, respectively.

In 1918, New York publishing magnate Joseph Knapp purchased Mackay Island as his own private hunting reserve. Knapp enjoyed many years of hunting in the expansive marshes, but he also recognized that waterfowl populations nationwide were suffering from the combined impacts of hunting and habitat loss. In 1930, he and two associates formed the More Game Birds in America Foundation "for the purpose of increasing the number of gamebirds and other game, fish, or wildlife in America." Knapp's foundation later became Ducks Unlimited, the premier organization devoted to preserving and restoring waterfowl nesting habitats in North America.

Following Knapp's death, Mackay Island passed through several owners. In 1961, the United States Department of the Interior purchased the property and designated it Mackay Island National Wildlife Refuge. Today, the refuge encompasses 8,024 acres of fields, marshes, and upland pine forests. Waterfowl, the principal attraction, can be viewed by car or by foot. N.C. 615, the main road through the refuge, crosses Great Marsh on a three-mile-long causeway. From here, you have a good chance of seeing king rails, least bitterns, and marsh wrens in summer and snow geese in late winter. An observation platform is located on the north side of the causeway on the eastern shore of Buzzards Bay. At the east end of the causeway, the **Great Marsh Trail** runs in a 0.3-mile loop that offers you a chance to get out of your car and see the birds mentioned above.

Farther south on N.C. 615, you will come to a refuge entrance at Mackay Island Road. The first 1.4 miles of this road, open to cars year-round, pass through fields, upland pine forests, pine and hardwood swamps, and brackish marshes. At the end of that distance, Mackay Island Road reaches a gate. The road and trails beyond this gate are open to pedestrian and bicycle travel from March 15 to October 15. A trail circles the East Pool, Middle Pool, and West Pool impoundments, a total distance of 6.5 miles, although you can shorten the hike by circling just one or two pools. These trails offer you a good chance of seeing wood ducks, American black ducks, and blue- and green-winged teals.

DIRECTIONS
From North Carolina, you can reach Mackay Island directly by taking a 45-minute ferry ride from the town of Currituck to Knotts Island; call 800-BY-FERRY for times. From the landing, drive north on N.C. 615 to the refuge entrance. By road, you can reach the refuge only by driving into Virginia. From the town of Currituck, drive north on N.C. 168 across the Virginia line. Approximately 1.8 miles past the state line, turn right on Galbush Road. Drive 1.6 miles, turn right on Indian River Road, go 5.6 miles to the T-intersection with Blackwater Road, turn left, drive 1.8 miles, and turn right on Pungo Ferry Road, which ends at Va./N.C. 615. Turn right and follow the signs to the refuge and the office/visitor center.

ACTIVITIES
Hiking, bird-watching, fishing, picnicking, hunting

FACILITIES
The refuge office has restrooms and displays.

DATES
The refuge office/visitor center is open from 8 A.M. to 4 P.M. weekdays through-

out the year. Portions of the refuge are open year-round, others from March 15 to October 15.

FEES

A fee is charged to ride the ferry.

CLOSEST TOWN

Currituck is 5.5 miles away by ferry.

FOR MORE INFORMATION

Mackay Island National Wildlife Refuge, P.O. Box 39, Knotts Island, N.C. 27950 (252-429-3100; http://mackayisland.fws.gov)

North River Game Land

Approximately 12 miles east of Elizabeth City, U.S. 158 traverses the head of a vast swamp bisected by the North River and stretching 20 miles down to Albemarle Sound. More than 17,000 acres of this swamp are protected by the state as the North River Game Land. The game land provides excellent waterfowl hunting and largemouth bass fishing and has also been designated a black bear sanctuary.

The southern portion of the game land is dominated by the brackish tidal basin of the North River. Salt marsh cordgrass, phragmites, and tall cordgrass grow thick along the shore. Farther north, freshwater marshes predominate, as evidenced by the diverse mix of bullrush, sedge, cattail, wild iris, pickerel weed, marsh gentian, and swamp milkweed. The tidally influenced freshwater marshes of the North River are considered the best examples of this community in North Carolina.

Starting in 1997, the North Carolina chapter of The Nature Conservancy helped the state acquire more than 7,000 acres along the North River in Camden and Currituck Counties. This includes a state-designated natural area known as **Indiantown Creek Cypress Forest**. The Nature Conservancy has also helped the state acquire some of the last remaining Atlantic white cedar stands along the North River. These stands contain some of the state's rarer Neotropical songbirds, including breeding populations of black-throated green warblers (*Dendrioca virens*), Swainson's warblers (*Limnothyypis swainsonii*), and worm-eating warblers

Fishing for bass and bowfin is popular on blackwater creeks like Indiantown Creek.

(*Helmitheros vermivorus*). The stands also harbor populations of a rare butterfly, the Hessel's hairstreak (*Mitoura hesseli*), the larvae of which feed exclusively on cedar foliage.

Exploring the North River Game Land is best done by boat, as there are no trails and the acreage is mostly swamp. East of Elizabeth City, a small blackwater stream known as **Indiantown Creek** offers adventurous kayakers and canoeists a great look at the wooded upper reaches of the game land. Upon setting out from any of the several access points, boaters are immersed in a fairy land of anvil-headed cypress trees and drooping Spanish moss. Water moccasins linger on the fringes of the stream, often coming out to challenge passing boaters. Indiantown Creek eventually feeds into the North River. However, it is a long way to any takeout, so most boaters paddle down to what is known as Thoroughfare Island, then return to the put-in, a good day trip.

Boaters can also explore the game land from the opposite (south) end by putting in at the public boat launch on the Intracoastal Waterway near the town of Coinjock. This canal runs south into the North River. The river here is wide and subject to winds, tides, and waves, so it is best explored using a powerboat. Boaters can cruise the shoreline looking for ospreys, eagles, wading birds, and ducks. Bass fishing in the upper reaches is reported to be excellent.

Elizabeth City

With the beginning of construction of the Dismal Swamp Canal in 1793, the North Carolina General Assembly directed that a town be established at "the Narrows of the Pasquotank," where port facilities and a customs office had opened in 1722. Elizabeth Town, as it was first called, was named the Pasquotank County seat, leading to the construction of a courthouse and a jail, followed by hotels, shops, and other commercial enterprises. The town's name was changed to Elizabeth City in 1801 to avoid confusion with Elizabeth Town in Bladen County. Elizabeth City thrived until the late 1850s, servicing the boat traffic that came down the Dismal Swamp Canal. But the completion of the deeper and shorter Albemarle and Chesapeake Canal to the northeast diverted boat traffic away from the city and devastated its economy.

The town enjoyed a brief revival during the first year of the Civil War, as the Union naval blockade of the North Carolina coast forced goods to be funneled through the sounds and the Dismal Swamp Canal. But when Union forces advanced on the town in 1862, fleeing citizens torched many of the homes and public buildings.

The arrival of railroad service in 1881 revived the city once again and led to unparalleled industrial, commercial, and residential growth. The city gained status as the only metropolitan area in a vast agricultural region. Farmers from the surrounding area brought their crops here to be processed and shipped. Soybeans were processed commercially for the first time in the United States in Elizabeth City in 1915.

In 1938, the United States Coast Guard opened an air station on the Pasquotank River just south of Elizabeth City. The base has been enlarged several times and now serves as the Coast Guard's largest aircraft repair and supply center, as well as the major search-and-rescue base for the coast of the Southeast. During World War II, the military constructed two giant hangars to accommodate blimps used to patrol the coastline. The larger hangar was destroyed by fire in 1995, but the smaller—a metal-clad dome with folding clamshell doors—still looms above the flatlands. Today, a private company that builds and services lighter-than-air craft owns and operates the blimp base.

Elizabeth City is gaining popularity as a tourist destination. The city has a stunning collection of 19th- and early-20th-century residential and commercial structures in a variety of architectural styles. Most are contained in a 30-block area designated as the **Elizabeth City Historic District**. The best way to tour this district is on foot. Free tour brochures are available from the **Elizabeth City Chamber of Commerce** (252-335-4365), located at 502 East Ehringhaus Street. Among the most impressive buildings are the Gothic Revival **Christ Episcopal Church**, built in 1857 at the corner of McMorrine and Fearing Streets; the Victorian-style **Pasquotank County Courthouse** at 206 East Main; the **Charles O. Robinson House**, an enormous Neoclassical Revival mansion directly across the street from the courthouse; and the **United States Post Office and Courthouse** at 306 East Main. Built in 1906, the courthouse features a magnificent two-story courtroom with hand-carved wainscoting and a 300-pound brass-and-glass chandelier. Another historic site worth visiting is the **Episcopal Cemetery**, located on Ehringhaus Street between Water and McMorrine Streets. Listed on the National Register of Historic Places, the cemetery has burial stones dating back to 1724. Except for the privately owned Charles O. Robinson House, all of the above sites are open to the public free of charge.

You should also be sure to visit **Mariners' Wharf** (252-335-4365), which parallels Water Street on the Elizabeth City waterfront. A destination for recreational boaters diverting from the Intracoastal Waterway, it offers complimentary dockage for 48 hours at its 14 boat slips. Following a tradition started by two local citizens in 1983, a group of people called the Rose Buddies offers the boaters a free rose and an invitation to explore the town as a gesture of hospitality.

For a taste of present-day culture, you should be sure to visit the **Pasquotank Arts Council Main Street Gallery** (252-338-6455), located at 609 Main Street. The gallery showcases the work of local and regional artists, and the gift shop sells a wide selection of arts and crafts. Across the Pasquotank River at 150 U.S. 158 East in Camden is the **Watermark** (252-338-0853), which displays and sells the works of the 700-member cooperative of the same name.

FOR MORE INFORMATION
Elizabeth City Chamber of Commerce, P.O. Box 426, Elizabeth City, N.C. 27909
(252-335-4365; www.elizcity.com)

The Charles O. Robinson House, one of Elizabeth City's many architectural gems

Museum of the Albemarle

Scheduled to relocate to a new 50,000-square-foot facility on Water Street in the fall of 2004, the Museum of the Albemarle is the flagship historical museum of the 13-county Albemarle region. The state-supported museum serves as the northeastern branch of the North Carolina Museum of History. Through films, lectures, and static and interactive displays, it traces the history of the Albemarle region from the days of the Native American through the colonial era, the Civil War, and into the present. Displays include locally manufactured crafts, weapons, tools, and textiles, as well as an early fire engine and a 1904 Alvirah Wright shad boat, an excellent example of the official state boat of North Carolina. The museum houses an auditorium, a library, meeting and conference rooms, and a deck with a view of the Pasquotank River.

DIRECTIONS

As of this writing, the museum is located at 1116 U.S. 17 South. The new facility is being constructed on the waterfront in downtown Elizabeth City at the intersection of Ehringhaus and Water Streets.

ACTIVITIES

Films, lectures, gallery tours

FACILITIES

Museum with an auditorium, a library, and meeting and conference rooms

DATES

The museum is open from 9 A.M. to 5 P.M. Tuesday through Saturday and from 2 P.M. to 5 P.M. on Sunday. It is closed on state holidays.

FEES

None

CLOSEST TOWN

Elizabeth City

FOR MORE INFORMATION

Museum of the Albemarle, 501 South Water Street, Elizabeth City, N.C. 27909 (252-335-1453)

RESTAURANTS IN ELIZABETH CITY

C & H Oyster Bar
1524 U.S. 17, Elizabeth City; 252-338-3300
Inexpensive

Housed in a double-wide manufactured building, this local favorite serves the best in fried seafood, most notably oysters, in a lively, unadorned atmosphere. It is open only during oyster season—that is, the months with an *r* in their names.

Marina Restaurant
35 Camden Causeway, Elizabeth City; 252-335-7307
Moderate

This restaurant specializes in fresh local seafood and steaks. Its upstairs oyster bar and outside deck offer great views of the Pasquotank River.

Mulligan's Waterfront Grill
Waterworks Building, 400 South Water Street, Elizabeth City; 252-331-2431
Moderate

Mulligan's offers fine dining with a view of the waterfront. Guests enjoy outdoor dining and entertainment on the dock in season. Specialties include blackened chicken breast smothered in salsa and shrimp sautéed with lemon, thyme, and basil, served over pasta.

LODGINGS IN ELIZABETH CITY

Elizabeth City Bed and Breakfast
108 East Fearing Street, Elizabeth City; 252-338-2177
www.bbonline.com/nc/elizabethcity
Moderate

This five-bedroom bed-and-breakfast is located in the two-story Victorian-style L. S. Blades Jr. House (1896) and the Fraternal Lodge (c. 1846) in the historic district across from the courthouse. All rooms have private baths and DSL connections. The Fraternal Lodge can accommodate groups of up to 50 people.

Hampton Inn
402 Halstead Boulevard, Elizabeth City; 252-333-1800
www.hamptoninn.com.
Moderate

Comfortable and clean, this hundred-unit motel features an outdoor pool, a hot tub, and free deluxe continental breakfast.

Hertford

Hertford is a beautiful riverside village with a main street largely unchanged from the turn of the 20th century. Approaching the town from the north, U.S. 17 Business crosses the Perquimans River on an S-shaped bridge, advertised by the town as the only such bridge in the country. Hertford, the county seat of Perquimans County, contains a host of historic buildings easily seen on a self-guided walking tour. Maps are available at the visitor center (252-426-1425), located at 118 West Market Street.

The central building in Hertford is the **Perquimans County Courthouse** at 128 North Church Street. Constructed in 1732 and renovated several times thereafter, this Federal-style courthouse is listed on the National Register of Historic Places. A monument to baseball great and Hertford native Jim "Catfish" Hunter stands on the courthouse lawn. Another notable structure is the **Church of the Holy Trinity** at 207 South Church Street. Constructed in 1850, this church has wooden buttresses, plaster ceiling decorations, and a working 1854 Jardine organ. The baptismal font was reputedly given to St. Paul's Parish in Edenton by Queen Anne in the early 18th century. The church is open only for Sunday services.

The business district along Church Street contains an assortment of antique shops and restaurants housed in buildings dating from the late 18th century through the early 20th century. At the corner of Hyde Park and King Streets is a monument to the African-American soldiers who fought in the Civil War, one of only two such monuments in the country.

Missing Mill Park and **Municipal Park**, both located along West Grubb Street, provide lovely views of the Perquimans River and the S-shaped bridge. Municipal Park has a public boat launch, while Missing Mill Park has a picnic pavilion, a covered fishing pier, and a canoe launch platform.

FOR MORE INFORMATION

Perquimans County Chamber of Commerce, P.O. Box 27, Hertford, N.C. 27944 (252-426-5657; www.perquimans.com)

The Newbold-White House

Though it appears at a distance to be a small, contemporary structure built in the middle of a large field, the Newbold-White House is actually the oldest brick home in North Carolina. Built around 1730, the house is significant not only for its age and its brick siding 18 inches thick, but also for the remarkable quality of the work. Catherine Bishir, author of the seminal architectural text *North Carolina Architecture*, had this to say about the house: "A display of brick-layers' skill amid the small wooden houses of the region offered a proud statement of exceptional success and status for the family and the artisans who built it. The vivacious pattern of glittering header bricks alternating with plain red stretchers transforms the clean, simple form into a sparkling checkerboard in the sunlight."

Inside, the house is furnished with period furniture and household goods that illustrate family life in the colonial era. Volunteers from the Perquimans County Restoration Association are available to conduct guided tours in season. The association also operates a visitor center beside the house. The center contains a gift shop and offers an orientation video, free literature, and displays.

DIRECTIONS

From U.S. 17 Bypass around Hertford, take Harvey Point Road heading south. The Newbold-White House is on the left after approximately 1.5 miles.

ACTIVITIES

Touring historical home, picnicking

FACILITIES

Visitor center with restrooms, exhibits, and gift shop

DATES

The house is open 10:00 A.M. to 4:30 P.M. Tuesday through Saturday and 2:00 P.M. to 5:00 P.M. on Sunday from March 1 to Thanksgiving. Tours are available by appointment. The gift shop is open year-round.

RESTAURANTS IN HERTFORD

Frankie's Hertford Café
127 North Church Street, Hertford; 252-426-5593
Inexpensive

> Located directly across from the courthouse, this classic old-time café prides itself on serving "home cooking as good as Grandma's."

Soundside Grill
The Albemarle Plantation, Holiday Island Road, Hertford; 252-426-2252
Moderate

> Located in a private residential, boating, and golfing community six miles south of Hertford, this restaurant offers a spectacular view of Albemarle Sound. Fresh seafood, Angus beef, and home-made breads and desserts are the specialties here. Reservations are recommended.

LODGINGS IN THE HERTFORD AREA

Lodgings in the Hertford area are limited to bed-and-breakfasts, albeit historical ones in beautiful settings.

Beachtree Inn
948 Pender Road, Hertford; 252-426-7815
Moderate

> Located five miles south of Hertford, this inn is a collection of 14 antebellum structures assembled by the Ben and Jackie Hobbs family and furnished with period antiques and reproductions made by Ben Hobbs. The cottages have cable TV, queen-sized beds, private baths, and fireplaces.

Covent Garden Inn
107 Covent Garden Road, Hertford; 252-426-5945
www.perquimans.com/covent
Moderate

This three-room inn is located in the historic Ruth Toms-Newby House, built around 1916. The guest rooms are furnished with vintage antiques and handmade quilts and linens. A gourmet breakfast is served in the ornate dining room.

Eagle and Anchor Bed and Breakfast
215 West Market Street, Hertford; 252-426-8382
Moderate

The Eagle and Anchor is located in the historic Colonel Francis Toms House, built around 1820. It features three rooms, including a two-bedroom family suite. All rooms have private baths and are furnished with vintage antiques. Fresh-baked breads are served with breakfast.

1812 on the Perquimans
Old Neck Road, Hertford; 252-426-1812
www.1812.qpg.com
Moderate

This five-room inn is located in the Fletcher-Skinner-Nixon House, one of the most outstanding Federal-style plantation dwellings in Perquimans County. From the front porch, guests have a view of wide pastures bordering the Perquimans River. Those traveling by boat can access the inn via a private mooring on the river. The owners offer a free continental breakfast or, for a small additional cost, a plantation breakfast including fish, spoon bread, fried green tomatoes, apples, grits, country sausage, and more.

Edenton

While all the towns on Albemarle Sound share a certain beauty by virtue of their waterfront locations and wealth of historic buildings, Edenton may well be the most beautiful of all. It is situated at the head of Edenton Bay and is bounded on the east and west by Queen Anne Creek and Pembroke Creek, respectively. South Broad Street, the main north-south avenue, is lined with a stunning collection of churches, homes, and businesses dating to the 1700s. Broad Street ends at the waterfront, where you can look out on a glassy bay dotted with bald cypress trees. A trio of Swiss cannons brought to Edenton in 1778 stands guard over the harbor, a reminder of the town's strategic past and the dedication of its citizens to preserving its place in history.

Edenton was founded in 1712. As the home of colonial governor Charles Eden, it served as the unofficial capital of North Carolina for many years. Upon Eden's death in 1722, the town was incorporated as Edenton in his honor. Edenton was considered one of the hotbeds of revolutionary fervor prior to the Declaration of Independence. In 1774, some 51 local ladies signed a resolution pledging their support for the First Provincial Congress's ban on the import and consumption of British tea and other highly taxed items. This is the earliest known instance of political activity on the part of women in the American colonies.

During the 18th century, Edenton flourished as a port city trading with the other American colonies, the West Indies, and England. Commerce and wealth fostered fine private and public architecture. However, a hurricane in 1795 silted up Roanoke Inlet and ended the easy access. The opening of the Dismal Swamp Canal to the north diverted more commerce, and Edenton gradually slipped into being a sleepy Southern enclave.

Bypassed by the battles of the Civil War, Edenton survived with most of its grand antebellum homes, churches, and civic buildings intact. Many of these are now listed on the National Register of Historic Places, and the town is enjoying a revival as one of the principal tourist destinations of the Albemarle region.

Edenton is home to some noteworthy cultural organizations. The **Rocky Hock Playhouse** (252-482-4621), located at the corner of Rocky Hock Church Road and Evans-Bass Road north of town, offers live indoor musical theater. The **Chowan Arts Council Gallery & Gallery Shop** (252-482-8005), located at 200 East Church Street, feature the work of both known and undiscovered area artists. More than a dozen antique and gift shops are in the downtown area.

Edenton Waterfront Park can be used as a put-in or takeout point for exploring several designated sections of the Albemarle Region Canoe and Small Boat Trails System. Paddlers can explore four miles of Pembroke Creek from the bridge at S.R.1208 down to the waterfront park. From there, they can paddle east past the town's historical section and up Queen Anne's Creek to the N.C. 32 bridge, a distance of two miles. A third water trail starts at the

A trio of Swiss cannons stands guard over Edenton's Waterfront Park.

culverts on S.R. 1120 beside the Trestle House Inn; the inn provides parking and rents canoes and kayaks. The trail follows a canal system through the Cape Colony subdivision for about a mile, then follows the edge of Albemarle Sound approximately three miles to Queen Anne Park.

You may want to stop at the **Edenton National Fish Hatchery** (252-482-4118) at 1104 West Queen Street. Authorized in 1898, this hatchery has raised and released millions of striped bass, American shad, and herring fingerlings over the past century. Tours of the small aquarium and hatchery ponds are offered by appointment.

> ### FOR MORE INFORMATION
> Edenton-Chowan Chamber of Commerce, P.O. Box 245, Edenton, N.C. 27932 (252-482-3400)

Historic Edenton

Most of the significant historic structures in Edenton are contained within a 16-block area. A good starting point for a tour of the district is the **Historic Edenton State Historic Site Visitor Center** at 108 North Broad Street. Here, you can arrange for guided walking tours or interpreted trolley tours, which depart at 9 A.M., noon, and 2 P.M. Tuesday through Saturday.

The historic buildings in Edenton are too numerous to mention in full. However, on the walking tour, one of the historic sites you'll want to see is the

Chowan County Courthouse National Historic Landmark, built in 1767 and restored several times since. This is one of the finest examples of Georgian public-building architecture in the nation. The oldest courthouse in continuous use in North Carolina, it is considered the most intact colonial courthouse in the nation. St. Paul's Episcopal Church, built in 1736, is the second-oldest church building in the state and another architectural gem. The 1757 Cupola House National Historic Landmark at 408 South Broad Street takes its name from the octagonal "lantern" atop its roof, used by the home's occupants to sight incoming ships. The Cupola House is furnished as a house museum of the mid- to late 18th century. Its gardens have been restored according to the 1769 Sauthier map of Edenton. The Barker House at 505 South Broad Street was once the home of Penelope Barker, the instigator of the Edenton Tea Party. Now a museum with period furnishings, it has been referred to by the *New York Times* as "Edenton's living room." The Barker House (252-482-7800) is open from 10 A.M. to 4 P.M. Monday through Saturday and from 1 P.M. to 4 P.M. on Sunday.

DIRECTIONS
From U.S. 17, exit on to N.C. 32 and drive south to its merger with Broad Street. Continue south on Broad. The Historic Edenton State Historic Site Visitor Center is at the corner of Broad and East Gale.

ACTIVITIES
Walking tours, trolley tours, special events and programs

FACILITIES
Information booth, restrooms, audiovisual program, exhibits, gift shop

DATES
From April 1 through October 31, the visitor center is open 9 A.M. to 5 P.M. Monday through Saturday and 1 P.M. to 5 P.M. on Sunday. From November 1 through March 31, it is open 10 A.M. to 4 P.M. Tuesday through Saturday and 1 P.M. to 4 P.M. on Sunday.

FEES
Fees are charged for guided walking tours and trolley tours.

FOR MORE INFORMATION
Historic Edenton State Historic Site, P.O. Box 474, Edenton, N.C. 27932 (252-482-2637; www.ah.dcr.state.nc.us/sections/hs/iredell/iredell.htm). This organization provides information on trolley tours.

Restaurants in Edenton

Harbor View Café & Harbor Side Restaurant
112 Water Street, Edenton; 252-482-0118
Moderate to expensive

This restaurant specializes in prime Angus steaks, fresh seafood, and homemade pasta dishes. The full bar includes an extensive selection of wines, domestic beers, and microbrews. Reservations are recommended.

Kramer's Garage
113 West Water Street, Edenton; 252-482-9977
Moderate

Located in a 1920s-era auto repair shop, Kramer's serves lunch, dinner, and Sunday brunch. Crab cakes are a specialty here. Live jazz is offered most Saturday nights.

Waterman's Grill
427 South Broad Street, Edenton; 252-482-7733
Moderate

Waterman's is located in the heart of the historic district. Fresh seafood is the specialty here.

Lodgings in Edenton

Edenton has several chain motels, but the principal attractions are the bed-and-breakfasts, most of which are located within the historic district.

Captain's Quarters Inn
212 West Queen Street, Edenton; 252-482-8945
www.captainsquartersinn.com.
Moderate

Located in a 1907 Colonial Revival home, the Captain's Quarters has eight guest rooms with modern baths and cable TV. A three-course gourmet breakfast is served Monday through Saturday.

Coach House Motel
823 North Broad Street, Edenton; 252-482-2107
*Inexpensive*_____

This traditional motel offers senior-citizen rates and commercial discounts.

Governor Eden Inn
304 North Broad Street, Edenton; 252-482-2072
www.governoredeninn.com
*Moderate*_____

Massive Ionic columns welcome guests to this turn-of-the-20th-century Neoclassical home. Each of the four bedrooms has a private bath, cable TV, and air conditioning.

Granville Queen
108 South Granville Street, Edenton; 252-482-5296
www.edenton.com/granvillequeen
*Moderate to expensive*_____

The nine bedrooms in this spectacular turn-of-the-20th-century home are decorated and furnished in unique styles ranging from early Egyptian to French country cottage. Guests are treated to a five-course breakfast and weekend evening wine tastings.

Hampton Inn
115 Hampton Inn Drive, Edenton; 252-482-3500
*Moderate*_____

This inn offers an outdoor pool, an exercise room, a business center, and meeting rooms.

Lords Proprietors' Inn
300 North Broad Street, Edenton; 252-482-3641
www.edentoninn.com
*Expensive*_____

This inn consists of three restored homes with a total of 20 fully equipped guest rooms. Dining is available in the Whedbee House in the center of the inn's grounds.

Travel Host Inn
501 Virginia Road, Edenton; 252-482-2017
Moderate

Located on U.S. 17 Bypass, this motel offers an outdoor pool and free continental breakfast. AARP, AAA, and corporate discounts are available.

Trestle House Inn
632 Soundside Road, Edenton; 252-482-2282
www.edenton.com/trestlehouse.
Moderate

Located on Albemarle Sound just outside the downtown area, this five-bedroom inn was built in 1972 with massive California redwood beams that were originally Southern Railway trestles. The inn overlooks a wildlife refuge on a private lake. The Trestle House is located along the North Carolina Biking Highway and the Albemarle Region Canoe and Small Boat Trails System. Canoes and bikes are available for rent.

Bennett's Millpond

Nestled in the farm country north of Edenton, Bennett's Millpond is one of the hidden gems of the sound country. Like Merchant's Millpond, it was formed by the damming of a creek to power a gristmill and has been in existence so long that it has created its own ecosystem. Bennett's Millpond is over a mile long and has lots of shoreline to explore. The Albemarle Learning Center, which manages the property in conjunction with Chowan County, has constructed several docks and a nature trail near the Rocky Hock Road entrance. The short nature trail leads through a bottom-land hardwood forest below the millpond dam, an entrancing environment were it not for the proximity of the highway.

To really appreciate the wildness of the millpond, you should explore it by canoe. The profusion of aquatic weeds growing on and under the surface can make it difficult to paddle the entire length of the pond. However, there is usually enough open water to make exploration of the lower end possible. Heading out from the boat ramp at the southern end of the pond, you will pass among cypress trees along the shore and in open water. The remains of duck

Bald cypress rise above Bennett's Millpond.

blinds nailed to many of these trees testify to the profusion of waterfowl that gathers here in fall. In spring and summer, ospreys nest in the tops of the cypresses. Herons squawk along the shore. Kingfishers dive from overhanging branches.

Mammals are common on the millpond as well. Nutrias (*Myocastor coypus*), large rodents native to South America, can be seen swimming along the shoreline and feeding on aquatic vegetation. Muskrats, beavers, and otters are also common.

DIRECTIONS
From U.S. 17 near Edenton, drive north on N.C. 32 for approximately four miles. Turn left on Rocky Hock Road. The entrance to the millpond is on the right just before the bridge over Rocky Hock Creek.

ACTIVITIES
Canoeing, hiking, bird-watching

FACILITIES
Boat ramp, dock, nature trail

DATES
Open year-round

FEES
None

CLOSEST TOWN
Edenton is five miles away.

FOR MORE INFORMATION
Albemarle Learning Center, 131 Morristown Road, Edenton, N.C. 27932 (252-482-5769)

 Windsor

Windsor, the county seat of Bertie County, is located at the junction of U.S. 13 and U.S. 17 on the banks of the Cashie (pronounced CASH-eye) River. Although the river seems altogether too small for such purposes today, tall ships from England used to sail up the Cashie to Windsor to load cargo and collect tannin-tinted river water for drinking. The highly acidic black water, a by-product of the peat-rich soil, inhibited the growth of bacteria, keeping the water fresh for the long voyage across the Atlantic.

Windsor's harbor and its key location on the highway between Edenton and Halifax led to a measure of prosperity, reflected in the town's stately homes and public buildings. The historic buildings are primarily in a 16-block area designated as the **Windsor Historic District**. Among the more prominent buildings is the **Bertie County Courthouse** at the corner of King and Dundee Streets, built in 1887 and added to several times since. The **Freeman Hotel**, built around 1840 at 102 North York Street, is a relatively rare survivor among the hotels once found in small, mid-19th-century eastern North Carolina towns. Moved to its present site in 1980, it serves as the home of the Windsor-Bertie County Chamber of Commerce. Free maps for a walking tour of the historic district are available here.

Another attraction in Windsor is **Livermon's Park and Mini-Zoo** (252-794-5553). Located at 102 North York Street across from the Freeman Hotel, this small zoo is ideal for school groups and young children. Its resident animals include Nubian goats, wallabies, miniature horses, and American bison.

Directly across from the Freeman Hotel and the zoo, the **Cashie Wetlands Walk** leads visitors atop a boardwalk running beside a canal and through a hardwood river-bottom wetland. Signs clearly identify the various trees, including bald cypresses, tupelo gums, red osier dogwoods (*Cornus stolonifera*), and overcup oaks (*Quercus lyrata*). An accompanying brochure provides information about wetland flora and fauna and the critical role wetlands play in maintaining water quality. Canoes are available for loan for those who wish to paddle out the canal and on to the Cashie River.

The **Roanoke/Cashie River Center** (252-794-2001), located at the corner of U.S. 17 and Sutton Drive, also has a river-front boardwalk and canoe ramp. Operated by the Partnership for the Sounds, the center features hands-on exhibits, a diorama of local bottom-land habitats, artifacts from the region's past, and educational wetland ponds. The center is open from 10 A.M. to 4 P.M. Tuesday through Saturday.

FOR MORE INFORMATION
Windsor-Bertie County Chamber of Commerce, P.O. Box 572, Windsor, N.C. 27983 (252-794-4277; www.albemarle-nc.com/windsor)

Hope Plantation, the magnificently restored home of North Carolina Governor David Stone

Hope Plantation

Four miles west of Windsor amidst the cotton fields of Bertie County, a remarkable plantation house has survived virtually intact through 200 years. The home of David Stone, a Princeton-educated lawyer, planter, and North Carolina governor, Hope Plantation reflects the prosperity of the slave-based tobacco-and-corn economy of northeastern North Carolina during the late 18th and early 19th centuries. Stone celebrated his prosperity in 1803 by building a grand

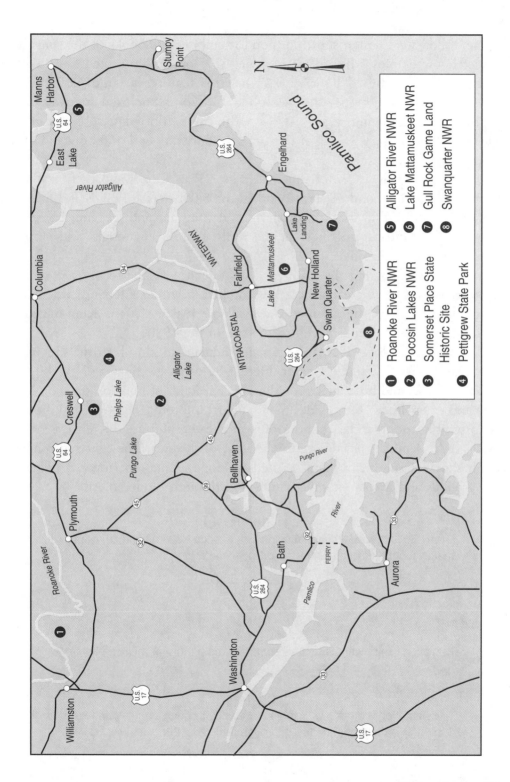

Legend

- ① Roanoke River NWR
- ② Pocosin Lakes NWR
- ③ Somerset Place State Historic Site
- ④ Pettigrew State Park
- ⑤ Alligator River NWR
- ⑥ Lake Mattamuskeet NWR
- ⑦ Gull Rock Game Land
- ⑧ Swanquarter NWR

N

Pamlico Sound

Stumpy Point

Manns Harbor

East Lake

Alligator River

Columbia

WATERWAY

INTRACOASTAL

Fairfield

Lake Mattamuskeet

Lake Landing

New Holland

Swan Quarter

Engelhard

94

U.S. 264

U.S. 264

Alligator Lake

Phelps Lake

Creswell

Pungo Lake

Plymouth

U.S. 64

U.S. 64

Roanoke River

Williamston

U.S. 17

Washington

Bellhaven

45

99

45

32

Bath

FERRY

92

Pungo River

Pamlico River

Aurora

33

33

U.S. 264

U.S. 17

home, following a design shown in popular architecture books of the time. The manor house employs the Palladian model of a square, hip-roofed block with a pedimented, two-tiered portico. The interior features a large parlor where guests were greeted before they were led up a long, enclosed stairway into a 20-by-30-foot drawing room. Also on the upper floor are a ballroom and Stone's private library, which at the time contained over 1,400 books in glass-fronted bookcases.

Like most plantations of the time, Hope Plantation was largely self-sufficient. More than a hundred slaves worked the 8,000 acres of fields and forest. A gristmill, a sawmill, a blacksmith shop, and spinning and weaving houses allowed for the creation of most of the tools, building materials, and clothing needed by the occupants.

Along with touring the main house, you can view the reconstructed dairy and meat house, a re-created detached kitchen, a winter kitchen, gardens, and an orchard. Also on the grounds and available for tour is the **King-Bazemore House**, built in 1763 and moved to the site in the 1980s.

Visitors to Hope Plantation are introduced to this historic site in the Roanoke-Chowan Heritage Center. Here, you can view films and exhibits and examine books and brochures providing background information on the plantation and its environs. Tour guides then conduct a tour of the home and grounds. An assembly room, a classroom, a 60-seat theater, and a conference room are available for seminars promoting the heritage of the area. The center also houses a gift shop offering many items related to Hope Plantation. You can picnic on the grounds and hike a 1.5-mile nature trail through Hope Forest.

DIRECTIONS
From U.S. 13 Bypass around Windsor, turn west on N.C. 308 and drive approximately four miles to the entrance to Hope Plantation.

ACTIVITIES
Touring historic homes, picnicking, hiking

FACILITIES
Reception center with assembly room, classroom, 60-seat theater, conference room, restrooms, and gift shop

DATES
The plantation is open 10 A.M. to 4 P.M. Monday through Saturday and 2 P.M. to 5 P.M. on Sunday from January 3 through December 20.

RESTAURANTS IN WINDSOR

Bunn's Barbecue
127 North King Street, Windsor; 252-794-2274
Inexpensive

This friendly, informal eatery is a must-see for visitors to Windsor. Located in a small wood-frame building constructed in the mid-19th century as a doctor's office, it was later converted to a gas station and, finally, a restaurant serving excellent pork barbecue, cornbread, and Coke in bottles. The walls are decorated with old photos of Windsor and gas-station memorabilia.

Crossroads Diner
129 U.S. 13/17 South, Windsor; 252-794-2078
Inexpensive

This local favorite serves home-cooked meals. It is open for dinner Thursday, Friday, and Saturday.

LODGINGS IN WINDSOR

King Street Bed and Breakfast
401 South King Street, Windsor; 252-794-2255
www.kingstreetbb.com
Moderate

This four-bedroom bed-and-breakfast is located in one of the oldest houses in Windsor. Built in 1790 and remodeled several times since then, it has been occupied by a number of renowned citizens, including Elisha Rhodes, a United States consul under President Van Buren; William Henry, one of the nation's first science-fiction writers; and David Outlaw, a pro-Union congressman before the Civil War. Each room is distinctly decorated and furnished with period antiques.

Williamston

Located at the intersection of U.S. 17 and U.S. 64, Williamston is considered the gateway to the northern half of the sound country. English colonists exploring the Roanoke River settled here in 1730. The town was incorporated as the Martin County seat in 1779 and thrived as a shipping port for nearly a century.

Several early homes and public buildings have been preserved as the **Williamston Historic District**. The former **Martin County Courthouse** at 215 East Main Street is one of the oldest courthouses in North Carolina. Constructed in 1885, it is considered an excellent blend of Italian and Victorian elements. The **Williamston Historic Commercial District** includes parts of the seven-block downtown area bounded by Main, Watts, Church, and Haughton Streets.

Just outside Williamston is the **Senator Bob Martin Eastern Agricultural Center** (252-792-5802), which sponsors horse shows, circuses, motocross races, and other events in its 108,000-square-foot indoor coliseum. It includes a convention center that can host meetings, receptions, and shows for up to a thousand people. Outside are dressage areas and cross-country courses.

FOR MORE INFORMATION
Martin County Travel and Tourism, P.O. Box 382, Williamston, N.C. 27892 (800-776-8566; www.visitmartincounty.com)

RESTAURANTS IN THE WILLIAMSTON AREA

R & C Restaurant
210 Washington Street, Williamston; 252-792-3161
Inexpensive

The R & C serves down-home country cooking in the heart of

the old mercantile district. The local tourism office encourages visitors to "try some great country cooking at R & C Restaurant." Dinner is offered Monday through Friday.

Sunny Side Oyster Bar
1105 Washington Street, Williamston; 252-792-3416
Moderate

Named for its sunny exposure, this restaurant is located in a small, gable-fronted wood structure built in 1935. Sunny Side specializes in oysters, shrimp, and scallops. It serves dinner only and is open only during oyster season—that is, the months with an *r* in their name.

Cypress Grill
1520 Stewart Street, Jamesville; 252-792-4175
Inexpensive

Featured in the December 2000 issue of *Smithsonian* magazine, the Cypress Grill is one of the last of the seasonal herring shacks still open in North Carolina. It serves fish and shellfish caught from the sound. The specialty is fried herring rolled in cornmeal and served with collard greens and hush puppies. The grill is open the second weekend in January through the last weekend of April.

LODGINGS IN WILLIAMSTON

Big Mill Bed and Breakfast
1607 Big Mill Road, Williamston; 252-792-8787
www.bigmill.com
Moderate

This two-bedroom inn overlooks a private pond and grape orchard.

Comfort Inn
100 East Boulevard, Williamston; 252-792-8400
www.choicehotels.com
Moderate

This 59-room motel offers continental breakfast and an exercise room.

Days Inn
103 West Boulevard, Williamston; 800-329-7466 or 252-792-4168
www.daysinn.com
Moderate

> The amenities at this 46-room motel include a swimming pool and an on-site restaurant.

Hampton Inn Williamston
1099 Hampton Court, Williamston; 252-809-1100
www.hamptoninn.com
Moderate

> Opened in 2002, this is the flagship of Williamston's motels. Amenities include an outdoor pool, a fitness center, and a game room. Guests enjoy a deluxe continental breakfast.

Holiday Inn
101 East Boulevard, Williamston; 252-792-3184
www.holiday-inn.com.
Moderate

> This motel features a swimming pool, a restaurant, and a lounge. Pets are accepted.

Lower Roanoke River Wetlands / Roanoke River Paddle Trail

For generations, the Lower Roanoke River and its labyrinthine network of forested tributaries, channels, and oxbows were known only to local hunters and fishermen. But beginning in the late 1990s, conservation groups worked together to build a network of canoe trails and camping platforms that provide adventurous paddlers with access to this natural oasis. The Roanoke River backwaters offer a swamp experience unlike any other in the mid-Atlantic.

The Roanoke River begins in the Blue Ridge Mountains of Virginia, traverses the Piedmont of that state and North Carolina, and settles into a wide, forested flood plain as it enters the coastal plain and merges with Albemarle Sound. The Lower Roanoke River wetlands contain the largest and least-disturbed complex of bottom-land and riparian forests on the eastern seaboard. River otters, white-tailed deer, black bears, bobcats, beavers, and minks thrive in these bottom lands. The flood plain supports the highest diversity of breeding birds in the North Carolina coastal plain, including some 44 species of Neotropical migrants. Wood ducks thrive in the forested flood plain. Barred owls are ever-present, their loud hooting echoing through the forests in winter and spring. The watershed is home to at least seven heron rookeries. The river itself is considered the state's most critical spawning area for striped bass. Springtime fishing for striped bass with spinning rod or fly rod is exceptional.

Beginning in the 1980s, the North Carolina chapter of The Nature Conservancy, in conjunction with the North Carolina Wildlife Resources Commission, the United States Fish and Wildlife Service, and the Georgia-Pacific Corporation (now Plum Creek Corporation), began to purchase land in the flood plain for the purpose of preserving this unique habitat. Today, more than 60,000 acres are protected by a combination of landowners. The federal government manages 18,000 acres as the **Roanoke River National Wildlife Refuge**. The state of North Carolina manages approximately 16,000 acres in various parcels as part of the **Roanoke River Game Lands**. Approximately 24,000 acres, including **Devil's Gut Preserve**, are managed by The Nature Conservancy.

To provide access to these wetlands, the nonprofit Roanoke River Partners, in conjunction with The Nature Conservancy and the former Georgia-Pacific

Canoeists pass cypress knees lining the shore of Gardner Creek, one of the Roanoke River Paddle Trails.

Corporation, developed the Roanoke River Paddle Trail, a system of high- and low-water trails through the heart of the bottom lands. As of this writing, seven wooden platforms have been erected along various creeks for overnight camping. Each platform accommodates six to eight people. Portable toilets are provided. When complete, this system will cover more than 200 miles of the Roanoke and its tributaries, eventually leading to Albemarle Sound. The best time to paddle the trail is during the spring, when the cypresses and tupelos are in bloom, the woods are filled with migratory songbirds, and the legendary barred owls are hooting. Ospreys, bald eagles, bright yellow prothonotary warblers, and a variety of wading birds are commonly seen on these outings. Fishing for bream, largemouth bass, crappie, catfish, and bowfin is usually quite productive. Fall is another good time, although hunters may be active in the area. You can paddle the trail on your own or with local guide services such as **Rock Rest Adventures** (919-542-5502). Water levels fluctuate over the course of the year with rainfall and the release of water through upstream dams, so it is important to know where and when you can travel. Advance reservations are required for use of the platforms.

DIRECTIONS
There are numerous access points to the Lower Roanoke River. The most popular put-in for canoeists is at Roberson's Marina on Gardner Creek. From the intersection of U.S. 64 and U.S. 17 Bypass in Williamston, drive approximately eight miles east on U.S. 64. Roberson's Marina is on the north side of the highway.

ACTIVITIES
Canoeing, camping, hunting, fishing

FACILITIES
Boat launches, camping platforms

DATES
The Roanoke River lands are accessible year-round.

FEES
A fee is charged to use the camping platforms.

CLOSEST TOWN
Williamston

FOR MORE INFORMATION

For a map of the river and the location of camping platforms, contact Roanoke River Partners, P.O. Box 488, Windsor, N.C. 27983 (252-794-2793). For platform reservations, call 252-794-6501 or visit www.roanokeriverpartners.org. For information on Roanoke River National Wildlife Refuge, contact P.O. Box 430, Windsor, N.C. 27983 (252-794-3808; http://roanokeriver.fws.gov). For information on the Roanoke River Game Lands, contact North Carolina Wildlife Resources Commission, 1701 Mail Service Center, Raleigh, N.C. 27699 (919-733-7291).

# Plymouth

Plymouth is one of those small towns that people tend to rush past on their way to the Outer Banks. By the looks of the buildings along U.S. 64, there is little here other than retail establishments, fast-food restaurants, and motels. Yet just a few blocks to the north on the banks of the Roanoke River lies a historical gem that is well worth visiting.

Plymouth is the oldest incorporated town in Washington County. During its heyday, it was the fifth-largest port in North Carolina. Active trade with Northern cities such as Baltimore bonded Plymouth's citizenry with the North. At the outbreak of the Civil War, Washington County citizens were split roughly equally between Confederate and Union sympathizers. This dual loyalty, combined with the town's key location, led to a significant battle during the Civil War.

In 1862, Plymouth fell to the naval forces of Union general Ambrose Burnside as part of his campaign to gain control of the coastline and impose a blockade on Confederate ports. Union forces held the town for two years, building a network of forts and entrenchments and mingling with the local citizenry. During their occupation, Union forces succeeded in recruiting more than 5,000 local boys into the Northern army, including more than 2,000 black troops.

In April 1864, unnerved by this Union force to his rear, General Robert E. Lee ordered General Robert F. Hoke to lead a joint army-navy expedition against the town. The Confederates built an ironclad ram, the CSS *Albemarle*, in a cornfield upstream to take on the wooden Union vessels anchored off Plymouth.

Moving in concert, 15,000 Confederate infantrymen assaulted the town on the afternoon of April 17. Under heavy bombardment from the Union navy, they were unable to make much headway. Then, in the early hours of April 19, the *Albemarle* arrived on the scene and rammed and sank the USS *Southfield*. The Union navy retreated, and Confederate troops took the town.

Six months later, the Union gained its revenge when an ingeniously designed steam launch rigged for silent running and outfitted with a torpedo on a 32-foot pole slipped past the Confederate pickets and rammed and sank the *Albemarle*. Union forces stormed the town a second time and held it through the end of the war.

As a result of the heavy bombardment, only half a dozen buildings in Plymouth survived the conflict. These and other structures are now included in the **Plymouth Historic District**, which may be easily seen by taking a walking tour. The district includes such notable buildings as **Grace Episcopal Church** (c. 1861) at 107 Madison Street, the **Latham House** (c. 1850) at 311 East Main Street, and the **Windley-Ausbon House** (c. 1861) at 302 Washington Street, which still contains Civil War bullet holes. On Water Street at the beautiful downtown waterfront, you can tour a reconstruction of the **Roanoke River Lighthouse**, which stood on this site from 1866 to 1885.

The town maintains public boating access and docking facilities on the Roanoke River.

FOR MORE INFORMATION
Washington County Chamber of Commerce, 701 Washington Street, Plymouth, N.C. 27962 (252-793-4804)

◯◯Port O'Plymouth Museum

Located in the old Seaboard Coastline Railroad depot on Water Street, this excellent museum contains a wealth of artifacts from the Civil War, and from the Battle of Plymouth in particular. Most of the weapons on display are from the actual battle. Letters sent by Union soldiers to their families describing life in Plymouth make fascinating reading. The original battle orders for the Confederate assault on Plymouth are on display, as is the Union flag that flew over the town. Curators even tracked down (in a house in Buffalo, New York) and secured the backup torpedo designed to sink the *Albemarle*.

Outdoors on the river, you can see a 63-foot-long replica of the *Albemarle*. During summer, staff take this boat out on the river at noon and fire off its cannon.

On the third weekend of April, as part of what is called Living History Weekend, the museum celebrates the Battle of Plymouth with reenactments by costumed soldiers, lectures by historians and authors, and torchlight tours. This increasingly popular event is a must-see for Civil War buffs.

DIRECTIONS
From U.S. 64 in Plymouth, turn north on Washington Street, follow it to its intersection with Water Street, and turn right. The museum is two blocks down Water Street.

ACTIVITIES
Touring museum, picnicking

DATES
During the summer, the museum is open 9 A.M. to 4 P.M. Monday through Saturday and 1 P.M. to 4 P.M. on Sunday. During winter, it is open 9 A.M. to 4 P.M. Tuesday through Saturday.

FEES
An admission fee is charged.

FOR MORE INFORMATION
Port O' Plymouth Museum, P.O. Box 296, Plymouth, N.C. 27962 (252-793-1377)

Restaurants in Plymouth

Ram *Albemarle* Restaurant
303 U.S. 64, Plymouth; 252-793-3388
Inexpensive

This restaurant specializes in home-style country cooking. It is open daily for breakfast and lunch and on Thursday and Friday for dinner.

LODGINGS IN PLYMOUTH

Four Gables Bed and Breakfast
109 West Main Street, Plymouth; 252-793-6696
www.fourgablesinn.com
Moderate

>Located in an 1870 Gothic Victorian home, the Four Gables stands in the heart of the Plymouth Historic District. Each of the four bedrooms is filled with period antiques. The backyard garden is shaded by magnolia, pecan, and Japanese maple trees.

Holiday Inn Express
840 U.S. 64, Plymouth; 252-793-4700
Moderate

>This 60-unit hotel has an outdoor pool and a fitness center.

Port O' Plymouth Inn
510 U.S. 64, Plymouth; 800-545-8548 or 252-793-5006
Moderate

>The amenities at this 61-room inn include an outdoor swimming pool and free continental breakfast. Fishermen are welcome.

Pettigrew State Park

In the heart of the table-flat coastal plain of the Albemarle-Pamlico Peninsula lie four large, oval lakes—Phelps, Pungo, New, and Mattamuskeet. Scientists have long puzzled over the origin of these lakes. They sit at the highest elevation in the area and are not fed by any natural rivers or streams. The most widely accepted theory is that they lie in depressions formed by wind and wave action when the ocean covered this section of North Carolina.

Lake Phelps is the second-largest of the four. The lake and much of its immediate shoreline are contained within Pettigrew State Park, named after Confederate brigadier general James Johnston Pettigrew, who was born and is buried here. Lake Phelps is most famous for the prehistoric Indian artifacts recovered from its bed since 1985, when a combination of drought and pumping to fight a nearby forest fire dramatically lowered the lake level. Fishermen and park personnel began noticing artifacts on the lake bottom, including pots, stone tools, and a large number of dugout canoes. Approximately 30 canoes have been discovered to date, the oldest of which has been carbon-dated to 2400 B.C. Two of these canoes are on display in a lakeside pavilion at the park.

Pettigrew State Park is also famous for the huge trees in the narrow band of virgin forest that rims the lake. Two national-champion trees—a swamp bay (*Persea palustris*) and a coastal plain willow (*Salix carolinina*)—have been recorded here. So, too, have the state-champion paw paw (*Asimina atriloba*), elderberry (*Sambucus canadensis*), devil's walking stick (*Aralia spinosa*), sweet bay (*Magnolia virginiana*), and buttonbush (*Cephalanthus occidentalis*). These trees are unmarked and not on any trail, so the best way to view them is to join the annual Big Tree Walk, which takes place the Sunday prior to Thanksgiving.

Pettigrew has a number of short but interesting hiking trails. Three trails of varying length lead from park headquarters to overlooks along the lakeshore. The **Bee Tree Trail** (1.3 miles one way) is excellent for birding on early mornings between late April and mid-June. Breeding species that are common and easy to see include yellow-billed cuckoos (*Coccyzus americanus*), Acadian flycatchers (*Empidonax virescens*), wood thrushes (*Hylocichla mustelina*), white-eyed and red-eyed vireos (*Vireo griseus* and *V. olivaceus*), Northern parulas (*Parula americana*), prothonotary warblers (*Prothonotaria citrea*), ovenbirds (*Seiurus aurocapillus*), and indigo buntings (*Passerina cyanea*). The **Moccasin Trail** (2.8 miles one way) follows the northern shore of the lake, passing through a section of forest that contains a number of state-champion trees. The **Moratoc Trail** (4.2 miles one way) begins at the end of the Moccasin Trail and travels along the northwestern lakeshore to Cypress Point. This trail is open to mountain bikers as well as hikers.

Among the wildlife along the wooded shores of Lake Phelps are black bears, white-tailed deer, opossums, gray foxes, bobcats, raccoons, minks, muskrats, and otters. A variety of owls and hawks frequent the forest, and kingfishers and bald eagles are commonly seen on the lakeshore. Waterfowl are largely absent from the lake in summer, but tundra swans and Canada geese are frequently seen in December. An observation tower for viewing winter waterfowl is on the south side of Lake Phelps at the end of Lake Shore Drive.

Lake Phelps is also known for its excellent fishing. Largemouth bass, yellow perch, and pumpkinseed are the favorite game fish. Boats on trailers can be launched from a boat ramp near the park headquarters. Cypress Point contains a canoe launch and a fishing pier. A fishing area is located beside the observation tower at the end of Lake Shore Drive.

Family camping and group camping are allowed in the park. Picnic tables are set up near the shore.

DIRECTIONS
From U.S. 64 at the town of Creswell, turn south on Main Street and drive to the intersection with Thirtyfoot Canal Road. Turn south on Thirtyfoot Canal Road, then east on Lake Shore Road. The park office is immediately on the right.

ACTIVITIES
Hiking, biking, camping, fishing, bird-watching, picnicking, boating

FACILITIES
The park office has restrooms. The outdoor pavilion has displays. Cypress Point also has restrooms.

DATES
The park is open daily from 8 A.M. to 6 P.M. November through February; from 8 A.M. to 7 P.M. during March and October; from 8 A.M. to 8 P.M. during April, May, and September; and from 8 A.M. to 9 P.M. June through August.

FEES
None

CLOSEST TOWN
Creswell is 6.5 miles away.

FOR MORE INFORMATION
Pettigrew State Park, 2252 Lake Shore Road, Creswell, N.C. 27928 (252-797-4475; http://ils.unc.edu/parkproject/ncparks.html)

Lake Phelps, where more than 30 prehistoric canoes have been recovered

⌒⌒Somerset Place State Historic Site

Within Pettigrew State Park just to the east of park headquarters is Somerset Place State Historic Site. One of the most complete collections of antebellum plantation buildings in North Carolina, it is well worth a half-day visit.

In 1785, wealthy Edenton merchant Josiah Collins joined with two other businessmen to purchase 100,000 acres adjoining Lake Phelps. Collins and his partners had previously failed in their attempt to drain Lake Phelps for conversion to agricultural land. But by constructing canals to drain the surrounding swamps, Collins now succeeded in creating one of the state's largest and most prosperous rice, corn, and wheat plantations. In addition to the drainage canals, slaves dug a six-mile-long canal connecting Lake Phelps with the Scuppernong River, so crops and hardwood timber could be shipped to Albemarle Sound, ensuring the plantation's commercial success. Lined with ancient cypresses, this canal is still visible as you approach the plantation.

In 1838, Collins's grandson, Josiah Collins III, built a magnificent 14-room Greek Revival mansion on the northeast shore of Lake Phelps. That mansion has survived intact and is now open for tours. Various outbuildings including a kitchen, a kitchen storehouse, and an icehouse surround the manor house. A smaller residence known as the Colony House, which served as a boarding school for the Collins children, is now the visitor center. A reconstructed slave cabin was opened in 1997.

The Collins family owned more than 300 slaves, all of whom lived on the grounds. Detailed records of them survive to this day. Those records have enabled the descendants of the slaves to trace their lineage back to Somerset and beyond. Since the summer of 1986, descendants of 21 slave families have held reunions at Somerset Place approximately every five years. The 1996 reunion drew more than 2,000 people.

The surviving buildings and records, along with ongoing archaeological digs on the grounds, have produced a veritable treasure trove of information about plantation life during the century leading up to the Civil War. You can gain an appreciation for the lifestyle through guided tours of the lavishly furnished manor house and the slave cabin, as well as from the displays and documents in the museum at the visitor center.

Pocosin Lakes National Wildlife Refuge

Pocosin Lakes National Wildlife Refuge encompasses a 113,600-acre patchwork of land in the center of the Albemarle-Pamlico Peninsula. Even finding the borders of this refuge can be a daunting prospect. The flat, largely treeless expanse offers few visual landmarks, and the destinations of the roads within the refuge are sometimes a mystery. Visitors may be forgiven if they think there is nothing here but acre upon acre of weeds with a couple of lakes somewhere in between. But for all its shortcomings as a tourist destination (remember, this is a refuge, not a park), Pocosin Lakes holds some great wildlife-viewing opportunities for those willing to be persistent.

Black bear cubs play on field roads in Pocosin Lakes National Wildlife Refuge.

Most of the refuge was once part of an enormous agricultural and mining operation known as First Colony Farms. During the energy crisis of the late 1970s, First Colony announced plans to mine peat from the land for conversion to methanol. Some peat was experimentally mined, but the project proved economically and environmentally unsound and was eventually abandoned. First Colony Farms went bankrupt, and the land was later purchased by the Richard King Mellon Foundation and the Conservation Fund. In 1990, the two foundations donated 93,000 acres of land to the United States Fish and Wildlife Service.

The refuge includes pocosins, lakes, marshes, second-growth forests, agricultural fields, and grasslands that have grown up on former cropland and timberland. A grid of dirt roads and drainage canals built by former commercial enterprises provides access to the refuge. However, these roads and canals also disrupt the natural movement of water, and the refuge managers are breaching certain canals in an attempt to restore some of that water flow. They are also seeking to reestablish native Atlantic white cedars on about 800 acres.

While refuge managers are returning some parts of Pocosin Lakes to their natural state, they continue to allow farmers to grow corn, soybeans, winter wheat, and milo on 1,200 acres in the Pungo Unit at the southern end of the refuge. A percentage of the crop is left as food for wintering waterfowl and resident wildlife, providing excellent opportunities for viewing. During summer evenings, you'll have a good chance of seeing black bears as they emerge from the woods to feed in the fields of corn and soybeans. These fields are also prime habitat for horned larks (*Eremophilia alpestris*), lapland longspurs (*Calcarius lapponicus*), and short-eared owls (*Asio flammeus*). Barred owls (*Strix varia*), great horned owls

(*Bubo virginianus*), red-shouldered hawks (*Buteo lineatus*), marsh hawks (*Circus cyaneus*), Cooper's hawks (*Accipiter cooperii*), sharp-shinned hawks (*Accipiter striatus*), American kestrels (*Falco sparverius*), screech owls (*Otus asio*), and black vultures (*Coragyps atratus*) are also common here. During the winter months, tundra swans, snow geese, and numerous species of ducks frequent the area in large numbers. Pocosin Lakes provides habitat for a number of threatened and endangered species, including red wolves, bald eagles, red-cockaded woodpeckers, and the occasional peregrine falcon.

The refuge allows hunting for white-tailed deer and small game. State seasons and bag limits apply. Archery hunting for deer is permitted in the Pungo Unit during state seasons, except for the month of October, when gun hunting is permitted. Check with the refuge office regarding permit hunts and other opportunities.

DIRECTIONS

There are numerous access points to the wildlife refuge. The refuge office and visitor center are located off-site at the Walter B. Jones Center for the Sounds on U.S. 64 in the town of Columbia. The Pungo Unit is accessible off N.C. 45 near its intersection with N.C. 99. Follow the signs to the refuge entrance.

ACTIVITIES

Wildlife observation, environmental education, hunting, fishing

FACILITIES

An observation tower and an information kiosk are located on the south side of Pungo Lake. The visitor center in Columbia includes a gift shop, an auditorium, laboratories, classrooms, and an outdoor classroom with an interpretive boardwalk along the Scuppernong River.

DATES

The refuge is open during daylight hours year-round. The office is open from 7:30 A.M. to 4:00 P.M. Monday through Friday.

FEES

None

CLOSEST TOWN

The visitor center is in Columbia.

FOR MORE INFORMATION

Pocosin Lakes National Wildlife Refuge, P.O. Box 329, Columbia, N.C. 27925 (252-796-3004; http://pocosinlakes.fws.gov)

Columbia

Like Plymouth, Columbia is a town that tourists tend to rush through on their way to the Outer Banks. Columbia, too, is well worth a stop.

You should first check in at the **Tyrrell County Visitors Center** (252-796-0723), located at the corner of U.S. 64 and South Ludington Drive on the banks of the Scuppernong River. The staff can provide a wealth of firsthand information and brochures on local attractions. Out the back door, the 0.75-mile **Scuppernong River Interpretive Boardwalk** leads through a bottom-land swamp along the cypress-lined banks of the Scuppernong. This handicapped-accessible walkway's overlooks and interpretive signposts make it easy to appreciate the local flora and fauna.

Beside the visitor center at 205 South Ludington Drive is the **Walter B. Jones Center for the Sounds** (252-797-4431). Opened in June 2002, the center serves as the headquarters for Pocosin Lakes National Wildlife Refuge. It contains mounted specimens of red wolf and black bear, as well as a gift shop, an auditorium, laboratories, and indoor and outdoor classrooms for the occasional outreach programs.

"Downtown" Columbia contains a host of attractive 19th- and early-20th-century homes and churches, most located within the **Columbia Historic District**. Maps for a walking tour of the district are available at the visitor center. The centerpiece of the historic district is the **Tyrrell County Courthouse** at the corner of Main and Broad Streets. This Italianate structure was built in 1903 and contains records dating to 1832.

Downtown is also home to a number of contemporary cultural attractions. **Pocosin Arts** (252-796-2787) is a studio that conducts classes in pottery, weaving, dance, blacksmithing, glassmaking, and more. The studio's directors incorporate art, history, and ecology in their programs by exploring local craft-making, Native American techniques, and native materials. Works by area artists are displayed and sold in the adjacent gift shop. The **Columbia Theater Cultural Resources Center** (252-766-0200) at 304 Main Street has displays on the history of fishing, farming, and forestry in Tyrrell County. Films and storytelling by locals such as "Hunter Jim" bring the heritage of the region to life.

The town of Columbia maintains docks along the Scuppernong River, where pleasure craft cruising Albemarle Sound or the nearby Intracoastal Waterway can tie up. The Scuppernong has been designated part of the Albemarle Region

Canoe and Small Boat Trails System. Canoeists and kayakers can put in at the visitor center for Pocosin Lakes National Wildlife Refuge and paddle as far as 17 miles upstream. The lower portion of the river is lined with beautiful cypresses and the upper portion with hardwood swamps. Several tributaries allow canoeists to penetrate deeper into the swamps.

FOR MORE INFORMATION
Tyrrell County Visitors Center, P.O. Box 55, Columbia, N.C. 27925 (252-796-0723; www.parternshipforthesounds.org)

RESTAURANTS IN COLUMBIA

McClees Restaurant
203 Main Street, Columbia; 252-796-1567
Inexpensive

Located in the heart of downtown, McClees serves basic home-cooked meals. It is open for lunch Monday through Saturday and for dinner on Saturday only.

LODGINGS IN COLUMBIA

Heart's Delight Bed and Breakfast
802 Green Street, Columbia; 252-796-1778
Moderate

This three-bedroom inn is located just outside the historic district. A full breakfast comes with the price of the room.

The River House Bed and Breakfast
Bridge and Water Streets, Columbia; 252-796-1855
www.river-house.com
Moderate

Located just off the Scuppernong River, this inn has three bedrooms and shared baths. Bikes, canoes, and fishing poles are available for loan. A three-course gourmet breakfast is included with the price of the room.

Alligator River
National Wildlife Refuge

For those who want to experience the feeling of being in the wild, Alligator River National Wildlife Refuge (ARNWR) is the place to go. The refuge is only a 13-mile drive from bustling Manteo, but visitors may feel they are in a distant land, especially when driving the lonely back roads at dusk. Having been timbered and mined in the recent past, ARNWR is not the most scenic refuge. But it is vast and offers a good chance to see wildlife, particularly black bears.

Located at the eastern end of the Albemarle-Pamlico Peninsula between the Alligator River and Croatan Sound, ARNWR is a patchwork of pocosins, wetlands, second-growth forests, and open fields. This land was hunted, timbered, and farmed for generations by a host of individuals and corporations. The Prudential Insurance Company was the latest corporate owner. In 1984, at the urging of the North Carolina chapter of The Nature Conservancy, Prudential donated 118,000 acres of timberland to the federal government. At the time, this constituted the largest gift of land (in terms of acreage) by a private corporation for conservation purposes in United States history. The Nature Conservancy purchased and donated additional plots totaling 25,000 acres. Together, these comprise ARNWR.

Today, the refuge contains 152,195 acres of some of the wildest land in eastern North Carolina. The interior grid of canals and dirt roads is a reminder of the large-scale timbering and farming that went on here in the recent past. The tangle of forest in between is so dense that local hunters say a deer has to pack a lunch to get across it. In 1987, the size and remoteness of the refuge prompted the United States Fish and Wildlife Service to choose this as the site for the reintroduction of the red wolf (*Canis rufus*), a smaller cousin of the gray wolf. Although a hundred or more of these animals roam the refuge today, they are extremely reclusive and are thus rarely seen. However, you can learn about and very likely hear the wolves by participating in one of the evening "wolf howlings" sponsored by refuge staff during the spring, summer, and fall. Contact the refuge at 252-473-1131, extension 243, or access its website for a schedule.

While you may not see any wolves, you will very likely see black bears if you come on a summer evening. Along Milltail, Long Curve, Grouse, and Bear Roads in the refuge, fields planted in corn and soybeans act as magnets for the normally shy bruins. Bears come out to feed on most summer evenings and can easily be photographed from a vehicle. Maps available at the information kiosk at the Milltail Road entrance indicate the best route for wildlife viewing.

Two short trails allow you to glimpse small portions of the refuge on foot. The **Creef Cut Wildlife Trail** (0.5 mile one way) is a paved, handicapped-accessible trail that overlooks a moist soil-management area to the south and a freshwater marsh to the north. A handicapped-accessible portable toilet and a fishing platform are located at the head of the trail. Interpretive plaques identifying and describing various aspects of the environment are scattered along the way. The **Sandy Ridge Wildlife Trail** (0.7 mile one way) follows an old roadbed along a man-made canal, then passes through a cypress swamp atop a 2,000-foot-long boardwalk. Sphagnum moss, carnivorous sundew plants (*Drosera capillaris*), and young Atlantic white cedars grow beside the boardwalk. The trail is handicapped-accessible and has a portable toilet at its head.

DIRECTIONS
From Manteo, drive west on U.S. 64 approximately 13.5 miles to the Milltail Road access point. The information kiosk and the Creef Cut Wildlife Trail are located at this entrance. The Buffalo City Road entrance is approximately 3.5 miles west on U.S. 64. Follow Buffalo City Road 2.2 miles to the Sandy Ridge Wildlife Trail and the lower Milltail Creek put-in.

ACTIVITIES
Wildlife viewing, canoeing, hiking, fishing, hunting, "wolf howling"

FACILITIES
An information kiosk and a handicapped-accessible portable toilet are located at the head of the Creef Cut Wildlife Trail. A portable toilet is also available at the head of the Sandy Ridge Wildlife Trail and the lower Milltail Creek put-in.

DATES
The refuge is open during daylight hours year-round.

FEES
No fee is charged to explore the refuge. Guided canoe tours are available during the warm months for a small fee.

CLOSEST TOWN
Manns Harbor is six miles away.

FOR MORE INFORMATION
Alligator River National Wildlife Refuge, P.O. Box 1969, Manteo, N.C. 27954 (252-473-1131; http://alligatorriver.fws.gov)

The Red Wolf

The rarely seen red wolf prowls the Alligator River National Wildlife Refuge.
©Jody Duggins

Red wolves (*Canis rufus*) once roamed the entire Southeast. But by the 1970s, they were reduced to a tiny population living in Louisiana and Texas. Fearing their impending extinction, the United States Fish and Wildlife Service captured the remaining animals and bred them in captivity to increase their numbers.

Wolves were first released into Alligator River National Wildlife Refuge in 1987. As with the reintroduction of gray wolves into Yellowstone Park, the red-wolf release sparked opposition from local residents, who feared the animals would threaten livestock, pets, and perhaps humans. While some attacks on livestock and pets were recorded early on, the wolves appear to have adapted to the wild. They feed primarily on deer, rodents, and raccoons.

Today, approximately a hundred red wolves roam the refuge and adjacent lands. They are rarely seen, but visitors can hear them by participating in one of the "wolf howlings" regularly sponsored by the refuge.

Milltail Creek Canoe and Kayak Trails

For those who want a more intimate view of ARNWR than is offered by roads or short foot trails, the Milltail Creek Canoe and Kayak Trails provide an excellent option. Two put-ins allow paddlers to explore the upper and lower reaches of the creek. The more popular put-in is at the end of Buffalo City Road. From here, you can explore a wide, slow stretch of Milltail Creek, looking for alligators and turtles among the lily pads and reveling in the songs of the more than 30 species of Neotropical migrants that breed in the forest.

Canoe trips of varying distances are possible, ranging from a two-mile one-way paddle to the end of Sawyer Lake to a 5.5-mile one-way trek to the bridge at Milltail Road. The latter trip can also be run in reverse by putting in at Milltail Road and paddling down to Buffalo City Road. If you're feeling truly adventurous, you can paddle down Milltail Creek into the wide expanse of the Alligator River. From here, you can paddle any distance north or south, exploring the various channels that flow in from the refuge.

Several outfitters, including **Kitty Hawk Sports** (800-948-0759) and **Kitty Hawk Kites/Carolina Outdoors** (877-359-8447), offer guided trips down Milltail Creek.

Lake Mattamuskeet National Wildlife Refuge

Lake Mattamuskeet appears as a misplaced sea amidst the vast agricultural plain of the Albemarle-Pamlico Peninsula. At 40,000 acres, it is the largest natural lake in North Carolina, yet it averages only 2.5 feet in depth. As with the other lakes in the region, its origin is a mystery. What is known is that it is a magnet for waterfowl, especially in early winter, when tens of thousands of ducks, geese, and swans descend on the lake. Tundra swans are the main attraction, but the list of other species that use the refuge—ducks, wading birds, land birds, and raptors—is practically endless.

Lake Mattamuskeet was not always valued as a waterfowl habitat. As early as 1789, drainage projects were undertaken to try to lower the lake's water level and convert its peat-rich bed into agricultural land. In 1911, the state sold the lake to the Southern Land Reclamation Company, which intended to drain it and divide the bed into farms and residential tracts, as was done at Haarlem Lake in Holland in 1853. Contractors dug a seven-mile-long outflow canal to Pamlico Sound, along with a vast network of feeder canals. They built a plant housing eight steam pumps capable of pumping 1.2 million gallons of water per minute. After changing its name to the New Holland Corporation, Southern Land laid out a town called New Holland, built a first-class hotel, and beckoned the world to come. The New Holland Corporation succeeded in partially draining the lake, but the pumps failed to perform as expected, and the soft canal banks caved in.

The North Carolina Farms Company took over the operation in 1918, building houses and stores in New Holland and constructing a 35-mile-long railroad to bring coal to the pumping plant. That company, too, was inadequately financed. It went bankrupt in 1923.

In 1925, New York real-estate developer August Hecksher purchased the land, completed work on the pumping station, completely drained the lake, and began farming the bed. By 1929, Hecksher's farm was the largest in the eastern United States, its 51 tractors tilling nearly 13,000 acres of land. Two years later, a heavy rain inundated the region, and the great pumps failed. Water poured over the canals and into the former lake bed, making harvesting impossible. Hecksher abandoned his project in 1933, leaving the last crop standing in the lake. With the pumps shut down, the lake gradually refilled, covering much of the town. In 1934, the federal government purchased 49,925 acres of the lake and its surrounding land, moved the town to higher ground (where it presently stands), and declared the lake a waterfowl sanctuary.

You can view wildlife in the refuge by car or on foot. The five-mile-long N.C. 94 causeway, which crosses the middle of the lake, is excellent for viewing waterfowl from mid-November to the first week in December. Tundra swans, Canada geese, dabbling ducks, and diving ducks often flock quite close to the causeway that time of year. At the southern end of the causeway, the refuge's entrance road forks off to the east. The impoundment to the right of the road is a good place to see wading birds in the summer and dabbling ducks, coots, and pied-billed grebes (*Podilymbus podiceps*) in winter. Beavers and muskrats are common here in the evenings year-round.

The entrance road ends at the rangers' office and **Lake Mattamuskeet Lodge**. After the government purchased New Holland Farms in 1934, Civilian Conservation Corps workers converted the pumping station into a rustic hunting and fishing lodge. They built a spiral staircase inside the old smokestack to create a 112-foot-tall observation tower. In 1981, the lodge was placed on the National Register of Historic Places. More recently, it served as a research facility and visitor center operated by the Partnership for the Sounds. In November 2000, however, architects discovered serious corrosion problems in the 85-year-old building. It has been closed indefinitely awaiting funds for renovation.

Beyond the pumping station, Wildlife Drive runs approximately two miles through brushy and wooded areas down to the lake. You're likely to see such species as bobwhite quails and prothonotary warblers on this drive.

At the eastern end of the refuge north of the Lake Landing community, a gravel road leads off U.S. 264. A parking area lies at the end of the road, and a path leads out to a network of fields and impoundments. In winter, these fields and impoundments may be covered with tundra swans, Canada geese, and snow geese. If the fields are wet, you may see common snipes, least sandpipers, and greater and lesser yellowlegs.

At the western end of the refuge, a limited-access dirt road parallels the Rose Bay Canal. The road passes through the northern edge of a wooded area known as **Salyer's Ridge Natural Area**, which is part of the refuge. This mature loblolly pine forest harbors a variety of woodpeckers and red-shouldered hawks and an occasional barred owl. Deer, otters, and bobcats are frequently seen here. One mile in, the road reaches the first impoundment. Depending upon the season, the impoundments may hold tundra swans, diving and dabbling ducks, and more.

DIRECTIONS
From the intersection of U.S. 264 and N.C. 94 in southern Hyde County, drive north on N.C. 94 for approximately 1.5 miles. The entrance road is on the right.

ACTIVITIES
Bird-watching, hiking, canoeing, fishing, hunting

FACILITIES
The Lake Mattamuskeet Lodge was closed as of the winter of 2001-2002. A restroom is available at the refuge office.

DATES
The refuge is open during daylight hours year-round. The office is open from 7:30 A.M. to 4:00 P.M. Monday through Friday; it is closed on holidays.

FEES
None

CLOSEST TOWN
Swan Quarter is 10 miles away.

FOR MORE INFORMATION
Mattamuskeet National Wildlife Refuge, 38 Mattamuskeet Refuge Road, Swan Quarter, N.C. 27885 (252-926-4021; http://mattamuskeet.fws.gov)

The Tundra Swan

The tundra swan (*Olor columbianus*), formerly called the whistling swan, is characterized by a white body and a black bill usually having a small yellow spot at the base of the upper mandible. The tundra swan is readily distinguished from the mute swan because it holds its neck straight up; the mute swan's neck settles into a graceful curve.

True to their name, tundra swans spend their summers in the arctic tundra of Alaska and northern Canada. Around mid-November, they descend en masse on Chesapeake Bay and the Albemarle-Pamlico Peninsula of North Carolina. One of their favorite wintering spots is Lake Mattamuskeet National Wildlife Refuge, where they can be seen by the thousands feeding in the planted fields and resting on the waters. On winter evenings, their mellow, reassuring calls wafting across the lake are unforgettable.

Lake Landing National Register Historic District

One of the most fascinating yet little-known historic districts in the sound country lies in the broad sweep of flatland south and east of Lake Mattamuskeet. This area was part of the Mattamuskeet Indian land in the early 18th century. European settlers received land patents or purchased land from the Indians starting around 1720 and began growing crops and building houses. Today, more than two dozens plantation homes and churches of exceptional architectural character remain within a 13,400-acre parcel known as the Lake Landing National Register Historic District. Most are not open to the public but can be seen from the road.

The best way to tour the district is to drive a circular route beginning along U.S. 264, heading north from its intersection with N.C. 94. The structures are generally situated along the south side of U.S. 264 against the backdrop of vast agricultural fields. Signs identify the homes by name and date of construction. The most impressive structure on this leg of the tour is **Amity United Methodist Church**. Visible for miles across open country, this Greek Revival church has a gabled front with fluted columns and an open belfry. The interior, unchanged since its 1850 construction, features a Neoclassical altar topped by a pediment with sunburst and finial. A particularly unusual home, and the only one open to the public, is the **Octagon House**. Built in the 1850s, this two-story, eight-sided structure is one of only two known antebellum examples in North Carolina of the form made popular by New York phrenologist Orson S. Fowler in his 1848 book, *A Home for All*.

To complete the circular tour, turn right off U.S. 264 at Farrows Fork and head south on S.R. 1114. At Middletown, turn right on S.R. 1108. Follow this road through the White Plains community, then turn left on S.R. 1110. At the town of Nebraska on the Burnt Ground Canal, you will catch a glimpse of a once-bustling fishing and agricultural center, now virtually a ghost town. Note the crab-processing houses and fishing boats on the south side of the canal. At the intersection with S.R. 1116, turn right and proceed along The Great Ditch to the intersection with U.S. 264. The Great Ditch was dug to drain Lake Mattamuskeet.

> ### FOR MORE INFORMATION
> Greater Hyde County Chamber of Commerce, P.O. Box 178, Swan Quarter, N.C. 27885-0178 (888-493-3826; www.albemarle-nc.com/hyde)

Fairfield

Frequently bypassed by travelers on their way to and from Lake Mattamuskeet, the village of Fairfield, located on N.C. 94 just north of the Mattamuskeet Causeway, contains a number of architectural gems.

Fairfield rose to prominence around 1860 with the completion of the Fairfield Canal, which linked this community to Albemarle Sound. For three decades after the Civil War, Fairfield thrived as a shipping center for agricultural products.

A number of small but impressive homes and churches in the picturesque

Carpenter Gothic and Italianate styles were built between 1850 and 1890. Many of them survive to this day. The centerpiece of the community is **Fairfield United Methodist Church**. As described in *A Guide to the Historic Architecture of Eastern North Carolina*, this is "an extraordinarily fine country church built in Gothic Revival style accented with Italianate touches." Other notable structures in Fairfield include the **Laura Blackwell House, All Saints Episcopal Church**, and the **Dr. Patrick Simmons House**.

FOR MORE INFORMATION
Greater Hyde County Chamber of Commerce, P.O. Box 178, Swan Quarter, N.C. 27885-0178 (888-493-3826; www.albemarle-nc.com/hyde)

Swan Quarter National Wildlife Refuge

Just south of Lake Mattamuskeet on the shores of Pamlico Sound lie Swan Quarter National Wildlife Refuge and Gull Rock Game Land. The wildlife refuge encompasses 15,501 acres of mostly marsh and open water. During the winter, it harbors an impressive number and variety of diving ducks, including canvasback, scaup, bufflehead, redhead, and ruddy ducks. The refuge contains a stand of old-growth cypresses that is used by great blue herons as a rookery. Egrets, ospreys, and other raptors also nest here.

A single road leads into the refuge from U.S. 264 about 1.5 miles west of its intersection with N.C. 45. This road ends at a fishing pier on Rose Bay, from which some waterfowl may be visible in winter. A better view can be enjoyed by riding the Swan Quarter-Ocracoke ferry, which travels from the town of Swan Quarter through the heart of the refuge.

DIRECTIONS
Swan Quarter National Wildlife Refuge lies south of U.S. 264 in Hyde County. The principal access point is from the refuge road 1.5 miles west of the intersection of U.S. 264 and N.C. 45 near Swan Quarter.

Gull Rock Game Land

Abutting Swan Quarter National Wildlife Refuge on the west is Gull Rock Game Land. Gull Rock includes more upland sites than Swan Quarter. The diverse habitats include brackish marshes, pond pine woodlands, non-riverine swamp forests, and low and high pocosins. The game land is home to 63 species of breeding birds, as well as black bears and American alligators. As with Swan Quarter, the best way to view Gull Rock is by boat. The game land is open to hunting, so visitors need to be aware of hunting seasons.

DIRECTIONS
Gull Rock Game Land can be accessed from several points. From U.S. 264 at the town of New Holland, drive south on S.R. 1164 for 4.3 miles. This dirt road becomes almost impassable after rainy days in winter, so four-wheel-drive vehicles are recommended that time of year.

ACTIVITIES
Bird-watching, hunting, canoeing, kayaking, hiking

Belhaven

Belhaven is a quaint community located at the junction of the Pungo and Pantego Rivers in Beaufort County. It is a popular destination for boaters by virtue of its several marinas and the nationally famous **River Forest Manor** (252-943-2151). This imposing Victorian mansion was built in 1904 by John Aaron Wilkinson, president of the J. L. Roper Lumber Company and vice president of the Norfolk & Southern Railway. Italian craftsmen were brought in to create the ornate ceilings, the mantels for the 11 fireplaces, the cut-glass windows, and the crystal chandeliers. After Wilkinson's death, the house passed through several owners, who developed it into the combination restaurant, hotel, marina, and shipyard that it is today. The manor is a popular stopping point for boats traveling the Intracoastal Waterway. Watching this boat traffic and talking with the passengers and crew are part of the attraction of staying at the manor.

The other main attraction in town is the **Belhaven Memorial Museum** (252-943-6817), located above the historic Belhaven Town Hall. Containing the eclectic collection of Mary Eva Blount Way, the museum has been described as being similar to "your grandmother's attic." But what a grandmother! Way was a prodigious collector, gathering curiosities from all over the world during her long life, which stretched from 1869 to 1962. Among the items on display are wreaths made from human hair, a dress worn by a 700-pound woman, a collection of skins from rattlesnakes killed by Mrs. Way, and two fleas dressed in formal wedding clothes. Each item seems to have a story behind it. Self-guided tours are available during regular operating hours (1 P.M. to 5 P.M. daily). Visitors are encouraged to ask the volunteers to provide background information.

FOR MORE INFORMATION
Belhaven Chamber of Commerce, P.O. Box 147, Belhaven, N.C. 27810 (252-943-3770)

RESTAURANTS IN BELHAVEN

The Helmsman
238 Pamlico Street, Belhaven; 252-943-3810
Inexpensive

This restaurant specializes in fresh-cooked seafood, including sea trout, shrimp, oysters, scallops, and crabs.

River Forest Manor
426 East Pantego Street, Belhaven; 800-346-2151
Inexpensive

During "busy season" (late spring, early summer, and fall), River Forest hosts a nightly buffet that is renowned throughout the sound country. The buffet features the staples of Southern cooking—fried chicken, ham, greens, and biscuits.

LODGINGS IN BELHAVEN

Belhaven Inn
402 East Main Street, Belhaven; 252-943-6400
Moderate

Located in a Victorian-style home in the heart of town, this attractive bed-and-breakfast offers three bedrooms with private baths.

River Forest Manor

426 East Pantego Street, Belhaven; 800-346-2151 or 252-943-2151
www.riverforestmarina.com
Moderate

River Forest offers eight bedrooms; most are in the manor house,
but two are in different outbuildings. The majority of the rooms
are decorated with antiques and offer views of the Pungo River.
The outdoor swimming pool is open during the summer.

Thistle Dew Inn

443 Water Street, Belhaven; 252-943-6900
www.bbonline.com/nc/thistledew
Moderate

This attractive bed-and-breakfast is located in a hundred-year-
old Victorian house overlooking the Pungo River. It has three
bedrooms decorated with antiques collected by the owners in their
travels through Finland, England, and the European continent.

# Bath

Standing on the quiet main street of Bath, it is hard to imagine that this
was once the preeminent town in North Carolina. Today, Bath is well off the
beaten path, but in 1705, when it was incorporated as North Carolina's first
town, it was a beehive of activity. The town stands on Bath Creek, a natural
harbor that leads to the Pamlico River, and from there to Ocracoke Inlet. During the colonial era, this was a favorite port of entry for ships crossing the Atlantic. Bath was also located on the post road extending from Portland, Maine,
to Savannah, Georgia. The local inns and taverns were alive with travelers and
merchants.

For much of the first half of the 18th century, Bath served as the unofficial
capital of North Carolina. The general assembly met here in 1743, 1744, and
1752. Bath also housed the first public library in North Carolina and possibly
the nation, a collection of a thousand books.

Bath was the home of John Lawson, surveyor general to the Crown and
noted explorer. Lawson was the author of *A New Voyage to Carolina*, published
in 1709, the earliest account of the natural history of the Carolinas. Bath
was also the home of Blackbeard the Pirate. Blackbeard settled here around

1712, building a house on Bath Creek with a view of the water, where he could observe the comings and goings of the merchant ships. Blackbeard struck up a friendship with townsman Charles Eden, who served as governor of North Carolina from 1714 to 1722. Rumor has it that Eden condoned Blackbeard's piracy so long as he brought the plunder back to North Carolina, where local merchants could buy and sell it cheaply without paying British tax.

Numerous structures from the colonial era are now included in the three-block area known as **Historic Bath**. The best way to view the historic area is to start at the **Historic Bath Visitor Center**, located at the corner of Carteret and Harding Streets. The state-owned center offers a free orientation film and maps for a walking tour. One stop on the tour is the **Palmer-Marsh House** at 104 South Main Street. Built in 1744, this is the oldest home in Bath and one of the oldest in the state. The massive wooden frame was built around a 50-foot-long center beam. The house, which features a 17-foot-wide double chimney on the eastern side, is open for guided tours. **St. Thomas Episcopal Church**, built in 1734, is the oldest church in North Carolina. Tucked beneath ancient cedar trees beside a small graveyard, it is still in use for church services and is open for tours. Several items of historical interest can be seen here, including a 1703 Bible and the church bell, cast in 1872. Other significant buildings in Bath include the **Van Der Veer House** (c. 1790) and the **Bonner House** (1830).

FOR MORE INFORMATION

Historic Bath, P.O. Box 148, Bath, N.C. 27808 (252-923-3971; www.pamlico.com/bath/history)

RESTAURANTS IN BATH

Old Town Country Kitchen & Grill
436 Carteret Street, Bath; 252-923-1840
Inexpensive

This restaurant offers basic country cooking (fried chicken and collard greens) during the week and serves fresh seafood on weekends.

LODGINGS IN BATH

Bath Harbor Marina and Waterfront Hotel
101 Carteret Street, Bath; 252-923-5711
www.bathharbor.com
Moderate

> This motel, located on Bath Creek, offers boaters a protected harbor and six-foot-deep water slips. It has four efficiencies with private decks overlooking the creek.

The Pirate's Den Bed and Breakfast
116 South Main Street, Bath; 252-923-9571
www.bbonline.com/nc/piratesden
Moderate

> Nestled among the historic homes of Bath, The Pirate's Den offers four rooms, three with views of Bath Creek.

Goose Creek State Park

Goose Creek State Park is sometimes referred to as "the best-kept secret in Beaufort County." Its proximity to the more famous Pocosin Lakes National Wildlife Refuge and Lake Mattamuskeet National Wildlife Refuge leaves it rarely visited and underappreciated. Yet this park offers good opportunities to hike, swim, fish, and view and photograph wildlife.

Prior to the state's purchasing the land in 1974, this property was owned and managed by the Weyerhaeuser Corporation as a pine plantation. Thus, most of the park is covered with uniform stands of young loblolly pines—not the most visually interesting habitat. Still, it can be an excellent place to view and photograph birds, especially pileated woodpeckers.

You should first stop at the excellent Goose Creek Environmental Education/Visitor Center for an orientation to the park and its wildlife. The center's Discovery Room contains mounted specimens of otter, beaver, black bear, and white-tailed deer, as well as live amphibians and reptiles. Other exhibits provide interesting details about the wetland environment found on the fringes of the park.

You can then explore a variety of habitats by following the more than half-dozen trails. From either of two parking lots at the southern end of the entrance road, you can hike a short distance to the Pamlico River. The **Live Oak Trail** leads to a sandy swimming beach graced with live oaks draped in Spanish moss. The **Ragged Point Trail** leads to a pristine estuarine area that has been declared a National Natural Landmark. The **Goose Creek Trail** traverses several swamp forests and offers excellent views of bald cypresses. The **Flatty Creek Trail**'s boardwalk crosses a shrub swamp and a brackish marsh, ending at an observation deck overlooking Flatty Creek. The **Ivey's Gut Trail** offers excellent views of Goose Creek and a good chance of seeing wood ducks.

If you bring a kayak, canoe, or motorboat, you can explore a whole other dimension of the park. A boat ramp at the end of Dinah's Landing Road provides access to the wide Pamlico River and the more intimate Goose Creek. Heading up Goose Creek from the landing, you will pass at least half a dozen osprey nests, active in spring and early summer. Within a mile, the tidal basin narrows to a winding stream, where pickerel weed, blue flag, and swamp rose bloom atop the tannin-stained waters. Otters and beavers frequent this part of the creek, as do assorted wading birds and an occasional bald eagle.

Downstream, Goose Creek opens immediately into the Pamlico River. The stumpy shoreline at the confluence of the waters provides excellent fishing for flounder and sea trout. Anglers should get plenty of action using lightweight spinning rods equipped with jigs.

Because of the intense summertime tick population, Goose Creek is best visited in the cool months.

DIRECTIONS
From the town of Bath, drive west on N.C. 92 to the merger with U.S. 264. Turn left on Camp Leach Road (S.R. 1334) and travel 2.5 miles to the park entrance.

ACTIVITIES
Hiking, picnicking, bird-watching, fishing, canoeing, kayaking, swimming, camping

FACILITIES
The Goose Creek Environmental Education/Visitor Center includes the Discovery Room, which has models and mounted specimens of local wildlife. Other facilities include a wet laboratory, an auditorium, a conference room for special educational programs, picnic areas, and camping areas.

The pristine shores of the Pamlico River at Goose Creek State Park

DATES

Goose Creek is open daily from 8 A.M. to 6 P.M. November through February; from 8 A.M. to 7 P.M. during March and October; from 8 A.M. to 8 P.M. during April, May, and September; and from 8 A.M. to 9 P.M. June through August.

FEES

A fee is charged for overnight camping.

CLOSEST TOWN

Bath is five miles away.

FOR MORE INFORMATION

Goose Creek State Park, Route 2, Box 372, Washington, N.C. 27889 (252-923-2191)

Washington

The town of Washington—or "Little Washington," as it is often called—includes a number of noteworthy architectural, cultural, and recreational sites. Founded as the "Forks of the Tar," the town changed its name to Washington in 1776 in honor of General George Washington. This port city at the head of the Pamlico River played a vital role during the Revolutionary War. As the British laid siege to the cities of Savannah, Charles Town, and Wilmington, Washington became a vital supply port for the Continental Army. After the war, it grew as a commercial and cultural center due to its prized location on navigable waterways.

During the Civil War, Union forces captured Washington early but caused minimal damage. However, when the Confederates recaptured the town in 1864, fleeing Union troops set it ablaze. Residents reconstructed the town, only to see it destroyed again in 1900, when a faulty stove flue sparked a fire that burned much of the business district. Residents rebuilt a second time. Much of the late-Victorian commercial architecture that graces the downtown area dates from this era.

Most of the significant homes, churches, and commercial buildings in town are located in the **Washington Historic District**. Maps for a walking tour are available from the Washington-Beaufort County Chamber of Commerce, located at 102 North Stewart Street. The tour begins and ends at the **Seaboard Coastline Railroad Depot** (c. 1934) at Main and Gladden Streets. The enormous brick depot once resonated with the rumble of passengers and freight but now echoes the calls of actors and the sounds of choirs performing at the Beaufort County Arts Council, which is headquartered here. The **Fowle Warehouse** at 112 Respess Street once housed naval stores and merchandise going to and coming from the West Indies. Built around 1825 on a foundation of ships' ballast stones, it has recently been converted to professional offices. The **Marsh House** at 210 Water Street is one of the oldest structures in Washington. Built in 1795, it housed Federal troops during the Civil War and still bears a war wound in the form of an unexploded cannonball lodged in its upper right facade. The **Old Beaufort County Courthouse** (c. 1786) at 158 North Market Street is the second-oldest courthouse in North Carolina and one of the oldest public buildings in the United

Architectural details of the DeMille Building in Washington

States. Graced by a 215-year-old, still-functioning wooden clock, the courthouse now houses the Beaufort-Hyde-Martin Regional Library.

Architecturally, Washington is best known for its churches. **First United Methodist Church** at 304 West Second Street is probably the most photographed building in town. This Neo-Gothic wonder looks like it was transported from some European province.

FOR MORE INFORMATION
Washington-Beaufort County Chamber of Commerce, P.O. Box 665, Washington, N.C. 27889 (252-946-9168; www.washingtonnctourism.com)

North Carolina Estuarium

The North Carolina Estuarium in Washington is dedicated to educating visitors about the importance of estuaries—how they function, how they have supported humans and animals for millennia, and what we must do to ensure their health. Estuaries are the zones where fresh water and salt water mix. In the flat terrain of the sound country's numerous creeks and rivers, there are thousands of square miles of estuaries. These are the nursery grounds for more than 90 percent of the seafood species—including blue crab, flounder, and shrimp—caught by North Carolina fishermen. Yet pollution and development along the shoreline are constantly threatening estuaries.

From the very start, you will understand that this is not a traditional museum. The elaborate wood-and-wire sculpture in the foyer, symbolizing the cycle of water, embodies the creative approach the estuarium's designers have taken. You'll find traditional aquariums, artifacts, and displays here, but the focus is on interactive displays and firsthand educational experiences. For example, the guided boat tour of the neighboring Pamlico and Tar Rivers is a favorite way to introduce visitors to the ecology and history of the region. On this one- to two-hour tour, guides discuss the roles of shipping, fishing, and lumbering in the development of Washington. As the boat cruises slowly up the feeder creeks, the talk turns to the local flora and fauna and the role that clean water plays in supporting them. Trips generally leave in the morning during the summer and in the afternoon during the cooler seasons. You might also enjoy the weekly program on native plants and coastal gardening and the special programs on wetlands, bears, birds, reptiles, crabs, and art.

RESTAURANTS IN WASHINGTON

Bill's Hot Dogs
109 North Gladden Street, Washington; 252-946-3343
Inexpensive

It's not haute cuisine, but people come from far and wide to have a hot dog and a Coke at this historic downtown eatery.

The Curiosity Shoppe
201 West Main Street, Washington; 252-975-1397
Moderate

Housed in the historic Fowle Warehouse, The Curiosity Shoppe serves creatively prepared steak, fresh seafood, quail, and duck. It is open for dinner only.

P. J.'s on Main Street
107 West Main Street, Washington; 252-946-9483
*Moderate*_____

> Located in the old Southern Furniture factory, P. J's serves gourmet sandwiches for lunch and pasta, chicken, and fresh seafood for dinner.

LODGINGS IN WASHINGTON

Washington has traditional motels, but the bed-and-breakfasts in the historic district allow visitors to enjoy the true flavor of this historic town.

Days Inn
916 Carolina Avenue, Washington; 252-946-6141
www.daysinn.com
*Moderate*_____

> Located a mile north of downtown, this 76-room motel includes an exercise room. Guests receive complimentary continental breakfast.

The Moss House
129 Van Norden Street, Washington; 252-975-3967
www.themosshouse.com
*Moderate to expensive*_____

> The Moss House is located in the historic district one block from the Pamlico River. The 1902 home is newly renovated. All rooms have private baths. The owners hail from New Orleans and specialize in full breakfasts with a southern Louisiana flavor.

Pamlico House Bed and Breakfast
400 East Main Street, Washington; 800-948-8507
www.pamlicohouse.com
*Moderate*_____

> Located in a turn-of-the-20th-century Colonial Revival home, Pamlico House offers four bedrooms with private baths. The classic Victorian parlor is decorated with family heirlooms.

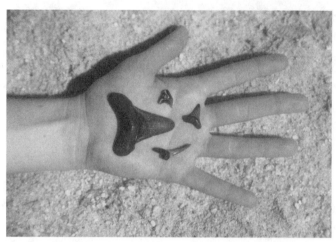

A typical day's find of fossilized shark's teeth at the Aurora Fossil Museum

Aurora Fossil Museum

Millions of years ago, the ocean covered much of eastern North Carolina. Marine animals, including whales, sharks, and all manner of crustaceans, lived and died here, their bones and exoskeletons sinking to the bottom, to be covered by layers of sand. Beginning in the 1960s, phosphate mining on the southern shores of the Pamlico River began to uncover remarkable fossils of these animals, many of which are now on display at the Aurora Fossil Museum in the tiny town of Aurora. The museum depicts ocean life from 5 to 15 million years ago and describes how phosphate mining has uncovered remnants of this life. It also has a display on Indian life in eastern North Carolina. An 18-minute video describes the geology of the coastal plain and demonstrates modern phosphate-mining processes and equipment. After completing a tour of the museum, you'll be invited to search for fossils, most notably sharks' teeth, in the piles of phosphate material deposited across the street. You're welcome to keep what you find. This is a great activity for children.

DIRECTIONS
Aurora is on N.C. 33 at the junction with N.C. 306 in central Pamlico County. From the traffic island in town, follow the signs to the museum, located at 400 Main Street.

ACTIVITIES
Touring museum, hunting for fossils, picnicking

Oriental

Located on the shores of the Neuse River where it empties into Pamlico Sound, Oriental is known as the sailing capital of North Carolina. The town, ideally situated just off the Intracoastal Waterway, offers excellent harborage at the convergence of six deep creeks. Dozens of fishing trawlers and more than a thousand sailboats call Oriental home. Many more boats stop by on their way up or down the waterway.

From a driver's perspective, the town is well off the beaten path, which has prevented it from being overrun by development. Oriental is a great place for walking and biking. The town is laid out in a simple grid with everything close at hand. The shady streets are lined with early-20th-century homes built in simple Victorian, Colonial Revival, and Bungalow styles. There are no stoplights, fast-food restaurants, or malls.

The principal reasons for visiting Oriental are to sail and fish. Sailing charters are available for both single-day and multi-day trips to destinations such as Beaufort, New Bern, and Cape Lookout. Those wanting to learn to sail should call the **Oriental School of Sailing** (252-249-0960). The school offers multiday classes from April through October. **Carolina Sailing Unlimited** (252-249-0850) also offers classes, as well as charter cruises aboard the 33-foot ketch *Puffin*. Sightseeing tours of Oriental's creeks are available on the **Oriental Water Taxi** (252-670-7117).

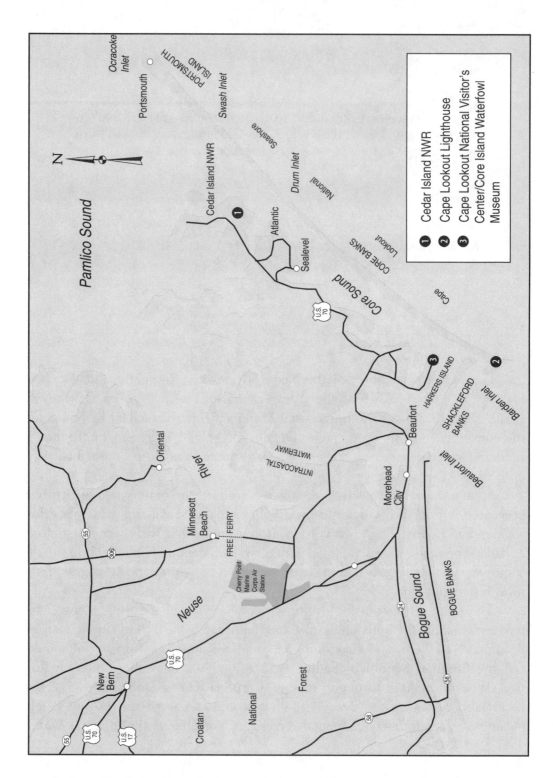

Kayaking has become increasingly popular along the creeks feeding into Oriental Harbor. If you want to explore these and other local waters, pick up a copy of *Paddle Trails of Pamlico County*, a set of four guides produced by the Pamlico County Rural Development Panel. The guides are available for free.

On land, you'll want to visit the **Circle Ten Art Gallery** on Broad Street. This gallery features the works of the Oriental Artists Cooperative. There are several gift shops in town, as well as marine-supply stores carrying items such as brass lanterns.

Oriental hosts half a dozen popular festivals, including the Croaker Festival, held each Fourth of July; the Spirit of Christmas, held the second weekend in December; the Oriental Rotary Tarpon Tournament (yes, tarpon do travel this far north), held in August; the Oriental Cup Regatta, held in mid-September; and the Running of the Dragon, held on New Year's Eve, an event featuring a huge, golden dragon that winds through the streets of town.

RESTAURANTS IN ORIENTAL

M & M's Café
205 South Water Street, Oriental; 252-249-2000
Moderate

A local favorite, this café is known for its excellent seafood and its meat dishes such as lamb chops and veal. Breakfast offerings include omelets made to order, burritos, and tortillas. Casual dining is available indoors or outside on the covered porch.

Oriental Marina Restaurant
Hodges Street, Oriental; 252-249-2204
Moderate

This restaurant features good food, a lovely view of Oriental Harbor, and live entertainment in its upstairs lounge on summer weekends. Specialties include "Seafood Nirvana," a puff pastry filled with shrimp, crabmeat, and scallops in a lobster cream sauce.

The Cartwright House
301 Freemason Street, Oriental; 888-726-9389 or 252-249-1337
www.cartwrighthouse.com
Moderate

> Located in the heart of town, this bed-and-breakfast is full of Victorian character and charm. Its porch offers views of the Neuse River. Each of the five bedrooms is individually decorated. Breakfast includes such delights as blueberry scones and crab or shrimp quiche.

The Inn at Oriental
508 South Church Street, Oriental; 800-485-7174 or 252-249-1078
www.innatoriental.com
Moderate

> Formerly the Tar Heel Inn, this newly renovated bed-and-breakfast has 12 rooms with private baths and cable TV. A full American breakfast is served.

Oriental Marina Motel
Hodges Street, Oriental; 252-249-1818
Moderate

> Part of the Oriental Marina complex, this harbor-side motel includes 14 deepwater rental slips. Guests enjoy the waterfront views, the deck, the swimming pool, and the tiki bar.

River Neuse Motel
South Neuse Drive and Mildred Street, Oriental; 252-249-1404
Moderate

> This 16-room motel offers a central location and excellent views of the Neuse River. Its private fishing pier makes it popular among fishermen.

New Bern

Of all the towns in the sound country, New Bern epitomizes recovery based on tourism. In the 1970s, many of New Bern's historic buildings were in disrepair, and its downtown area was forlorn. In 1979, the town gave Swiss Bear, Inc., a nonprofit organization of civic leaders, the authority to revitalize the downtown. Today, it is a hub of activity. Restaurants, art galleries, and specialty shops line the streets. Trolleys packed with tourists circumnavigate the historic district. The renovation of Union Point Park is bringing people to the waterfront, where the Trent and Neuse Rivers merge.

This prime location was what attracted Baron Christophe de Graffenried, an enterprising Swiss businessman looking for land in the New World on which to establish a colony. In 1710, Graffenried purchased 19,000 acres at the junction of the two rivers and brought over a group of Swiss immigrants. He named his settlement New Bern, in honor of his native city of Bern, Switzerland.

In 1711, Graffenried and author-explorer John Lawson were venturing up the Neuse River when they were captured by Tuscarora Indians. Although the details of the encounter remain unclear, the Tuscaroras released Graffenried with the warning that they were massing for war against the whites. The Indians tortured and killed Lawson. War did indeed follow, the Tuscaroras killing hundreds of whites in the Neuse-Pamlico region before being defeated.

Although Graffenried returned in despair to Switzerland, New Bern gradually recovered from the war and a subsequent plague of yellow fever to become the preeminent town in the region. In 1770, British colonial governor William Tryon built a lavish mansion here on the banks of the Trent. Tryon Palace is where delegates gathered in 1777 for the first meeting of the state legislature. The palace burned in 1798, but the city thrived as a hub in the triangular trade route among the Caribbean islands, coastal North Carolina, and Northern ports. New Bern became the largest town in the state.

As was the case with many other port cities in the sound country, New Bern was captured early in the Civil War, in 1862. It is because Union forces occupied the town for the remainder of the war that most of the town's buildings have been preserved, while many of those in other Southern cities were destroyed. The historic buildings are centered within the magnificent **New Bern Historic District**. A good way to tour this district is by trolley. The 90-minute, narrated **New Bern Historic District Trolley Tour** (252-637-7316) begins and ends at the ticket office for Tryon Palace, located at 712 Pollock Street. You can also take a self-guided walking tour by following one of the several published tour guides available at area gift shops and historic sites.

The historically significant houses in New Bern are too numerous to mention, and not all are open to the public. However, there are several must-see public buildings. **New Bern City Hall** at 300 Pollock Street is an eclectic blend of the Romanesque Revival and High Victorian Gothic styles. The central structure was built in 1895 by the United States Treasury Department. The distinctive tower with its illuminated, four-faced clock was added in 1910. The copper bears projecting above the entrances were installed in 1936. **St. John's Masonic Lodge** (c. 1801, enlarged c. 1904) at 516 Hancock Street is renowned for its second-floor lodge room, which features intricate woodwork by local craftsmen John Dewey and Asa King and walls painted in trompe l'oeil Masonic emblems. **New Bern Academy** (c. 1806-1810), located at Hancock and New Streets, was North Carolina's first incorporated school. It houses historical displays on local architecture and the history of the school and town.

New Bern is famous for its historic churches. One of the most photographed is **First Presbyterian Church** (c. 1819-1822) at 412 New Street. Its Federal-style design is similar to that of many New England churches but is unusual in North Carolina. Thanks to its four-faced clock atop a tall steeple, **Christ Episcopal Church** (1875) at 320 Pollock Street is one of the identifying landmarks of the downtown skyline. Inside, you can view a 1752 *Book of Common Prayer*, a huge 1717 Bible, and a five-piece silver communion service given to Christ Church by King George II.

If you love old graveyards, be sure to visit **Cedar Grove Cemetery**, located at the corner of Johnson and Queen Streets. Note the wall and the arched gateway made of marl, a mixture of fossilized seashells. You'll find numerous fascinating tombstones beneath the moss-draped cedars, as well as the city's monument to Confederate soldiers killed during the Civil War.

The **New Bern Fireman's Museum** (252-636-4087) at 408 Hancock Street is well worth a visit by anyone interested in antique vehicles. This museum has a superb collection of old firefighting equipment, including an 1879 Atlantic steamer, an 1884 Button steamer, and a 1927 Seagrove ladder and pumper truck in use until 1977.

FOR MORE INFORMATION
Craven County Convention and Visitors Bureau, 314 South Front Street, New Bern, N.C. 28563 (252-637-9400; www.visitnewbern.com)

The kitchen garden at Tryon Palace

Tryon Palace

In the colonial era, North Carolina was not known for its palatial dwellings. Most settlers, even the prosperous ones, lived in relatively simple dwellings, as evidenced by the modest Newbold-White House in Hertford (see page 137). However, Royal Governor William Tryon wanted to build a residence that would suitably impress visitors from around the world and serve as a meeting place for the colonial assembly. From 1766 to 1770, Tryon erected a brick palace on the banks of the Trent River in New Bern that had no equal in the colony.

Designed by English architect John Hawks, Tryon Palace employed a tripartite villa design with a large central building measuring 82 feet by 59 feet. Curved colonnades led to "offices" on either side containing a kitchen and stable. Inside, the rooms were finished with Georgian woodwork including pedimented doors and window frames integrated into the wainscoting. The expense of the palace infuriated many colonists, especially the farmers of the back country already disgruntled over tax issues and abuses of Crown authority. But visitors were suitably impressed, including Venezuelan traveler Francisco de Miranda, who called the building "the best edifice of all, and one that really merits the educated traveler's attention."

Tryon Palace served as the State Capitol until 1794, when the capital was moved to Raleigh. After that, the palace fell into disrepair and was destroyed by fire in 1798.

In the 1940s, New Bern native Maude Moore Latham and the state raised funds for the reconstruction of the palace. Following Hawks's original plans, the palace was completed in 1959 and furnished with 18th-century English and American antiques reflecting the world of Royal Governor Tryon during the decade of the American Revolution.

Today, the palace and grounds are open for regular tours led by costumed guides. Avid gardeners should be sure to visit the kitchen garden, resplendent with vegetables, herbs, and fruit trees. The tour includes the adjacent **John Wright Stanly House**, the **Dixon-Stevenson House**, and the **New Bern Academy Museum**. Special events include the Decorative Arts Symposium in March, the Gardener's Weekend and the Historic Homes and Gardens Tour in April, historical drama tours in summer, the Chrysanthemum Festival in October, and the Christmas Celebration in December.

DIRECTIONS
From U.S. 70, exit on to U.S. 17 North and follow the signs to downtown New Bern and Tryon Palace. The palace is located at 610 Pollock Street.

ACTIVITIES
Touring historic homes and gardens

FACILITIES
The palace is the main attraction. A museum shop is located in the adjacent Jones House, and a crafts and garden shop is located behind the kitchen office.

DATES
The palace is open from 9 A.M. to 4 P.M. Monday through Saturday and from 1 P.M. to 4 P.M. on Sunday. It is closed Christmas and Thanksgiving.

FEES
An admission fee is charged.

FOR MORE INFORMATION
Tryon Palace Historic Site and Gardens, 610 Pollock Street, New Bern, N.C. 28560 (800-767-1560)

Restaurants in New Bern

The Berne Restaurant
2900 Neuse Boulevard, New Bern; 252-638-5296
Inexpensive

A favorite among locals, The Berne Restaurant features country-style cooking. Dinner specialties include pork barbecue and a large selection of seafood.

The Chelsea—A Restaurant and Publick House
325 Middle Street, New Bern; 252-637-5469
Moderate

The Chelsea is located in the restored 1912 building that was the drugstore of pharmacist Caleb Bradham, the inventor of Pepsi-Cola. This popular nightspot serves specialty sandwiches and burgers, along with a wide variety of domestic and imported beers and wines. Live entertainment is often featured.

Fred and Claire's
247 Craven Street, New Bern; 252-638-5426
Inexpensive

Located in the heart of the historic district, Fred and Claire's offers diverse fare at reasonable prices. Specialties include cheese and broccoli casserole, shepherd's pie, and crab quiche.

Henderson House Restaurant
216 Pollock Street, New Bern; 252-637-4784
Expensive

The ultimate in fine dining, the Henderson House offers such specialties as tournedos of beef, pheasant in port wine, and shrimp amandine. Appropriate dress and reservations are required.

Lodgings in New Bern

New Bern has half a dozen bed-and-breakfasts in the historic district and a wide selection of motels, several with river views and docking facilities.

The Aerie

509 Pollock Street, New Bern; 800-849-5553 or 252-636-5553
www.aerieinn.com
Moderate

This seven-bedroom bed-and-breakfast is located in an 1880s Victorian-style home in the heart of the historic district. Each room has a private bath. A full country breakfast is served each morning.

BridgePointe Hotel

101 Howell Road, New Bern; 800-228-2828 or 252-636-3637
www.bridgepointehotel.com
Inexpensive to moderate

This hotel is located just across the river from the downtown historic district. Each of the 116 rooms offers a river view. BridgePointe has a riverside restaurant and lounge with live entertainment.

Comfort Suites Riverfront Park

218 East Front Street, New Bern; 800-228-5150 or 252-636-0022
www.choicehotels.com
Moderate to expensive

Comfort Suites is located in the downtown historic district on the edge of the Neuse River. Many of the hundred suites have balconies with river views. Amenities include an outdoor pool, an outdoor heated whirlpool, a fitness center, and boat slips.

Harmony House Inn

215 Pollock Street, New Bern; 800-636-3113 or 252-636-3810
www.harmonyhouse.com
Moderate to expensive

This home was built around 1809 and has been added on to several times. The inn offers nine guest rooms and one suite, all with private baths and decorative fireplaces.

Howard House Bed and Breakfast

207 Pollock Street, New Bern; 800-705-5261 or 252-514-6709
www.howardhousebnb.com
Inexpensive

Located in a restored Victorian home in the heart of the historic district, Howard House offers four guest rooms, each with a private bath and period antiques.

King's Arms Inn
212 Pollock Street, New Bern; 800-872-9306 or 252-638-4409
Expensive

Built in 1847, the King's Arms Inn was named for a New Bern tavern said to have hosted members of the First Continental Congress. The inn has eight guest rooms, each with a private bath and antique and reproduction furniture.

New Berne House
709 Broad Street, New Bern; 800-842-7688 or 252-636-2250
www.newbernehouse.com
Inexpensive

This seven-room bed-and-breakfast is located in a Colonial-style home one block from Tryon Palace. All rooms have private baths.

Sheraton Grand New Bern
100 Middle Street, New Bern; 800-326-3745 or 252-638-3585
www.newbernsheraton.com
Expensive

Located on the waterfront, the Sheraton Grand New Bern offers luxury and convenience in the heart of the historic district. Amenities include a 120-slip marina, a pool and patio, an exercise room, a restaurant, a café, and three lounges.

Croatan National Forest

The North Carolina coast is not known for hiking opportunities. There are simply not enough long-distance trails and variations in terrain to make it interesting. Croatan National Forest is the one exception to this rule, offering a 26-mile trail and several shorter ones, along with opportunities for canoeing, camping, fishing, and bird-watching. Lying astride the fast-developing U.S. 70 corridor between New Bern and the Crystal Coast, Croatan is an island of respite.

Through the colonial era and beyond, forest products were key to North Carolina's prosperity. Longleaf pine forests—from which workers extracted or processed timber, tar, pitch, and turpentine—dominated the sound country. After years of tapping, the longleaf pines produced less and less sap. Most died or were cut down. The trees failed to regenerate due to the suppression of fire, which is necessary for longleaf pine germination and the elimination of competing hardwoods. In Croatan National Forest, Civilian Conservation Corps workers planted thousands of loblolly pine seedlings, which became the staple of the Southern timber industry due to their rapid growth rate.

Today, the variety of forest types within Croatan's 160,000 acres includes loblolly pine forests, lowland and upland hardwood forests, pocosin swamps, and a few remnant stands of longleaf pines. As the demand for outdoor recreation has grown, forest managers have sharply decreased commercial timber harvests in Croatan and increased such practices as controlled burning to encourage longleaf pine regeneration. All of this makes Croatan a more interesting destination for nature lovers than it has been in years past.

Croatan harbors the full spectrum of sound-country wildlife, including white-tailed deer, black bears, and wild turkeys. Its lakes support a decent population of alligators, making Croatan the northernmost site where these reptiles can be reliably seen. Endangered red-cockaded woodpeckers (*Picoides borealis*) are making a comeback in the longleaf pine-wiregrass savannas. These areas also support populations of carnivorous plants such as the Venus flytrap, the sundew, and the pitcher plant. You'll have your best chance to see wildlife by slowly driving the interior roads in the early-morning or late-evening hours. Red-cockaded woodpeckers are most prolific along Little Road between Catfish Lake Road and Riverdale Road. Trees with active nest cavities are marked with blue paint.

Another good birding area is **Millis Road Savanna** in the southern end of the forest. The forest service burns this area every few years to maintain the longleaf pine-wiregrass community. This is a good area to see Bachman's sparrows (*Aimophila aestivalis*) in summer. Pygmy rattlesnakes (*Sistrurus miliarius*) also inhabit this area, so bird watchers should take care if they walk through the thick grass.

Croatan contains a host of trails and campgrounds. These are located primarily in the northeastern and southwestern corners of the forest bordering the Neuse and White Oak estuaries. The **Neuse River Recreation Area**, locally known as Flanners Beach, is a popular drive-in campground and swimming and picnic area on the banks of the four-mile-wide Neuse River estuary. The **Cedar Point Recreation Area** on the White Oak River provides fishing, boating, hiking, and

A view of tidal marshes from the Cedar Point Tideland Trail in the Croatan National Forest

camping opportunities. Both areas have electrical hookups, flush toilets, warm showers, and drinking water.

The interior of the forest contains a number of freshwater lakes popular for fishing and waterfowl hunting. Catfish Lake and Great Lake are accessible by gravel road; four-wheel-drive vehicles are recommended after heavy rains. Both lakes have boat ramps. The lakes are surrounded by the Sheep Ridge, Pond Pine, and Catfish Lake South Wilderness Areas. Comprised largely of pocosins and devoid of trails and roads, these areas are virtually impenetrable.

Neusiok Trail

The signature hiking trail in Croatan National Forest is the Neusiok Trail, which begins at the **Pine Cliff Recreation Area** on the banks of the Neuse River and runs for 26 miles through a variety of terrains down to the Newport River. This trail is best hiked from late October to early June to avoid bugs and high humidity. Shorter options are available by leaving a car at one of the various forest-road access points along the way. Most people do not hike the full trail, but rather limit themselves to the 5.5-mile leg from the recreation area to N.C. 306, which includes most of the major forest types found in Croatan.

The first mile of the trail runs west along a hard sand beach and offers an excellent view of the three-mile-wide Neuse River estuary. In the 1990s, the Neuse gained notoriety as the site of major fish kills variously caused by low dissolved oxygen and the depredations of a microscopic flesh-eating dinoflagellate named *Pfiesteria piscicida*. During summer, the Lower Neuse River suffers from periodic algal blooms caused by a combination of low flow, warm temperature, and over-enrichment of nitrates and phosphates from urban development and agricultural operations (including hog farms) upstream. As these thick mats of algae die, they are consumed by bacteria, which themselves consume oxygen. Dissolved oxygen levels can drop so low that fish begin to die. *Pfiesteria*, a normally benign single-cell organism, appears to be stimulated to attack fish when they are in a stressed condition, possibly linking this behavior to water pollution. The state is seeking to reduce pollution in the Neuse by imposing tougher restrictions on municipal sewage-treatment plants in the watershed, requiring 50-foot vegetative buffers alongside all watercourses, and banning the construction of new hog farms in the flood plain.

From the beach, the trail turns inland (south), passing through forests of loblolly pines and mixed hardwoods, cypress-palmetto swamps, pocosins, and salt marshes. It terminates at the Newport River estuary a scant five miles from the ocean.

Among the wildlife you may see along this trail are red-cockaded woodpeckers, bald eagles, alligators, otters, white-tailed deer, black bears, and wild turkeys.

∞ Cedar Point Tideland Trail

The Cedar Point Tideland Trail, located in the southwestern corner of Croatan National Forest, provides an interesting hike through varied terrain. The trail offers two loop options—one 0.5 mile long and the other two miles long. The first portion of the trail passes pine and upland hardwoods forests. The low, shrubby woods on the western side of the trail are frequented by prairie warblers and the occasional painted bunting (*Passerina ciris*). Farther along, the trail opens on to a salt marsh that offers views of the White Oak River estuary. It then enters a boardwalk along which wooden blinds have been erected to allow an undisturbed look at the marsh and the wading birds that frequent it.

This is also an excellent place to watch the sunset.

To reach the trailhead from the intersection of N.C. 24 and N.C. 58 in Cape Carteret, drive north on N.C. 58 for 0.7 mile, turn left on S.R. 1114, proceed 0.5 mile, turn left on F.R. 153-A, and follow it to the camping area, the boat ramp, and the trailhead.

Island Creek Forest Walk

The Island Creek Forest Walk, located at the northern end of Croatan National Forest, provides a short but interesting hike through a variety of habitats. This 0.5-mile loop trail runs along Island Creek, then through a mature upland hardwood forest. Island Creek is unusual for Croatan in that it has steep banks with outcrops of limestone and a swift current much of the year. The upland hardwood forest, more reminiscent of the Piedmont than the coastal plain, is a good area for woodpeckers, especially pileated (*Dryocopus pileatus*) and hairy (*Picoides villosus*) woodpeckers. A pamphlet available at the ranger station provides a key to the numbered stops along the trail.

To reach the trailhead, take U.S. 70 south from New Bern. Turn right at the first sign for Craven Regional Airport on to William Road. Go past the airport to the stop sign and turn left on S.R.1004. The trailhead parking lot is on the right after 7.5 miles.

Brice Creek Canoe Trail

For an up-close look at a freshwater wetland and creek, you can paddle a canoe or a kayak down Brice Creek at the northeastern tip of Croatan National Forest. This blackwater creek passes from high ground dominated by sweet gums, red maples, and white oaks through a freshwater marsh to its confluence with the Trent River. Brice Creek has been designated a canoe trail by the forest service and the Craven County Recreation and Parks Department. Numbered markers have been erected along the trail to identify significant natural features, all of which are explained in detail in a trail guide available at the ranger station.

Brice is a flat-water creek that can be paddled either upstream or downstream from various points. A brochure and map giving directions to the put-ins and takeouts can be obtained from the **Craven County Recreation and Parks Department** (252-636-6606). To reach the put-in farthest upstream, follow U.S. 70 south from New Bern. Approximately 4.5 miles after crossing the Trent River bridge, turn right on West Thurman Road. Turn left on Old Airport Road, then right on S.R. 1111 to reach the bridge over Brice Creek. From here, it is a five-mile paddle to the public boat ramp off F.R. 121-A. You can proceed another four miles to the takeout at Merchants Grocery Store or continue into the Trent River to Lawson Creek Park in New Bern. This would make a total trip of 12 miles.

DIRECTIONS
Croatan National Forest lies east and west of U.S. 70 south of New Bern and north of Newport. To reach the rangers' office, drive south from New Bern on U.S. 70 for approximately eight miles. Turn left on East Fisher Avenue. The head-quarters for the national forest is immediately on the left.

ACTIVITIES
Hunting, fishing, hiking, swimming, camping, picnicking

FACILITIES
The national forest contains boat ramps, camping facilities, dump stations, picnic tables, and restrooms at various locations. A kiosk outside the rangers' office provides maps and brochures on the forest.

DATES
The rangers' office is open from 8:00 A.M. to 4:30 P.M. Monday through Friday.

FEES
A fee is charged for camping.

CLOSEST TOWN
New Bern is eight miles away.

FOR MORE INFORMATION
Croatan National Forest, 141 East Fisher Avenue, New Bern, N.C. 28560 (252-638-5628; www.cs.unca.edu/nfsnc)

Cedar Island National Wildlife Refuge

Cedar Island may be the most visited but least appreciated of the sound country's national wildlife refuges. Whether they know it or not, everyone driving to or from the Cedar Island-Ocracoke ferry passes through the refuge along N.C. 12. The refuge begins shortly after N.C. 12 forks off U.S. 70 at the eastern end of Carteret County. The road leaves the pinewoods and runs atop a causeway through a vast plain of black needlerush that is breathtaking in its expanse yet frustrating for its inaccessibility. Indeed, the only way to properly tour the refuge is by boat. There are no trails or campgrounds here. Neither is there a permanent ranger station, as the refuge is administered by the Lake Mattamuskeet staff.

Approximately 10,000 of the refuge's 14,611 acres are salt marsh—the largest tract of unaltered, irregularly flooded (by wind, not lunar tides) salt marsh in the state. Public boat ramps are located at the southern end of the refuge where N.C. 12 crosses Thorofare Creek and at the end of Lola Road on the eastern shore of Cedar Island. By kayak, canoe, or shallow-draft motorboat, you can cruise the edges of the refuge looking for black, clapper, and Virginia rails, as well as seaside sparrows and marsh wrens. Without a boat, you may be able to hear these birds by pulling off the N.C. 12 causeway anywhere north of the Thorofare Creek bridge. Listen for the *zhur-zeee* call of the seaside sparrows and the *kakkakkak* of the clapper rails.

DIRECTIONS
From Beaufort, drive north on U.S. 70 for approximately 24 miles. Turn left on N.C. 12 and follow the signs to the refuge.

ACTIVITIES
Bird-watching, canoeing, kayaking

FACILITIES
None

DATES
The refuge is open year-round.

FEES
None

CLOSEST TOWN
Beaufort is 30 miles away.

Harkers Island

Between Cedar Island and Beaufort, U.S. 70 skirts the edge of Core Sound at the eastern end of Carteret County, an area locally known as "Down East." Inland, there is almost no habitation, only swamps and agricultural fields. But along the shore, you'll find a host of small communities, including Atlantic, Sea Level, Davis, Marshallberg, and Harkers Island. For generations, the inhabitants of these communities made a living as boatbuilders, fishermen, and guides. Isolated from the rest of the state, they developed distinct expressions and pronunciation. As these traditional trades have declined and "outsiders" have moved in, the unique language and skills have begun to fade. Still, you'll enjoy spending a day driving this scenic stretch of U.S. 70 and dropping in on the various communities, Harkers Island in particular.

Harkers Island was settled by Tuscarora Indians, evidence of whom can be seen in the large mound of shells at the eastern end of the island, said to be the start of a walkway out to Core Banks. White settlers established a community here in the 1700s that eventually included schools, churches, and businesses.

Today, Harkers Island contains two principal tourist attractions—the Core Sound Waterfowl Museum and the Cape Lookout National Seashore Visitor's Center (see the Outer Banks chapter). The island is the closest point of departure for those wanting to visit Cape Lookout and its famous lighthouse, visible on the horizon four miles away. The North Carolina Wildlife Resources Commission operates a free public boat ramp on Island Road just past the bridge on to Harkers. Sea kayaks can be launched from the picnic area across from the visitor center at the end of Island Road. Water taxis can be found all along this road, announced by assorted signs and banners.

Harkers Island is a prime destination for recreational fishermen pursuing game fish in the productive waters around Cape Lookout. Fly fisherman in particular are drawn here in November to hunt the infamous false albacore (*Euthynnus*

Sunset at Core Sound

alletteratus), or little tunny. Pound for pound one of the best fighting fish in the ocean, false albacore occur in schools close to shore. Those around Cape Lookout seem to be particularly large. Harkers offers lodgings and restaurants geared toward anglers, as well as a surfeit of guides.

FOR MORE INFORMATION

Crystal Coast Visitor Center, 3409 Arendell Street, Morehead City, N.C. 28557 (800-786-6962; www.sunnync.com)

Core Sound Waterfowl Museum

For the better part of two centuries, hunting waterfowl with dog and gun has been an important part of sound-country life. Generations of families have made an honorable, if modest, living as hunting guides, decoy makers, and boatbuilders. Waterfowl hunting is still very much alive in the sound country, but since the advent of mass production and modern materials, the demand for handcrafted decoys and boats has faded. The Core Sound Waterfowl Museum on Harkers Island is dedicated to preserving these Down East traditions, as well as celebrating the people and places from which they sprang.

Moved to a stunning new facility in 2001, the museum includes a large collection of decoys dating back to the early 1900s. Some were carved by legendary decoy makers of old, others by members of the Decoy Carvers Guild, formed in 1987 to renew the craft and develop the museum. Visiting artists and carvers offer regular demonstrations of wood carving and painting. Each December, the museum hosts the Core Sound Decoy Festival. Blue-ribbon pieces from all the past festivals are on display.

In addition to decoys, the museum includes displays on boat building and life in Down East communities such as Harkers Island. Just outside the museum, you can watch wild ducks and wading birds up close from the wooden blind overlooking Willow Pond.

DIRECTIONS
From Beaufort, follow U.S. 70 approximately nine miles north to the Otway community. Turn right on Island Road and drive to the end of Harkers Island. The museum is located at 1205 Island Road.

ACTIVITIES
Viewing displays, educational demonstrations, and live waterfowl

FACILITIES
Museum, gift shop, educational area, library

DATES
The museum is open from 10 A.M. to 5 P.M. Monday through Saturday and from 2 P.M. to 5 P.M. on Sunday.

FEES
None

FOR MORE INFORMATION
Core Sound Waterfowl Museum, 1205 Island Road, Harkers Island, N.C. 28531 (252-728-1500; www.coresound.com)

RESTAURANTS ON HARKERS ISLAND

The Ruddy Duck
980 Island Road, Harkers Island; 252-728-5252
Inexpensive

This restaurant is known for its hearty sandwiches—Philly cheese steaks, Reubens, and cheeseburgers. It is open year-round from 10 A.M. to 10 P.M.

Lodgings on Harkers Island

Calico Jack's Inn and Marina
1698 Island Road, Harkers Island; 252-728-3575
Inexpensive

Calico Jack's has comfortable beds and an outside porch with a great view of Core Sound. The marina offers a boat ramp, diesel fuel, supplies, and a tackle shop. Boats are available for fishing and tours of the Cape Lookout area.

Harkers Island Fishing Center
1002 Island Road, Harkers Island; 252-728-3907
Inexpensive

Harkers Island Fishing Center offers clean, no-frills accommodations and easy access to a marina and boat ramp. Fishing guides and water taxis are available for those who wish to access Cape Lookout.

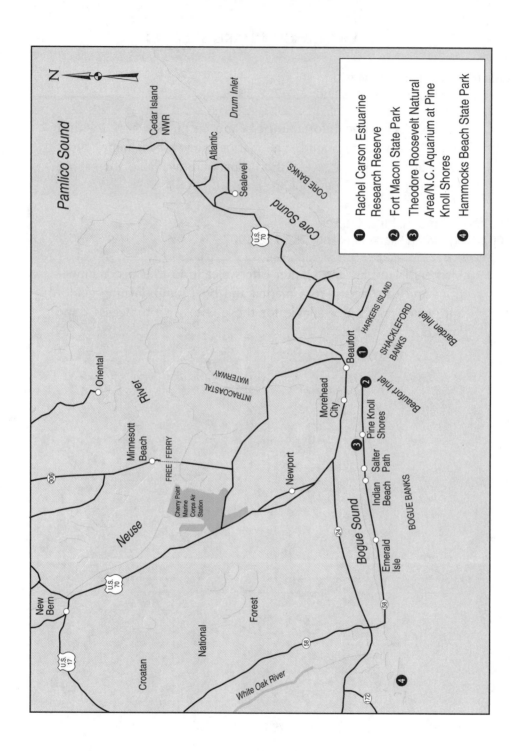

The Southern Coast

Brown Pelican

South of Cape Lookout, the North Carolina coast undergoes a dramatic change. Gone are the expansive sounds and their distant offshore banks. Barrier islands still exist, but they hug the shoreline, sometimes separated from the mainland only by the channel of the Intracoastal Waterway. Bogue Banks in Carteret County is the southernmost landmass in North Carolina to carry the name *banks*. From here to the South Carolina border, all offshore landmasses are referred to as islands. The change in name reflects a change in the underlying geology. While the Outer Banks are made of relatively thick sheets of recently deposited sand over sedimentary underpinnings less than 5 million years old, North Carolina's southern islands are made of thin sheets of recent sand covering sedimentary underpinnings at least 24 million years old.

There is no single name for the 150-mile stretch of coast running from Cape Lookout to the South Carolina line. Various sections are locally referred to by distinctive names. Carteret County calls its seaside area "the Crystal Coast." Topsail Island tourism officials refer to their region as "the Treasure Coast." New

Hanover County and eastern Brunswick County are dominated by the Cape Fear River and a shallow ridge of hundred-million-year-old sediment known as "the Cape Fear Arch." This area is commonly referred to as "the Cape Fear Coast." From here to the South Carolina line lie what are known as "the South Brunswick Islands."

Owing in part to their proximity to the mainland, the southern islands have a longer history of development than the Outer Banks. The towns along these islands often bear the name *beach*, in recognition of their raison d'être—catering to summertime tourists. Warmed by the Gulf Stream, the ocean waters along the southern coast heat up sooner in the year and stay warm longer than the Outer Banks waters, which are subject to gyres of the colder Labrador Current. Most people find it comfortable to swim on the southern coast from late May into October, whereas the ocean off the Outer Banks is still cold in June.

Of course, there is more to the southern coast than just the beaches. Brunswick County is home to more endangered plant and animal species than any other county in the state. Wilmington, the largest city on the North Carolina coast, contains a wealth of cultural, historical, and recreational attractions. Some of the finest golf courses in the state are located on the southern coast. And there are countless blackwater rivers, marshes, and swamps waiting to be explored.

Beaufort

Off the southern coast of Carteret County, the barrier islands draw close to the mainland, narrowing the intervening sounds to a few miles in width. Bogue is the southernmost of the waterways to bear the title of "sound," and thus is considered the end of the sound country.

The two cities—Beaufort and Morehead City—that dominate this portion of the coast are connected by a bridge over the Newport River. Beaufort is far and away the older town. In 1713, it was laid out in a neat grid, and the streets were named after British royalty (Queen Anne) and local statesmen (Moore, Pollock, Turner). Thanks to its immediate access to the sea via Beaufort Inlet, Beaufort developed into a renowned shipbuilding and fishing center. It was also an important base for privateers, including Blackbeard. In 1997, a ship presumed to be Blackbeard's *Queen Anne's Revenge* was discovered lying just offshore.

Toward the end of the 19th century, Beaufort began to blossom as a seaside resort with boardinghouses and a boardwalk along the waterfront. That trend continued through the 20th century, as the warehouses and docks of the commercial fishing trade were gradually torn down and replaced by restaurants, art galleries, and gift shops. Today, the Beaufort waterfront is a major tourist destination. Front Street is a delightful place to stroll, dine, and perhaps catch a glimpse of the wild horses on nearby Carrot Island. A magnificent collection of late-18th- to early-20th-century houses faces the sound along the 100 block of Front Street. Noted for their wraparound, two-tiered porches, these served as boardinghouses for tourists more than a century ago. Front Street is also a good place to catch a boat ride to Cape Lookout or Shackleford Banks, to take a sunset cruise of the harbor, or to join a "guaranteed dolphin watch."

The tree-lined residential area just back from the waterfront is filled with homes and churches dating to the 18th century. Through the efforts of the Beaufort Historical Association, a hundred of these structures have been permanently protected as **Historic Beaufort**. The best place to start a tour of the historic district is the **Beaufort Historic Site** (800-575-7483 or 242-728-5225) at 138 Turner Street. This two-acre tract contains 10 structures moved to the site and restored by the Beaufort Historical Association. These include the **Apothecary Shop** (c. 1859), which features a collection of early medical instruments; the Carteret County Courthouse (c. 1796); and the **Old County Jail** (c. 1859), which has brick walls two feet thick. The **Robert W. and Elva Faison Safrit Historical Center** at the historic site welcomes visitors and provides information on Beaufort. From here, you can head out on a walking tour of the district or take a driving tour on the center's famous double-decker English bus. On the bus tour, a costumed guide relates interesting details of the historic structures and some of the infamous characters who lived in them.

The **Old Burying Ground**, bounded by Ann, Craven, and Broad Streets, is another popular destination. Shaded by ancient live oaks and filled with lichen-encrusted headstones dating to the mid-1700s, this is one of the oldest and loveliest cemeteries in the state. Among the notable graves are that of Captain Otway Burns, a naval hero from the War of 1812 whose tomb is surmounted by a cannon from his ship, and that of an unnamed child buried in a barrel of rum.

FOR MORE INFORMATION
Beaufort Historic Site, 138 Turner Street, Beaufort, N.C. 28516 (800-575-7483 or 252-728-5225; www.nccoastline.com/BHA)

Beaufort's Old Burying Grounds contains headstones dating back to the mid–1700s.

∞North Carolina Maritime Museum

Lovers of things nautical will be entranced the moment they step into the North Carolina Maritime Museum on the Beaufort waterfront. From the building itself, designed in the style of the 19th-century lifesaving stations, to the fully rigged wooden skiffs and sailboats on the display floor, the museum immerses visitors in maritime history. It houses an impressive collection of model ships, decoys, hand tools, fossils, shells, saltwater aquariums, and lifelike dioramas. There are exhibits on the United States Life Saving Service, outboard motors, poisonous reptiles, and deep-sea diving. Artifacts recovered from what is presumed to be Blackbeard's *Queen Anne's Revenge* are also on display.

In the **Harvey W. Smith Watercraft Center**, you can watch experts constructing and restoring wooden boats. The center offers classes in boat building, carpentry, oar making, lofting, tool making, and half-modeling. It also houses the **John S. MacCormack Model Shop**, where scale models of a variety of vessels are constructed.

The museum sponsors special programs throughout the year, including the Wooden Boat Show, held the first weekend in May; a summer science school for children; and the Cape Lookout Studies Program for adults, which includes dolphin and turtle workshops conducted at the museum's outpost at Cape Lookout.

DIRECTIONS
From U.S. 70 in Beaufort, turn south on Turner Street, then right on Front Street.

Rachel Carson Estuarine Research Reserve

Across Taylor Creek from the Beaufort waterfront lies a cluster of small islands, salt marshes, and spoil banks created by the dredging of the Beaufort channel. This estuarine system is home to a broad spectrum of flora and fauna. More than 200 bird species have been recorded here, including piping plovers, oystercatchers, and terns. Feral horses roam the larger islands, feeding on the grasses that grow in the salt marsh.

In the 1940s, scientist and author Rachel Carson conducted research on these islands and through her writing made people aware of their ecological importance. However, the privately owned islands were slated for development in the 1970s, and it was only through the action of the Beaufort Land Conservation Council, working in concert with The Nature Conservancy, that they were saved. Today, they are managed by the state of North Carolina as the Rachel Carson component of the North Carolina Estuarine Research Reserve.

The public is welcome to visit the reserve, although camping is not allowed. This is a great place for beachcombing, swimming, sunbathing, and clamming. On the west side of the reserve, an 0.5-mile interpretive trail meanders through mud flats, uplands, and salt marshes, illustrating the various environments found in estuarine systems. Guided tours are offered through the North

Carolina Maritime Museum. Or you can simply paddle a canoe or kayak over from the Beaufort waterfront.

DIRECTIONS
The reserve's islands lie approximately a hundred yards across the channel from the Beaufort waterfront.

ACTIVITIES
Bird-watching, beachcombing, hiking, picnicking, swimming

FACILITIES
None

DATES
The reserve is open year-round.

FEES
None

CLOSEST TOWN
Beaufort

FOR MORE INFORMATION
North Carolina Estuarine Research Reserve, Rachel Carson Component, P.O. Box 1040, Beaufort, N.C. 28516 (252-728-2170)

RESTAURANTS IN BEAUFORT

Beaufort Grocery
117 Queen Street, Beaufort; 252-728-3899
Expensive

Located in a quaint former grocery store in the heart of Beaufort's historic district, the Beaufort Grocery wins consistent praise as one of the area's finest restaurants. Lunch offerings include gourmet sandwiches and salads. Dinner includes fresh seafood, steaks, free-range chicken, veal, and lamb.

Clawson's 1905 Restaurant
429 Front Street, Beaufort; 252-728-7459
Moderate

Housed in a former general store, this is a popular eatery for tourists visiting the Beaufort waterfront. Clawson's is famous for its seafood bisque. It also has an excellent beer selection and coffee bar.

The Sandbar
232 West Beaufort Street, Beaufort; 252-504-7263
Moderate

This elegant, candlelit restaurant offers fine dining with a view of Town Creek. Among the specialties are fresh seafood, "Duck Grand Marnier," and filet mignon wrapped in bacon.

LODGINGS IN BEAUFORT

Beaufort Inn
101 Ann Street, Beaufort; 800-726-0321 or 252-728-2600
www.beaufort-inn.com
Expensive

This first-class inn is located on the banks of Taylor Creek on the edge of the historic district. Amenities include an exercise room, an outdoor hot tub, and boat slips. Bicycles are available for loan.

The Cedars by the Sea
305 Front Street, Beaufort; 252-728-7036
www.cedarsinn.com
Expensive

Comprised of two historic homes facing the Beaufort waterfront, The Cedars gives guests a true feel for this historic town. All 11 rooms are beautifully furnished with period pieces.

Inlet Inn
601 Front Street, Beaufort; 800-554-5466 or 252-728-3600
www.inlet-inn.com
Expensive

Located on the Beaufort waterfront, the Inlet Inn includes 37 rooms, many with private porches offering views of the sound.

Pecan Tree Inn
116 Queen Street, Beaufort; 252-728-6733
www.pecantree.com
Moderate to expensive

> This seven-room inn is located in an 1860s-era Victorian home in the heart of the historic district. Each room is individually decorated.

Morehead City

Morehead City had a much later start than Beaufort but soon surpassed it in population and economic vitality. The town was begun in 1853 by John Motley Morehead, governor of North Carolina from 1841 to 1845. Morehead purchased the strip of land bounded by Bogue Sound and the western bank of the Newport River, anticipating that it would become the eastern terminus of the Atlantic and North Carolina Railroad and a deepwater port. Both of those dreams were eventually realized, though not to the degree Morehead hoped. The state developed a sprawling port facility here in the 1950s, and at least one oceangoing freighter can usually be seen loading or unloading at the docks. However, the ports of Wilmington to the south and Norfolk, Virginia, to the north have overshadowed Morehead City.

Mostly developed in the 20th century, Morehead City lacks the architecture of Beaufort, but it has a vibrant commercial scene, including a variety of bars, restaurants, and lodgings. The town is best known as the home of the North Carolina Seafood Festival, which is held the first weekend in October and features three days of live music, tours of the state port, fireworks, and plenty of seafood.

The **Carteret County Museum of History and Art** (252-247-7533) at 100 Wallace Drive is worth a visit to understand how life in Carteret County has changed through the ages. The museum has a large collection of Indian artifacts and clothing worn by coastal residents in the 1800s. One room is a Victorian parlor complete with antique furniture, glassware, and artwork. The museum's research library contains an impressive collection of local and national history and genealogy, as well as the best collection of Civil War research materials in eastern North Carolina. The museum is open from 1 P.M. to 4 P.M. Tuesday through Saturday.

With its ready access to the ocean, Morehead City is a center for sailing, fishing, and scuba diving. It is the favored point of departure for divers wanting to explore the many wrecks in the warm waters of the lower North Carolina coast. The **Olympus Dive Center** (800-992-1258 or 252-726-9432) at 713 Shepard Street was voted the number-one dive center in North America by *Rodale's Scuba Diving* magazine in early 2001. Olympus is a full-service dive facility that offers charters, classes, sales, and service.

FOR MORE INFORMATION
Crystal Coast Visitor Center, 3409 Arendell Street, Morehead City, N.C. 28557 (800-786-6962; www.sunnync.com)

Restaurants in Morehead City

Anchor Inn Restaurant and Lounge
2806 Arendell Street, Morehead City; 252-726-2156
Inexpensive to moderate

The Anchor Inn is famous for its lavish breakfasts, which include omelets, waffles, fruits, pancakes, quiches, biscuits, and muffins. At dinner, guests enjoy fresh seafood, Angus beef, and prime rib.

Captain Ottis' Waterfront Restaurant
709 Shepard Street, Morehead City; 252-247-3474
Moderate

This restaurant specializes in fresh seafood delivered daily from the captain's own boats. Steamed clams and shrimp are always available; oysters are available in season. The dockside bar offers live entertainment and a great view of the sound.

Sanitary Fish Market & Restaurant
501 Evans Street, Morehead City; 252-247-3111
Inexpensive

Legend has it that this combination market and restaurant owes its name to the original owners' promise to their landlord to keep the rented premises neat and clean. Opened in 1938, the restaurant has earned fame for serving fresh seafood broiled, steamed, grilled, or fried.

Wreck-Diving off the North Carolina Coast

   With more than a thousand shipwrecks lying off its coast, North Carolina is one of the favorite wreck-diving spots in the country. Many wrecks lie in relatively shallow water (40 to 70 feet) and are thus accessible to beginning and intermediate divers. However, these wrecks are generally in poor condition, often no more than piles of debris scattered on the ocean floor. The best specimens lie in deeper water (80 to 130 feet), where visibility is good and the wrecks are undamaged by draglines and waves.

   The most popular wreck is the *U-352*, a German U-boat sunk during World War II in 115 feet of water 25 miles southeast of Beaufort Inlet. The *Papoose*, a tanker lying in 130 feet of water 37 miles from Bogue Inlet, is a favorite among photographers because of the clarity of the water and the wealth of colorful reef fish around it.

LODGINGS IN MOREHEAD CITY

Best Western Buccaneer Inn
2806 Arendell Street, Morehead City; 800-528-1234 or 252-726-3115
www.bestwestern.com
Moderate to expensive

   This 91-room motel is located next to Morehead Plaza a short drive from Atlantic Beach. Golf, diving, fishing, and outdoor-drama packages are available.

Comfort Inn
3012 Arendell Street, Morehead City; 800-422-5404 or 252-247-3434
www.moreheadhotels.com
Moderate

   The Comfort Inn is close to the Crystal Coast Civic Center and Atlantic Beach. An outdoor swimming pool is among the amenities. Guests enjoy a complimentary deluxe continental breakfast.

Hampton Inn
**4035 Arendell Street, Morehead City; 800-467-9375 or 252-240-2300;
www.hamptoninn.com**
Expensive

> This 119-room inn located on Bogue Sound offers beautiful views
> of the Intracoastal Waterway and Bogue Banks. Amenities include
> an outdoor pool and deck, an exercise room, and two restaurants.

Shackleford Banks

Just to the northwest of Cape Lookout lies Shackleford Banks, the smallest
of the barrier islands that make up Cape Lookout National Seashore. Shackleford
is situated on an east-west axis, perpendicular to the prevailing winds, and is less
buffeted by winds and waves than the islands lying north. This contributes to
Shackleford's having a taller dune system and a larger maritime forest than any
other island in the national seashore.

At one time, some 500 people lived on Shackleford Banks, fishing, farming,
and raising livestock. But the island was devastated by a series of major storms at
the end of the 19th century, and when an 1899 hurricane inundated houses and
fields with salt water, the remaining residents left.

Shackleford Island was added to the national seashore in 1985. At that time,
sheep, goats, cows, and horses ran wild on the island. The National Park Service
proposed removing this livestock to return the island to its natural state. Local
citizens didn't object to the banishment of the sheep, goats, and cows, but they
argued that the horses added to the picturesque atmosphere of the Banks and
ought to be allowed to stay. The Park Service acquiesced. Today, a herd of about
a hundred horses remains on the island.

Shackleford lies barely 0.25 mile off the mainland and is easily accessed by
kayak or water taxi operating out of Beaufort or Harkers Island. People wander
the south-facing beach in search of shells, stroll through the maritime forest on
the sound side of the island, and visit the graveyard where the inhabitants of the
19th-century town of Diamond City are buried.

There are no facilities on the island, so visitors must bring everything they
want. Shackleford is notorious for its terrible chigger and tick population, making bug repellent a must.

Bogue Banks

Bogue Banks is a 24-mile-long barrier island lying just off the Carteret County mainland. It is accessible at the east end via a causeway from Morehead City and at the west end by a bridge from Cape Carteret. Before heading to Bogue Banks, you may want to stop at the **Crystal Coast Visitors Center** (252-726-8148) at 3409 Arendell Street (U.S. 70) in Morehead City. The visitor center, open daily from 9 A.M. to 5 P.M., contains a wealth of brochures on area attractions, accommodations, and services. Among its amenities are restrooms, a gift shop, and a public boat ramp providing access to Bogue Sound.

Bogue Banks offers a variety of natural and man-made attractions. The island has a near-perfect east-west orientation, which allows sunbathers to get the perfect tan while facing the sea. A single road, N.C. 58, runs the length of the island; green milepost markers identify building addresses. Although the island is heavily developed, its scattered wooded areas provide a refreshing break from the stark glare of pavement and sand. Bogue Sound, lying between Bogue Banks and the mainland, supports healthy populations of fish and shellfish and provides a sheltered environment for recreational boating.

There are four incorporated communities on Bogue Banks.

Atlantic Beach is the oldest, having started in 1887 as a seaside pavilion for the Atlantic Hotel in Morehead City. Guests were originally transported to the site by sailboat. In 1928, a toll bridge was built across Bogue Sound from Morehead City, and the area began to blossom as a resort. Today, the permanent population of Atlantic Beach is around 3,000, and the summer population swells to more than 35,000. Atlantic Beach, the most heavily developed portion of Bogue Banks, has an abundance of motels, retail stores, and amusements. As its name implies, the town has an extensive beach. There are three fishing piers along the ocean: **Oceanana Fishing Pier** (252-726-0863) at the end of Oceanana Drive, **Sportsman's Pier** (252-726-3176) at the end of Money Road, and **Triple "S" Fishing Pier** (252-726-4170) at the end of Henderson Boulevard. On the sound side, half a dozen marinas provide dockage and service for recreational boaters. Approximately 16 sportfishing charter boats operate out of these marinas, making this a favorite departure point for deep-sea anglers.

Pine Knoll Shores is located in the middle of Bogue Banks. When he landed on this part of the island in 1524, Italian explorer Giovanni da Verrazano became the first European to reach North Carolina's shores. A marker at the corner of N.C. 58 and Roosevelt Boulevard commemorates that event. Pine Knoll Shores began in the 1950s as a planned community on property owned by the wife and four children of President Theodore Roosevelt. The Roosevelts wanted to ensure that the delicate maritime-forest ecology was respected as the island was developed, a policy the town has followed to a large degree. Homes are tucked beneath the canopy of wind-swept live oaks and loblolly pines. Development here tends to be more upscale than in the other communities on Bogue Banks. There is one fishing pier, **Iron Steamer Pier** (252-247-4213) at Milepost 6.5 on N.C. 58.

Indian Beach abuts Pine Knoll Shores to the west and surrounds the unincorporated community of Salter Path. Families that fled Diamond City on Shackleford Banks in the wake of successive hurricanes settled Salter Path in 1893. Indian Beach was incorporated in 1973. With its intermingling of trailer parks, condominiums, and old and new cottages, this is perhaps the most economically diverse community on the island. Salter Path has several campgrounds that offer access to sound and shore. Most popular is the **Salter Path Family Campground** (252-247-3525) at Milepost 11.5 on N.C. 58. This campground offers tent and RV sites in the shade of live oaks. Amenities include a swimming pool, a boat basin and ramp, bathhouses with hot showers, a laundromat, a playground, and a freshwater fishing pond.

Emerald Isle was also settled by refugee families from Diamond City. Originally known as Middletown, the community remained fairly small until 1971, when the high-rise Cameron Langston Bridge was built across the western end of Bogue Sound. Emerald Isle owes its name to the lush vegetation that once thrived at this end of Bogue Banks. Unfortunately, hurricanes and attacks by the Southern pine beetle (*Dendroctonus frontalis*) have severely diminished the greenery. Emerald Isle is densely developed and sparsely vegetated at its narrow eastern end, where the houses run from sound to shore. The island widens at the western end, where development is tucked among the remaining maritime forest. A cinema complex and a pair of amusement parks at this end of the island provide entertainment for vacationers. **Bogue Inlet Fishing Pier** (252-247-2919) at the end of Bogue Inlet Drive is a gathering place for fishermen and sightseers.

FOR MORE INFORMATION
Carteret County Tourism Authority, 3409 Arendell Street, Morehead City, N.C. 28557 (252-726-8148; www.sunnync.com)

Fort Macon State Park

Hunkered below the horizon at the eastern end of Bogue Banks is one of the best-preserved 19th-century brick fortifications on the East Coast. Completed in 1834, Fort Macon was one of a series of forts constructed at the edge of Beaufort Inlet to defend the port of Beaufort. Fort Macon was designed by General Simon Bernard, formerly Napoleon's military engineer. He was assisted by Captain William Tell Poussin, another French émigré officer. Bernard's distinctive sunken, pentagonal design maximized the field of fire for the fort's cannons while minimizing its exposure to naval bombardment. In the 1840s, Robert E. Lee, then an engineer with the United States Army, designed a series of stone jetties to help minimize erosion along the inlet.

Fort Macon was never attacked by a foreign power, but it did see action during the Civil War. In April 1861, Confederate troops seized it from the Union without a fight. Only one Union soldier was stationed here at the time. A year

The sunken, pentagonal-shaped design of Fort Macon maximized its field of fire while minimizing its exposure to naval bombardment.

later, Federal forces recaptured it after an 11-hour battle. Though the fort was considered indestructible at the time of its construction, the development of rifled cannons enabled the Union to blast right through the four-foot-thick brick walls with relative ease.

Having outlived its usefulness for coastal defense, Fort Macon served as a federal prison during the decade after the Civil War. It was briefly regarrisoned during the Spanish-American War, then officially closed in 1903. In 1924, the federal government sold the fort to the state of North Carolina for one dollar. It subsequently became North Carolina's second state park.

Today, Fort Macon is the most visited state park in North Carolina. People come to wander the labyrinth of rooms surrounding the interior yard and to gaze from the ramparts at Beaufort Inlet. The brickwork in the fort is considered exceptional, as are the ironwork and woodwork. Guided tours are offered, or you can take a self-guided tour using one of the free maps. The museum on the grounds includes exhibits that will acquaint you with the fort. Reenactments are scheduled periodically from spring to fall. In addition to the fort itself, Fort Macon State Park includes a large public beach facing the Atlantic Ocean. The beach includes a bathhouse, a refreshment stand, and a picnic area. Use of all facilities is free.

The park also has a 0.4-mile loop nature trail named after Elliot Coues, a physician assigned to the fort in 1869. A keen admirer of birds, Coues took every opportunity to observe and collect the birds he saw around the fort. He used the information gathered at Fort Macon and other sites to publish his *Key to North American Birds*, an illustrated guidebook widely admired by ornithologists. The

Elliot Coues Nature Trail starts at the entrance to the fort and runs through a thicket of red cedar, yaupon, and wax myrtle. This is a good place to see boat-tailed grackles, Carolina wrens, Northern cardinals, rufous-sided towhees, gray catbirds, and brown thrashers. Leaving the thicket, the trail emerges on to a series of low sand dunes overlooking Beaufort Inlet. The towering cranes and massive storage facilities of the state port at Morehead City are visible to the north, and beyond them is the humble waterfront of historic Beaufort. The trail then runs on to the beach and parallels the inlet heading south. A variety of terns are usually present on the beach during summer. In the winter, brown pelicans, double-breasted cormorants, red-breasted mergansers, and common loons often join them. You can follow the beach for as long as you want or take the loop trail back to the parking lot.

DIRECTIONS
From U.S. 70 (Arendell Street) in Morehead City, take the Morehead Avenue causeway out to Atlantic Beach. Turn left on N.C. 58 and follow the signs to the state park.

ACTIVITIES
Touring fort, swimming, picnicking, hiking, bird-watching

FACILITIES
Museum, bookstore, bathhouse, restrooms, refreshment stand, picnic area, observation deck

DATES
The park is open daily from 9:00 A.M. to 5:30 P.M.

FEES
None

CLOSEST TOWN
Atlantic Beach

FOR MORE INFORMATION
Fort Macon State Park, P.O. Box 127, Atlantic Beach, N.C. 28512 (252-726-3775)

North Carolina Aquarium at Pine Knoll Shores / Theodore Roosevelt Natural Area

To appreciate the ecology of the Crystal Coast, be sure to visit the North Carolina Aquarium and Theodore Roosevelt Natural Area, located side by side in the community of Pine Knoll Shores. The North Carolina Aquarium at Pine Knoll Shores, one of three state aquariums along the coast, is located within Theodore Roosevelt Natural Area, a 265-acre park that preserves the last significant tract of maritime forest on Bogue Banks.

The aquarium will give you a close look at the marine life that exists in abundance in the sea and sounds but is often hidden from view. The main gallery features a darkened room illuminated with porthole-shaped windows. Behind these windows swim a variety of fish common to local waters. "Close Encounters," a water-filled "sandbox," contains live horseshoe crabs, whelks, and starfish that visitors are allowed to handle under the guidance of a staff member. One display is a series of tanks holding young loggerhead sea turtles hatched from nests on nearby Shackleford Banks. The display on hurricanes features dramatic photos of storm damage along the North Carolina coast. "Salt Marsh Safari" leads out the back of the aquarium to a boardwalk overlooking a real salt marsh. Here, you can see egrets, herons, and other wading birds stalking fish and crabs in the tidal creek. The two observation decks with telescopes are excellent viewing areas.

From the end of the boardwalk, you can return to the aquarium or take an extended trek into Theodore Roosevelt Natural Area along the **Alice B. Hoffman Nature Trail**. This maritime forest is dedicated to the family of Theodore Roosevelt, who originally owned the property and sought to preserve it in an environmentally sensitive fashion. The 0.5-mile loop trail follows the crest of an old dune ridge through a forest of loblolly pines and laurel oaks. The forest has been severely battered by hurricanes and a blight of pine beetles, but most of the low-growing trees remain intact. Especially beautiful are the American holly trees, whose bark is splotched with bright red lichen. The low swales to either side of the ridge support a forest of red ash and red maple trees. Virginia chain ferns grow thick in the moist soil, while yaupon seedlings, poison ivy, and partridgeberry thrive on higher ground. This is a "snaky" area; hikers are warned to be on the lookout for the half-dozen species found here—the yellow rat snake (*Elaphe obsoleta*), the black racer (*Coluber constrictor*), the banded water snake (*Nerodia fasciata*), the copperhead (*Agkistrodon contortrix*), the cottonmouth (*Agkistrodon*

Visitors observe an American egret from an overlook on the Alice B. Hoffman Nature Trail.

piscivorus), and the canebrake rattlesnake (*Crotalus horridus atricaudatus*). After climbing a high dune, the trail loops back to the boardwalk.

At the south end of the parking lot, a second trail allows for a more extended trek through the natural area. This unnamed trail runs out and back along another dune ridge for a total distance of 1.2 miles. The forest here is in better shape than the one around the Alice B. Hoffman Nature Trail, and the trail is used more sparsely. At the end of the trail, you'll be rewarded with a great view of Bogue Sound.

DIRECTIONS
From Atlantic City, follow N.C. 58 west to Milepost 7. Turn right at the stoplight on to Pine Knoll Boulevard, then turn left on Roosevelt Drive.

ACTIVITIES
Touring aquarium, bird-watching, hiking, picnicking

FACILITIES
Museum, boardwalk, observation decks, picnic tables

DATES
The aquarium and the natural area are open 9 A.M. to 5 P.M. from Labor Day to Memorial Day. The summer hours are 9 A.M. to 7 P.M.

FEES
A fee is charged to enter the aquarium.

CLOSEST TOWN
Pine Knoll Shores

RESTAURANTS ON BOGUE BANKS

Bogue Banks has nearly 40 restaurants covering every style and price range. Most are on N.C. 58; their locations are identified by milepost. Below is a selection from each of the towns.

Crab's Claw Restaurant
201 West Atlantic Beach Boulevard, Atlantic Beach; 252-726-8222
Moderate

Easily identified by its turquoise walls and prominent location, Crab's Claw offers casual dining with an oceanfront view. The restaurant is noted for its conch fritters, seafood specials, and oyster bar.

Paradise Bar & Grill
Sheraton Oceanfront Resort, Milepost 4, N.C. 58, Atlantic Beach; 252-240-1155
Moderate

Paradise is famous for its Saturday-night seafood buffet and its Sunday champagne brunch. A la carte dinner selections include shrimp and grits, flounder stuffed with lobster, and prime rib. Reservations are recommended for the Saturday-night buffet.

Clamdigger Restaurant
Ramada Inn, Milepost 8, N.C. 58, Pine Knoll Shores; 252-247-4155
Inexpensive

A favorite among locals, the Clamdigger is noted for its breakfast omelets, soft-shell crab sandwiches, and seafood and steak dinners.

Tradewinds
Royal Pavilion Resort, Milepost 5.5, N.C. 58, Pine Knoll Shores; 252-726-5188
Moderate

Tradewinds is an elegant dining facility within an oceanfront resort and conference center. The varied dinner menu includes grilled fish, blackened fish, prime cuts of beef, veal, pasta, and chicken. Theme menus are offered in the fall and winter.

Crab Shack
Milepost 10, N.C. 58, Salter Path; 252-247-3444
Moderate

Specializing in steamed crab and shrimp, the Crab Shack captures the laid-back atmosphere of the beach. The restaurant actually hangs over Bogue Sound. Diners appreciate the outside deck, which lets them enjoy the summer air.

Frank & Clara's Restaurant and Lounge
Milepost 11, N.C. 58, Salter Path; 252-247-2788
Moderate

Frank & Clara's is a handsome lounge beneath the live oaks. Specialties include seafood au gratin, homemade crab cakes, and "Angels on Horseback"—oysters or scallops wrapped in bacon.

Plum Tree
Milepost 9, N.C. 58, Salter Path; 252-808-3404
Moderate

A popular lunch spot and deli, the Plum Tree serves a variety of seafood, beef, and chicken delicacies. It is famous for its crab-cake sandwich, made of lump crabmeat folded on to a croissant with spicy dressing, provolone, lettuce, and tomato. The Plum Tree offers a quiet dining atmosphere, serving dinner by candlelight. Reservations are recommended.

Bushwhackers Restaurant
100 Bogue Inlet Drive, Emerald Isle; 252-354-6300
Moderate

Located at Bogue Inlet Fishing Pier, Bushwhackers is a great place to bring the family. It serves fresh seafood, steaks, and pasta in a lively atmosphere with an excellent view.

Lodgings on Bogue Banks

Bogue Banks has more than 20 motels available for nightly stays and hundreds of beach homes and condominiums available for weekend or weekly rentals. Below is a selection covering a variety of styles and price ranges.

Caribbe Inn
Milepost 1.5, N.C. 58, Atlantic Beach; 252-726-0051
www.caribe-inn.com
Inexpensive to moderate

The Caribbe is a small, family-operated inn located on a side channel to Bogue Sound. The rooms feature colorful aquatic decor. The boatslips, dock, and fish-cleaning area make this a favorite choice of anglers.

Oceanana Family Resort Motel and Pier
700 East Fort Macon Road, Atlantic Beach; 252-726-4111
www.insiders.com/crystalcoast/wwwads/oceanana
Moderate to expensive

Billing itself as "Carolina's most complete family resort motel," the Oceanana is ideal for families with children. Amenities include an outdoor pool, an oceanfront grass recreation area, and free pier fishing.

Sheraton Atlantic Beach Oceanfront Hotel
Milepost 4.5, N.C. 58, Atlantic Beach; 800-624-8875 or 252-240-1155
www.sheratonatlanticbeach.com
Expensive

This full-service oceanfront hotel has a restaurant, a beach-side bar and grill, a fishing pier, indoor and outdoor swimming pools, meeting rooms, a whirlpool, and a fitness center. During summer, a director engages children in a full day of activities.

Atlantis Lodge
Milepost 5, N.C. 58, Pine Knoll Shores; 800-682-7057 or 252-726-5168
www.atlantislodge.com
Moderate to expensive

One of the first motels on Bogue Banks, Atlantis has a loyal following. Advertising itself as "the quiet place," it is set amidst a maritime forest with a view of the ocean. Pets are allowed.

Royal Pavilion Resort
Milepost 5, N.C. 58, Pine Knoll Shores; 800-533-3700 or 252-726-5188
www.rpresort.com
Moderate to expensive

The Royal Pavilion has 156 rooms, most with an ocean view. Amenities include an on-site restaurant, private beachfront, two outdoor pools, a heated indoor pool, and a fitness center.

Harborlight Guest House
332 Live Oak Drive, Cape Carteret; 252-393-6868;
www.harborlightguesthousenc.com
Expensive

Named one of America's "Top Undiscovered Inns" by bedandbreakfast.com in 2002, this guest house offers stunning views of Bogue Sound. Harborlight features seven suites, each with a Jacuzzi and/or a fireplace. A gourmet breakfast is served daily in the waterfront dining room.

White Oak River

Many blackwater rivers course through the coastal plain of North Carolina, but few rival the White Oak for sheer beauty. The river offers boaters two distinctive experiences. The upstream portion is a narrow, winding passage through a swamp forest. Canoes and kayaks are the best craft for exploring this section. The downstream portion consists of a wide channel bordered by a progressively more treeless marsh leading into a broad tidal basin. Sea kayaks and motorboats are best suited to these open waters.

As of this writing, Gibson Bridge Road just north of U.S. 17 near the town of Maysville is the farthest point upstream where you can put in on the White Oak. The river here is narrow as it winds through a beautiful swamp forest. This is a good place to see beavers and other wildlife, as it is well away from roads and houses. The run from Gibson Bridge to the U.S. 17 bridge is approximately 5.5 miles and takes one to two hours.

The run from U.S. 17 to the takeout at Haywood Landing is another popular paddling route. It requires four to five hours and covers approximately nine miles. (Note: a closer takeout is being planned for Dixon Field Road, which will cut this distance in half.) Paddlers will encounter an anomaly just downstream from the bridge—a two-foot ledge that is easily run at normal water levels but that requires a short portage at low water. This sudden drop, unusual for a coastal-plain river, may be the easternmost rapid in the state. The White Oak then enters a series of interconnected man-made lakes, the remnants of a now-defunct marl-quarrying operation. Though not the prettiest environment, this is a good place to see beavers and kingfishers. Beyond the lakes, the White Oak narrows again as it enters a swamp forest dominated by cypresses, gums, willow oaks, and red maples. The shady environs are easy on the eyes, and the low banks allow a view far into the surrounding forest. If you're quiet, you may see a barred owl in the overhanging trees or spook a wild turkey or a white-tailed deer. Where Holston Creek merges in from the east, the White Oak widens and the canopy opens. Wax myrtle and yaupon grow thick on the banks, while arrowroot and pickerel rush dot the shore. Yellow-bellied sliders bask on logs, and a few alligators cruise the banks. A prominent ridge of hardwoods and loblolly pines to the east signals the approach of Haywood Landing. Here, you will find a cement ramp for launching boats on trailers and a picnic area with chemical toilets.

The run from Haywood Landing to the takeout at Stella covers eight miles. Much of this is open water and should be attempted only by sea kayak, as winds and waves can be strong. Swamp forests and freshwater marshes continue to dominate the shoreline for several miles below Haywood Landing. Gradually, the scenery changes as salt water mixes with fresh. The flood plain widens, and trees dwindle. Head-high stands of tall cordgrass line the shore. The skeletons of pines along this stretch of river are evidence that the sea is rising and exposing the vegetation to increasingly salty water. The bridge crossing at Stella is the takeout for this stretch of the river.

Alligators frequent the rivers and ponds of the southern coast, but disappear at the first sight of people.

Note: Beyond Stella, the White Oak enters a wide estuary subject to high winds and waves. This area is not recommended for paddle craft.

Canoe rentals and guided trips down the White Oak are available through several outfitters, including **White Oak River Outfitters** (910-743-2744), **The Boondocks** (252-393-8680), and **Barrier Island Kayaks** (252-393-6457). The Boondocks also offers tent camping and a bunkhouse overlooking the river.

DIRECTIONS

To reach Gibson Bridge from Maysville, drive north on N.C. 3 and turn left on Gibson Bridge Road. There are two access points near the U.S. 17 bridge crossing. With permission, you can park at the private campground beside the bridge or at the quarry just south of the bridge; the latter is the preferable put-in at low water. You can reach the North Carolina Wildlife Resources Commission boat ramp at Haywood Landing by driving south from Maysville on N.C. 58. Approximately 7.2 miles south of town, turn right on F.R. 157 (Loopy Road) and follow the signs to the landing. To reach the bridge crossing at Stella, continue south on N.C. 58, turn right on Kuhns Road, then turn right on Stella Road.

ACTIVITIES

Canoeing, fishing

FACILITIES

There are boat ramps, picnic tables, and toilet facilities at Haywood Landing.

DATES

Open year-round

FEES

A fee is charged to put in at the quarry.

CLOSEST TOWN

Maysville is one mile away.

FOR MORE INFORMATION

Contact the outfitters listed above.

Swansboro

Situated on the bluffs overlooking the mouth of the White Oak River, Swansboro is considered by many to be one of the best-kept secrets on the coast. It's a quiet town with a great location and an attractive, if little-known, historic district.

Swansboro was settled in the 1730s by the Green and Weeks families, who moved south from Falmouth, Massachusetts. Theophilus Weeks laid out the town on his plantation, known as Weeks Wharf. At the town's incorporation in 1783, the North Carolina General Assembly christened it Swannsboro (the second *n* was later dropped) in honor of Samuel Swann, former speaker of the North Carolina House of Representatives and a longtime Onslow County resident.

Swansboro prospered as a port through the Civil War, exporting lumber, tar, and pitch derived from the nearby pine forests. Though its importance as a port city faded after the war, its easy access to sea and sound has made it an active center for commercial fishing and recreational boating. Several large marinas line the waterfront. Old mercantile buildings along South Front Street have been converted to antique shops, restaurants, and coffee houses.

Bike riders may want to pedal the **Swansboro Bicentennial Bicycle Trail**. This 25-mile loop trail follows a marked route along the lightly traveled back roads of Onslow and Carteret Counties. It begins at Bicentennial Park at the Swansboro waterfront, crosses the White Oak River, follows N.C. 24 to Cape Carteret, then winds through Croatan National Forest and back across the river to Swansboro.

The nearby 2,000-seat, waterfront **Crystal Coast Amphitheater** (800-662-5960) offers an outdoor performance of the drama *Worthy Is the Lamb* during the summer. This drama portrays the life of Christ. Call the theater for directions, performance times, and prices.

FOR MORE INFORMATION
Swansboro Area Chamber of Commerce, P.O. Box 122, Swansboro, N.C. 28584 (910-326-1174)

Restaurants in Swansboro

Captain Charlie's Restaurant
N.C. 24 and Front Street, Swansboro; 910-326-4303
Moderate

Captain Charlie's has a loyal following among locals and vacationers from the nearby beaches. Fresh seafood, legendary hush puppies, and high-quality steaks keep them coming back.

The Gourmet Café
99 Church Street, Swansboro; 910-326-7114
Moderate

Located on the second floor of a waterside building, The Gourmet Café offers fine dining and wonderful views of the White Oak River. Dinner specialties include rack of lamb and flounder amandine. The Sunday champagne brunch is highly popular.

Riverside Steak & Seafood
Main Street and N.C. 24, Swansboro; 910-326-8847
Moderate

The Riverside offers a cozy lodge-type atmosphere of natural wood. Game fish are mounted on the walls. The chefs are proud of their Angus steaks, grouper, soft-shell crabs, fried shrimp, and oyster baskets.

White Oak River Bistro
206 West Corbett Street, Swansboro; 910-326-1696
Moderate to expensive

Housed in a white wood-frame building with porches overlooking the river, the White Oak River Bistro serves fine European cuisine, with an emphasis on Italian food. For an appetizer, try the fresh clams or mussels in the shell, mixed with olive oil, garlic, oregano, basil, onions, and diced plum tomatoes. Follow this with a seasoned entrée of veal, chicken, seafood, or beef.

Yana's Restaurant
119 South Front Street, Swansboro; 910-326-5501
Inexpensive

This is the place to go for a cheeseburger, onion rings, and a milk shake. Yana's is housed in an old drugstore in the historic downtown. Its 1950s theme includes barstools, a jukebox stocked with 45 rpm records, and lots of Elvis memorabilia.

LODGINGS IN SWANSBORO

Waterway Inn
160 Cedar Point Boulevard, Swansboro; 252-393-8027
www.waterwayinn.net
Moderate

Situated on the Intracoastal Waterway right next door to Barrier Island Kayaks, the Waterway Inn is ideal for recreational boaters. It offers nine boatslips and 16 rooms, some with refrigerators and microwaves.

Hammocks Beach State Park

Although most of the islands along the southern part of the North Carolina coast have been developed or are off-limits to the public, one—**Bear Island**—is both pristine and accessible. Bear Island is the crown jewel of Hammocks Beach State Park, which includes a 33-acre tract on the mainland near the town of Swansboro and a smaller back-bay island, Huggins Island. For those interested in tent camping on the beach, Bear Island is the place to go.

The mainland site houses the park's headquarters, a visitor center, and a ferry dock providing access to Bear Island. You can either ride the ferry 2.5 miles out to Bear Island or paddle a sea kayak or a canoe. Guided trips and kayak rentals are available from **Barrier Island Kayaks** (252-393-6457) and **The Boondocks** (252-393-8680).

A marked trail guides paddlers along a protected channel among marshy islands dominated by salt cordgrass. Low marsh all but fills the channel between the barrier islands and the mainland, a feature common from this point to the South Carolina border. These marshes owe their presence to a ready supply of fine-grained sediment from the barrier islands' ancient substrata (the Cape Fear

Arch) and tidal currents sufficient to move the sediments. In addition to providing greenery, the marshes are hunting grounds for a variety of wading birds, crabs, otters, and raccoons, which you're likely to encounter on your trip out to Bear Island. The dolphins that frequent these channels may come quite close—an experience you will not soon forget.

The ferry lands on the backside of Bear Island. From there, you can hike a half-mile to the beach. Kayakers and canoeists can land anywhere, but tend to prefer the low spit at the eastern end of the island. Tall dunes anchored by sea oats form the backbone of Bear Island. Grasslands and thickets lie in between. In fact, Bear Island has the most extensive dune field of any island on this part of the coast. On the ocean side, the dunes taper to a wide, flat beach ideal for swimming and wading. A variety of gulls and terns nest just behind the beach, as do endangered loggerhead turtles. Nesting sites are marked by flags and should be strictly avoided.

There are no buildings on Bear Island. The state has marked off 14 campsites, which are available on a first-come, first-served basis. There are no facilities, so campers must bring in (and take out) everything they need. Fresh water is available at the ferry landing, but it may be a long hike from there to your campsite. Overnight camping on Bear Island is a rare treat, especially in fall and early winter, when the bugs are gone. Even a day trip to the island is worthwhile to see what the coastline was like before it was developed. The booming of artillery fire at nearby Camp Lejeune Marine Base is an unfortunate reminder of the island's proximity to civilization, but otherwise, this is as close to a wilderness experience as you will find on this part of the coast.

DIRECTIONS
From Cape Carteret, drive west on N.C. 24, cross the bridge into Swansboro, and turn left on Hammocks Beach Road. The road ends at the state park.

ACTIVITIES
Camping, canoeing, kayaking, picnicking, swimming, fishing, bird-watching

FACILITIES
The Hammocks Beach State Park Visitor Center in Swansboro includes an auditorium, displays, a gift shop, restrooms, a gazebo, a picnic area, a ferry landing, and a public boat launch. The facilities on Bear Island include restrooms, a spigot for drinking water, an outdoor cold shower, and a telephone.

Bear Island offers spectacular coastal scenery untouched by development.

DATES

The visitor center is open from 8 A.M. to 6 P.M. Memorial Day through Labor Day and from 8 A.M. to 5 P.M. other times. The ferry runs from the first weekend in April to the last weekend in October. It departs hourly during April and May and every half-hour other times.

FEES

A fee is charged to ride the ferry.

CLOSEST TOWN

Swansboro

FOR MORE INFORMATION

Hammocks Beach State Park, 1572 Hammocks Beach Road, Swansboro, N.C. 28584 (910-326-4881; www.ncparks.net)

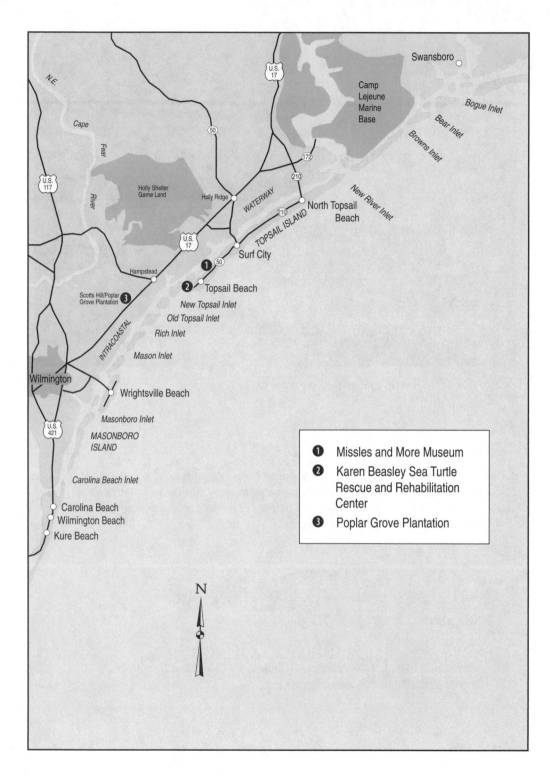

Topsail Island

Topsail Island is a narrow, 26-mile-long barrier island lying half in Onslow County and half in Pender County. A favorite destination for family vacationers, Topsail offers a wealth of houses and condominiums for rent on both the ocean side and the sound side. Many of the island's oceanfront homes were destroyed by wind and storm overwash during Hurricane Fran in 1996, demonstrating the vulnerability of development along the coast. However, most of the homes have since been rebuilt, a testament to the equally strong human desire to remain on the beach.

Topsail Island contains three towns with a total year-round population of around 3,500 and a summertime population swelling to 35,000. **North Topsail Beach**, as its name implies, is the northernmost town on the island. This is a new community of oceanfront condominiums and cottages scattered on the low ground bordering the sound-side marshes. **Surf City**, located on both the mainland and the island, serves as the commercial hub of the greater Topsail area. It provides a variety of restaurants and retail establishments both on and off the island. **Topsail Beach**, at the southern end of the island, has a large selection of rental cottages, several motels and condominiums, and a few small stores and restaurants.

Visitors to the area may first want to call or visit the **Greater Topsail Island Chamber of Commerce and Tourism Bureau** (800-626-2780), located at Treasure Coast Landing off N.C. 50 in the mainland portion of Surf City. The chamber can provide a wealth of brochures and firsthand information on area attractions and lodgings.

Swimming and fishing are the favorite activities at Topsail Beach. The island has three oceanfront fishing piers, although their presence from year to year is never guaranteed, due to the ravages of nor'easters and hurricanes. From north to south, these are **Seaview Pier** (910-328-3171) at New River Inlet Road in North Topsail Beach, **Surf City Ocean Pier** (910-328-3521) at South Shore Drive in Surf City, and **Jolly Roger Pier** (910-328-4616) at 803 Ocean Boulevard in Topsail Beach. **Topsail Soundside Pier** (910-328-3641) at 1522 Carolina Boulevard in Topsail Beach offers fishing on the sound side. Those who want to view the sound-side creeks and marshes from the water can take a ride with *LuLu* Boat Tours (910-328-5071) aboard a 26-foot tug. From April through October, the *LuLu* departs several times a day from the Breezewood Motel dock.

Golfers will enjoy Topsail's proximity to a wide selection of mainland golf courses. Foremost among these is **North Shore Country Club** (910-327-2410), located on N.C. 210 in Snead's Ferry. North Shore has a four-star rating from *Golf Digest*. Its numerous water hazards surround heavily bunkered bent-grass greens.

Like many islands on this part of the coast, Topsail is migrating south and west, driven by longshore currents and rising seas. This is evidenced by the encroaching channel of New River Inlet at the north end of the island and, correspondingly, the wide spit of sand extending beyond the last line of homes at the south end. Much of the north end is now protected from storm overwash only by an artificial dune bulldozed along the oceanfront. After strong nor'easters, this dune is often chopped off, making access to the beach difficult. Before renting a cottage or booking a motel room, check on the status of the property and the beach nearby.

It is a happy accident of nature that Topsail Island is a wonderful hunting ground for fossils. As the meandering New River Inlet wears away the north end of the island, it exposes old fossil-bearing sediments and washes 30-million-year-old sharks' teeth and clamshells on to the beach. Fossilized sharks' teeth are distinguished from "modern" teeth by their jet-black color, which develops when objects made of calcium carbonate are buried in sediments that have no free oxygen.

FOR MORE INFORMATION
Greater Topsail Island Chamber of Commerce and Tourism Bureau, P.O. Box 2486, Surf City, N.C. 28445 (800-626-2780; http://members.tripod.com/topsailjo/society.html)

∞Missiles and More Museum

Since its economy and infrastructure are dedicated almost exclusively to tourism, it's hard to imagine that Topsail Island was once a center for the development and testing of rockets. This and other interesting facets of local history are celebrated in the Missiles and More Museum, located in the Assembly Building at Topsail Beach.

On the heels of World War II, the American military recognized the need to develop a rocket that could travel at supersonic speeds and hit targets at long distances. Working in conjunction with the Johns Hopkins University Applied Physics Laboratory, the United States Navy launched a secret project known as Operation Bumblebee to develop this technology. It chose Topsail Island, then an uninhabited spit of sand, as the key testing ground. A concrete rocket assembly building and eight observation towers were constructed. From 1946 through 1948, the navy fired several hundred missiles from the island. The rockets employed ramjet engines, predecessors of modern jet engines. On this basis, military historians say Topsail Island is to jet propulsion what Kitty Hawk is to propeller flight.

Although the navy's presence is long gone from Topsail Island, the Topsail Island Historical Society felt the island's role in aviation history ought to be celebrated. The Missiles and More Museum opened in 1993 in the building where the rockets were assembled. The museum contains models of three different types of rockets tested on the island and shows a rare video of launches undertaken at that time. It also recalls the history of Camp Davis, a United States Army antiaircraft artillery training facility located in the nearby community of Holly Ridge. Of particular interest is the display on the WASPs—Women's Air Force Service Pilots—who flew airplanes out of Camp Davis during World War II.

The museum also addresses the early history of Topsail Island. Numerous arrowheads and pottery shards are on display, artifacts from Algonquian and Tuscarora Indians who hunted and fished on the island. An impressive artifact is the 18th-century Indian sailing craft made from a cypress log, which was recovered from a local marsh.

DIRECTIONS
Arriving on Topsail Island at Surf City, turn right on N.C. 50 and proceed to the town of Topsail Beach. The museum is located in the Assembly Building at 720 Channel Boulevard.

ACTIVITIES
Viewing displays

FACILITIES
Museum, gift shop

DATES
The museum is open 2 P.M. to 4 P.M. on Monday, Tuesday, Thursday, Friday, and Saturday from April through October.

FEES

Donations are encouraged.

CLOSEST TOWN

Topsail Beach

FOR MORE INFORMATION

Greater Topsail Island Chamber of Commerce and Tourism Bureau, P.O. Box 2486, Surf City, N.C. 28445 (800-626-2780; http://members.tripod.com/topsailjo/society.html)

Karen Beasley Sea Turtle Rescue and Rehabilitation Center

Each year, large numbers of sea turtles are found sick or injured along the North Carolina coast, victims of collisions with boats, dragging by nets, and natural causes such as shark attack. The citizens of Topsail Island have responded to this situation by building and staffing a sea-turtle rescue and rehabilitation center, one of the few in the nation and the only one in North Carolina.

Located in a small cinder-block building behind Topsail Beach's town hall, the Karen Beasley Sea Turtle Rescue and Rehabilitation Center takes in sick and injured sea turtles from along the East Coast and nurses them back to health. As many as 20 turtles may be in residence at any one time, including loggerhead, green (*Chelonia mydas*), and Kemps ridley (*Lepidochelys kempi*) turtles. As soon as the turtles are capable of surviving on their own, they are released back into the wild. Volunteers staff the entire effort, cleaning and feeding the turtles each day and sanitizing the tanks.

This is strictly a rehabilitation facility, not a museum or an aquarium. During the summer, the public is allowed to visit and see the turtles. The building is small, and lines can be long, so visitors are encouraged to come on Monday or Tuesday. People can also volunteer to walk the beach in search of turtle nests, to guard identified nests during incubation periods, or to help out in the hospital, which requires a minimum two-week commitment. Many tourists plan their vacations around these volunteer activities. Others come to witness the turtle releases, which typically occur in mid-June. This is a rare opportunity to get involved in a truly worthwhile effort.

A loggerhead turtle recovers at the Karen Beasley Sea Turtle Rescue and Rehabilitation Center.

DIRECTIONS

Driving south on N.C. 50 in the town of Topsail Beach, turn right on Cruise Street and follow it to the intersection with Carolina Boulevard.

ACTIVITIES

Visitors can view sea-turtle rehabilitation activities and beach hatchings. Volunteers may participate after receiving the proper training.

FACILITIES

Hospital

DATES

The center is open to the public from 2 P.M. to 4 P.M. during the summer. It is closed Wednesdays and Sundays.

FEES

Donations are encouraged.

CLOSEST TOWN

Topsail Beach

FOR MORE INFORMATION

Karen Beasley Sea Turtle Rescue and Rehabilitation Center, P.O. Box 3012, Topsail Beach, N.C. 28445 (910-328-3377; www.seaturtlehospital.org)

Restaurants on Topsail Island

Paliotti's at the Villa Capriani
790 New River Inlet Road, North Topsail Beach; 910-328-8501
Moderate

Paliotti's serves fine Italian food amidst the glamorous surroundings of a villa-style hotel. Pasta is the specialty, accompanying such entrées as veal parmigiana and shrimp scampi.

Mollie's Restaurant
107 North Shore Drive, Surf City; 910-328-0505
Moderate

Mollie's is open year-round for breakfast, lunch, and dinner. Lunch offerings include crab-melt sandwiches and specialty salads. Prime rib, pasta, and fresh seafood are available for dinner.

Soundside & Sounds Edge
209 North New River Drive, Surf City; 910-328-0803
Moderate

Soundside offers fine dining with a view of the Intracoastal Waterway. Its old standby is broiled seafood, but it also serves specialties such as pan-seared halibut with citrus vinaigrette and broiled jumbo shrimp with creamy polenta and black bean sauce. The Sounds Edge bar presents live jazz and blues every Friday.

Latitude 34
1520 Carolina Boulevard, Topsail Beach; 910-328-3272
Moderate

Latitude 34 serves gourmet meals in elegant surroundings with a wonderful view of Topsail Sound. Appetizers include such delights as yellowfin tuna served with a creamy mixture of Parmesan and herbs. Dinner entrées include seafood étouffée, prime rib, and Atlantic salmon and halibut served with a rosemary champagne cream sauce. Reservations are recommended.

Lodgings on Topsail Island

Topsail Island offers motels, condominiums, and cottages for daily or weekly rental in a variety of price ranges.

St. Regis Resort

2000 New River Inlet Road, North Topsail Beach; 800-682-4882 or 910-328-4975
www.ncvacations.com
Expensive

This ocean-side vacation resort offers one-, two-, and three-bedroom condominiums for rent by the week in peak season (June 9 through August 12) and for shorter periods other times. Amenities include a private ocean beach, indoor and outdoor pools, a fitness center, a sauna, tennis courts, shuffleboard courts, and volleyball courts. A pizza restaurant and a convenience store are on the premises.

Villa Capriani

790 New River Inlet Road, North Topsail Beach; 800-934-2400 or 910-328-1900
www.ncvacations.com.
Expensive

Built in the style of a large Italian villa, this luxurious resort offers one-, two-, and three-bedroom units by the week or for a two-night minimum. Villa Capriani has private beach access, two swimming pools, tennis courts, and an on-site restaurant.

Surf Side Motel

121 North Shore Drive, Surf City; 877-404-9162 or 910-328-4099
www.surfsidemotel.net.
Moderate

The Surf Side offers basic motel-style rooms right on the beach. The motel is within easy walking distance of Surf City's pier, restaurants, and gift shops. A large deck overlooks the ocean and the town.

Breezeway Motel and Restaurant

636 Channel Boulevard, Topsail Beach; 800-548-4694 or 910-328-7751
www.breezewaymotel.com.
Moderate

Located on Topsail Sound at the southern end of Topsail Island, the Breezeway is a family-oriented motel with such amenities as an on-site restaurant, a swimming pool, a fishing pier, a boat dock, and a direct walkway to the beach.

Holly Shelter Game Land

Holly Shelter Game Land encompasses approximately 50,000 acres in southeastern Pender County between the Northeast Cape Fear River and U.S. 17. As its name implies, the game land is set up primarily for hunting, offering seasons for white-tailed deer, black bears, wild turkeys, doves, and small game. Hunting limits the chances of seeing these animals, but the game land is still worth a visit for its diversity of plant and bird life. The time to come is on non-hunting days (Tuesdays, Thursdays, Fridays, and Sundays) in the cool parts of the year.

Holly Shelter has been referred to as "the land that no one wanted." The state seized the property during the Great Depression for nonpayment of taxes and, in accordance with the law at the time, offered it to the North Carolina Board of Education. The board had no use for it, so it was passed on to the North Carolina Department of Conservation and Development to become the state's first public game land. The department employed the Civilian Conservation Corps to build a hunting lodge and 70 miles of sandy roads. The lodge no longer stands. Hunting is still allowed, but the state is now focusing on managing the land to promote wildlife conservation.

While Holly Shelter may appear at first to be a monotonous landscape, it contains a diversity of unique ecosystems, including longleaf pine savannas and pocosins. A gated entry off U.S. 17 provides access to the eastern end of the game land. The high ground here supports one of the best longleaf pine and wiregrass savannas in the state. This is an excellent place to see Bachman's sparrows and red-cockaded woodpeckers. Trees with active woodpecker cavities are identified with double white ribbons. Fox squirrels are also common in the longleaf pine savannas, where they can be seen feeding on the large pine cones. Insectivorous plants, including Venus flytraps (*Dionaea muscipula*), pitcher plants, and sundews, grow in the nutrient-poor soil of the game land, though they have been reduced in number by poaching. Be advised that it is against the law to dig these up.

At the western edge of the game land, you'll find boat access and a parking lot beside the Northeast Cape Fear River. A trail leads from the parking lot along a tree-covered dike paralleling the river. This is an excellent place to see protho-notary warblers, Northern parulas, and other Neotropical migrants during the breeding season, which runs from late April to June. Fishing for sunfish, pickerel, warmouth, and catfish is also popular here.

Across Shaw Highway from the boat ramp lies the western entrance to the game land. The gated entry is open to vehicles from September 1 to March 1 and from April 1 to May 15. It is closed at other times, although you may park and walk in as far as you like. Lodge Road starts out through a mixed forest of longleaf pines and turkey oaks that transitions into a pocosin swamp. It is possible to see black bears here, along with white-tailed deer and wild turkeys. The swamp con-tinues for miles, covering some 30,000 acres of the game land.

In May 2002, The North Carolina Nature Conservancy purchased 38,000 acres of land bordering Holly Shelter to the north. Biologists plan to restore the natural longleaf pine forests and wiregrass on what are now loblolly pine forests planted by the former owner, International Paper Company. As of this writing, the land is not open to the public, though it may be in the future.

The Red-Cockaded Woodpecker

The red-cockaded woodpecker is distinctive for a number of reasons, one being that it will nest only in large, live pine trees. Other woodpeckers chisel their nesting cavities out of the soft, rotting wood of dead trees. The red-cockaded insists on boring into the hard heart-wood of living pines, a process that can take a year or more. Scientists theorize that red-cockaded woodpeckers prefer live trees because they evolved in fire-prone pine savannas, where dead trees often go up in flames.

As old-growth longleaf forests became rare, so did the red-cockaded woodpecker. It landed on the endangered species list in 1970. Today, foresters are conducting controlled burns to encourage the growth of longleaf pines, and the outlook for this bird is improving.

Venus flytraps are one of the hidden treasures in the Holly Shelter Game Land.

DIRECTIONS

From Interstate 40 heading south toward Wilmington, take Exit 408 and turn left on N.C. 210. Approximately 0.6 mile after crossing the Northeast Cape Fear River, turn left on Shaw Highway (S.R. 1520). Continue 7.3 miles until you see a North Carolina Wildlife Resources Commission boating access sign. Turn left to access the boat ramp, the parking area, and the dike trail. Continue 0.2 mile north to access the Lodge Road entrance. The eastern entrance is on U.S. 17 approximately 4.4 miles north of its intersection with N.C. 210, just past Topsail Baptist Church.

ACTIVITIES

Hunting, hiking, bird-watching

FACILITIES

None

DATES

The game land is open year-round to pedestrian traffic and from September 1 to March 1 for vehicular traffic.

FEES

None

CLOSEST TOWN

Surf City is approximately eight miles from the eastern gate.

Poplar Grove Plantation

Located on U.S. 17 north of Wilmington, Poplar Grove offers a unique look at 19th-century coastal plantation life and architecture. The 628-acre plantation was once worked by 64 slaves, who raised peas, corn, beans, and swine. In the depressed economy that followed the Civil War, owner Joseph T. Foy managed to keep the plantation afloat by raising peanuts, a novelty at the time.

The Greek Revival plantation house, listed on the National Register of Historic Places, features a high basement and a rear-porch configuration designed to provide relief from the hot, humid coastal climate. Notable outbuildings include a brick smokehouse, a frame carriage house, a tenant house, and sheds.

Today, the house and grounds are open for visitation. Craftspeople demonstrate traditional skills such as weaving, spinning, basket making, and blacksmithing. Poplar Grove also offers classes, workshops, exhibits, and special events throughout the year.

DIRECTIONS
From Wilmington, drive nine miles north on U.S. 17 to Scotts Hill.

ACTIVITIES
Touring home and grounds

FACILITIES
Restaurant, picnic and play area, facilities for weddings and parties

DATES
The plantation is open from 9 A.M. to 5 P.M. Monday through Saturday and from noon to 5 P.M. on Sunday. It is closed Easter Sunday and Thanksgiving Day and from the week of Christmas to the first Monday in February.

FEES
An admission fee is charged.

Wilmington

Of all the cities on the North Carolina coast, Wilmington offers the most museums, historic architecture, restaurants, and nightlife. Boasting a population of more than 90,000, it is the largest city on the North Carolina coast. Wilmington is also highly accessible, lying at the eastern terminus of Interstate 40 and having an airport served by several domestic carriers. Visitors should plan on spending several days here touring the city and its nearby attractions.

Wilmington traces its origins to 1729, when English settlers with an eye to creating a port were drawn to this high ground on the east bank of the Cape Fear River. For the next century and a half, Wilmington served as a key outlet for agricultural and timber products in the southeastern portion of the state. Tar, turpentine, and pitch derived from the region's vast pine forests were major exports, as were lumber and cotton. At one time, Wilmington was the site of the largest cotton exchange in the world.

From 1840 to 1910, Wilmington reigned as the largest city in the state. During that time, a wealthy merchant class, infused with ideas from Northern immigrants and traders, built elaborate homes, churches, and public structures in a variety of architectural styles. Many of these buildings survive to this day.

Wilmington was the Confederacy's most important port during the latter stages of the Civil War. Protected by Fort Fisher at the mouth of the Cape Fear, Wilmington defied Union attempts at a blockade for four years. Fort Fisher finally fell in January 1865, becoming the last Confederate fort to surrender to the Union. Wilmington fell soon thereafter.

During the 20th century, Wilmington's prominence declined. The ports of Charleston to the south and Newport News to the north developed better facilities and siphoned off much of the region's trade. As late as 1990, truckers could access Wilmington only via a two-lane road. While the suburban areas grew, the

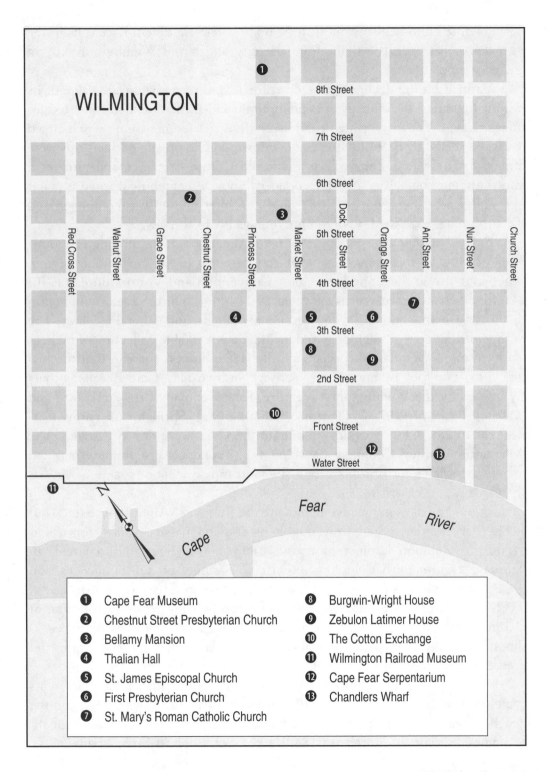

WILMINGTON

8th Street

7th Street

6th Street

5th Street

4th Street

3rd Street

2nd Street

Front Street

Water Street

Red Cross Street
Walnut Street
Grace Street
Chestnut Street
Princess Street
Market Street
Dock Street
Orange Street
Ann Street
Nun Street
Church Street

N

Cape Fear River

1 Cape Fear Museum
2 Chestnut Street Presbyterian Church
3 Bellamy Mansion
4 Thalian Hall
5 St. James Episcopal Church
6 First Presbyterian Church
7 St. Mary's Roman Catholic Church
8 Burgwin-Wright House
9 Zebulon Latimer House
10 The Cotton Exchange
11 Wilmington Railroad Museum
12 Cape Fear Serpentarium
13 Chandlers Wharf

downtown fell into neglect, and historic homes were shuttered. Race riots in the early 1970s hastened the flight from the city and tarred Wilmington with an unsavory reputation.

Alarmed by the decline of the downtown, and recognizing the value of its historic buildings, the citizens of Wilmington decided the time had come to turn things around. The city created the Historic District Commission, which aimed to restore the many beautiful homes downtown. Public-private partnerships were formed to renovate buildings such as the old Cotton Exchange and turn them into shopping complexes. Movie producer Dino De Laurentiis opened a major film studio near the airport in 1983. In 1990, Interstate 40 was completed and the airport was expanded, vastly improving access to the city.

Today, Wilmington is a major tourist destination with a thriving economy. To get an idea of the many sites of interest here and in the surrounding region, begin your visit at the **Cape Fear Coast Convention and Visitors Bureau** (910-341-4030; www.cape-fear.nc.us), located at 24 North Third Street. Wilmington supports a vibrant shopping scene, restaurants, hotels, and cultural facilities. The historic district covers 230 blocks and includes a remarkable collection of meticulously restored Victorian, Georgian, and Italianate homes. You can tour the historic district on foot, by horse-drawn carriage, or by trolley. Guided walking tours are offered by the **Wilmington Adventure Tour Company** (910-763-1785) and **Walking Tours of Old Wilmington** (910-602-6055). **Springbrook Farms Carriages** (910-251-8889) provides 30-minute tours via horse-drawn carriage. The **Wilmington Trolley Company** (910-763-4483) conducts a 45-minute narrated tour that includes historic mansions, TV and movie locations, and Civil War shipyards.

Among the most impressive homes are the **Burgwin-Wright House** (c. 1700) at 224 Market Street, noted for its double piazzas and massive ballast-stone foundation; the **Zebulon Latimer House** (c. 1853) at 126 South Third Street, an Italianate townhouse that employs a remarkable variety of stylistic devices; and the **Bellamy Mansion** (c. 1860), a four-story, 22-room Greek Revival palace at 503 Market Street. The mansion now houses the **Bellamy Mansion Museum of Design Arts** (910-251-3700), which hosts multimedia traveling exhibits, workshops, films, and lectures on regional architecture, landscaping, preservation, and decorative arts. Each of these homes is open to the public for a fee.

Nowhere is Wilmington's urban eclecticism better displayed than in its churches. Fires in the 1830s and 1840s destroyed vast swaths of the city, and the new buildings that went up were of a far more elegant style than the originals. **St. James Episcopal Church** (c. 1840) at 25 South Third Street, built in the

Wilmington is a treasure trove of antebellum architecture.

Gothic Revival style, was considered prime among the new monuments of progress. **St. Mary's Roman Catholic Church** at 412 Ann Street was executed in the Spanish Baroque style with elaborate tiling and stained-glass windows. The tiny **Chestnut Street United Presbyterian Church** at 710 North Sixth Street originally served a congregation of slaves and later a long list of prominent African-American citizens. **First Presbyterian Church** at 125 South Third Street blended the Gothic and Renaissance styles. The church features a stone spire topped with a metal rooster (a sign of the Protestant Reformation), a 1928 E. M. Skinner organ, and intricate stained-glass windows.

Be sure to visit the Wilmington waterfront. The heart and soul of the port city for the better part of a century, this area was spruced up in the 1980s and 1990s to attract tourists. **The Riverwalk**, located along Water Street, offers great views of the Cape Fear River and its commercial and recreational boat traffic. It also provides access to some of the town's best dining, lodging, and shopping. **The Cotton Exchange**, located at 321 North Front Street, houses a variety of shops inside a complex of eight buildings that once comprised the busiest cotton exchange in the world. **Chandlers Wharf**, located at Ann and Water Streets, recreates the heyday of the riverside mercantile district with wooden sidewalks and a cobblestone street. Its renovated warehouses and homes house a number of fine restaurants and shops. You can also tour the Cape Fear River by boat. **Captain Maffit Sightseeing Cruise** (910-343-1611) offers 45-minute cruises aboard a converted World War II navy launch. **Cape Fear**

Riverboats (910-343-1611) offers lunch, dinner, and moonlight cruises aboard its three-tiered paddleboat, the *Henrietta III*.

South of the downtown area on U.S. 421, **Greenfield Lake and Gardens** is a wonderful place for picnicking, walking, and jogging. A paved path runs around a beautiful lake shaded by live oaks and filled with herons, egrets, and ducks. This metropolitan park is open year-round.

FOR MORE INFORMATION
Cape Fear Coast Convention and Visitors Bureau, 24 North Third Street, Wilmington, N.C. 28401 (910-341-4030; www.cape-fear.nc.us)

Battleship North Carolina

The battleship USS *North Carolina* is a must-see attraction for anyone visiting this part of the coast. Berthed in a man-made canal across the Cape Fear River from Wilmington, the 728-foot-long ship is an impressive sight, bristling with nine 16-inch guns, an array of antiaircraft guns, and a deck-mounted seaplane. The *North Carolina* was commissioned in 1941 and saw action in virtually every major campaign in the Pacific, including Guadalcanal, the Solomon Islands, Iwo Jima, and Okinawa. It earned 15 battle stars, more than any other United States battleship in World War II.

To appreciate the genius of the *North Carolina*, take the self-guided tour both above and below decks. The upper deck contains the battle control areas, such as the bridge, the admiral's cabin, the combat information center, the chart house, and the gun turrets. Below decks, you'll find a miniature city housing such support services as a barbershop, a galley, sick bays, and crew's quarters. In the plotting room, you can even see the analog computers used to control the firing of the guns.

The battleship memorial is also a good place to see wildlife. A 12-foot alligator named Charlie has lived in the canal since the 1960s. In the adjacent marshes are wading birds, turtles, and fish.

DIRECTIONS
The battleship is located on U.S. 421 just north of its junction with U.S. 17/74 and U.S. 76. Look for the signs.

Cape Fear Museum

If you want to gain a clear understanding of the Cape Fear region's role in history, don't miss this excellent museum in downtown Wilmington. Starting with prehistory and moving to modern times, the museum highlights key events, technologies, and trade practices characteristic of each era along the way. Whether it's an Indian carving out a canoe, an African-American tapping a longleaf pine for resin, or a model of a blockade runner, the displays are easy to understand and appealing to the eye. Quotes from early explorers provide firsthand accounts of what the region was like in times past.

The ecology of the region is covered in the Michael Jordan Discovery Room. Kids will enjoy the many interactive displays, including a beaver lodge they can climb through. Basketball fans will like the display on native son Michael Jordan, which features such memorabilia as Jordan's college term paper—marked and graded—on the 1984 Olympics.

The museum maintains a steady rotation of temporary exhibits, so there is always something new to see.

Cape Fear Serpentarium

Opened in the fall of 2002, the Cape Fear Serpentarium features a truly remarkable collection of reptiles drawn from the private collection of Wilmington native Dean Ripa. Housed under one roof are some 80 species of snakes from around the world. These include large and deadly spitting cobras, green and black mambas, Gaboon vipers, fer-de-lances, and bushmasters. An eight-foot-long Nile crocodile and a four-foot-long water monitor lizard round out the collection.

As impressive as the reptiles themselves are the displays in which they are housed. Through the use of stone walls, waterfalls, and artificial Mayan ruins, local movie-set designer John Girard has created habitats suggestive of the environments in which the reptiles are found. A soundtrack of jungle drums completes the exotic mood of this museum.

You'll also enjoy the display of African art at the entrance to the serpentarium. Museum-quality masks and statues collected by Wilmington art dealer Charles Jones are available for sale.

The Cape Fear Serpentarium in Wilmington is a must-see for nature lovers.

DIRECTIONS

From Market Street in downtown Wilmington, drive west to Water Street. Turn left on Water Street and left on Orange Street.

ACTIVITIES

Viewing displays

DATES

The serpentarium is open daily from 10:30 A.M. to 9:00 P.M. in summer and from 11:00 A.M. to 5:00 P.M. in winter.

FEES

An admission fee is charged.

FOR MORE INFORMATION

Cape Fear Serpentarium, 20 Orange Street, Wilmington, N.C. 28401 (910-762-1669; www.bushmastersonline.com)

Thalian Hall

City Hall-Thalian Hall

Wilmington's principal civic monument surviving from the antebellum period is City Hall-Thalian Hall at 310 Chestnut Street. Completed in 1858, the L-shaped building has municipal offices in front and a theater behind. It was designed by New York's leading theater architect, John Trimble, and modified by Robert and John Woods, Massachusetts-born brothers who executed many of the fine buildings in Wilmington. The Woods brothers' touch is evident in the towering Corinthian portico. Trimble's is born out in the sweeping interior galleries, supported by iron columns decorated with spiraling grapevines.

In its time, Thalian Hall has brought countless great performers to its stage. The hall was renovated and expanded in the 1980s and renamed the **Thalian Hall Center for the Performing Arts**. Today, the center consists of two theaters—the Main Stage and the Studio Theater—plus a ballroom that doubles as the city council's chambers. Check local listings for upcoming performances. In addition, backstage tours are available Monday through Friday by appointment.

FOR MORE INFORMATION
Thalian Hall Center for the Performing Arts, 310 Chestnut Street, Wilmington, N.C. 28401 (800-523-2820 or 910-343-3664; www.thalianhall.com)

EUE/Screen Gems Studios

In 1983, Hollywood producer Dino De Laurentiis chose Wilmington as the site to build a major film studio. Now under the direction of Frank Capra, Jr., EUE/Screen Gems Studios is the largest full-service film lot in the United States outside of California. The studio, which covers 32 acres across from the Wilmington airport, includes nine sound stages and five production suites.

Over the years, dozens of hit movies like *Firestarter, Teenage Mutant Ninja Turtles*, and *Sleeping With the Enemy* have been filmed here, as was the network television series *Dawson's Creek*. In addition to providing work for many local actors and support staff, the studio has brought a host of big-name actors and actresses to town. These include Bruce Willis, Kim Basinger, Alec Baldwin, and Dennis Hopper. The frequent sitings of Hollywood stars in local bars and restaurants have been an added draw for tourists.

Regardless of whether you get to see a movie star, you'll want to take advantage of Screen Gems' weekend studio tours. Stage sets change over time; the tour currently includes the *Dawson's Creek* school, a $1.5 million castle built for the movie *Black Knight*, and a screening room. For an additional charge, you can watch a stunt production featuring a full-body fire burn; a flame-spewing jet truck; various motorcycle, ATV, and car stunts; and a high fall into an air bag.

DIRECTIONS
The studios are located at 1223 North 23rd Street, across from Wilmington International Airport.

ACTIVITIES
Touring studios, viewing stunt shows

FACILITIES
Film studios, back lots

DATES
Tours start the first weekend in April and run through November. They are held on Saturdays and Sundays at 10 A.M., noon, and 2 P.M.

FEES
A fee is charged.

Louise Wells Cameron Art Museum

The Louise Wells Cameron Art Museum opened in 2002 to take the place of the downtown-based St. John's Museum of Art. Located on 17th Street, the Cameron is dedicated to collecting, preserving, and exhibiting the art of North Carolina. It features permanent collections of the works of such artists as Claude Howell, Francis Speight, Mary Cassatt, Maud Gatewood, and Romare Bearden. Here, you'll see original versions of some of the artwork that decorates the walls of bed-and-breakfasts, hotels, and restaurants throughout the Cape Fear region.

The museum houses a popular atrium restaurant, The Forks, which overlooks a sculpture garden. It has an expansive gift shop where visitors can purchase beautiful crafts (many by North Carolina artists) at reasonable prices. Located on the grounds are restored Confederate defensive mounds built during the Battle of the Forks Road, fought in the last days prior to the fall of Wilmington during the Civil War.

DIRECTIONS
From the end of Interstate 40 in Wilmington, continue on College Road for five miles. Turn right on 17th Street and proceed one mile to the museum entrance.

ACTIVITIES
Touring museum

FACILITIES
Auditorium, museum shop, restaurant

DATES
The museum is open from 10:00 A.M. to 5:00 P.M. Tuesday, Wednesday, Thursday, and Saturday; from 10:00 A.M. to 9:00 P.M. on Friday; and from 10:30 A.M. to 4:00 P.M. on Sunday.

Wilmington Railroad Museum

Much of Wilmington's prosperity in the mid-19th century was due to the construction of the Wilmington and Weldon Railroad, which allowed goods brought into the port city to be shipped inland and sold at a profit. At the time of its completion in 1840, the Wilmington and Weldon was considered the world's longest rail line.

The key role that railroads played in the city's development is celebrated in the Wilmington Railroad Museum, located in the former Atlantic Seaboard freight traffic office at 501 Nutt Street. Just outside the entrance are a 1910 Baldwin steam locomotive and a red caboose. Inside, you'll find all manner of railroad memorabilia, including vintage lanterns, postcards, and photos of historic train wrecks. Those who remember riding the rails in the 1940s, 1950s, and 1960s will especially enjoy the old menus and place settings. Upstairs, the museum houses an enormous model railroad diorama maintained by the Cape Fear Model Railroad Club. Kids will enjoy participating in the club's scavenger hunt, in which they are challenged to find such things as "woman throwing out dirty water" and "man in outhouse"among the hundreds of scale model figures.

DIRECTIONS

From Market Street in downtown Wilmington, drive west to Water Street at the Cape Fear River. Turn right on Water Street and drive to the end of the street.

ACTIVITIES

Viewing displays, operating model trains, climbing on rolling stock

DATES

From March 15 through October 14, the museum is open from 10 A.M. to 5 P.M. Monday through Saturday and from 1 P.M. to 5 P.M. on Sunday. From October 15 through March 14, it is open from 10 A.M. to 4 P.M. Monday through Saturday.

FEES

An admission fee is charged.

FOR MORE INFORMATION

Wilmington Railroad Museum, 501 Nutt Street, Wilmington, N.C. 28401 (910-763-2634; www.wilmington.org/railroad)

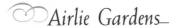

Airlie Gardens

The Wilmington area is renowned for its spectacular springtime floral displays. Nowhere are these better seen than at Airlie Gardens, a 67-acre Eden bordered by Bradley Creek and the Intracoastal Waterway. Now operated by New Hanover County, Airlie Gardens was originally the private garden of Sarah and Pembroke Jones. Beginning in the early 1900s, they planted a quarter-million to a half-million azaleas, thousands of camellias, and numerous magnolias and live oaks. The azaleas flower from March to April, the magnolias in summer, and the camellias from October through April, assuring that something is blooming here every month. Other attractions on the grounds include the 450-year-old Airlie Oak, a stone pergola built in the 1920s, and numerous statues and fountains. Approximately 10 acres of lakes dot the grounds, attracting a variety of waterfowl. Self-guided tours are available using maps available at the front gate.

DIRECTIONS

From the intersection of College Road (N.C. 132) and Oleander Drive (U.S. 76) in Wilmington, drive east on Oleander, following the signs for Wrightsville Beach. Just before the bridge over the Intracoastal Waterway, turn right on Airlie Drive. The main gate is on the right after 1.3 miles.

ACTIVITIES

Touring gardens

FACILITIES

Restrooms

RESTAURANTS IN WILMINGTON

Wilmington is chock-full of excellent restaurants and cafés. Below is a sampling of those in the downtown area.

Caffe Phoenix
9 South Front Street, Wilmington; 910-343-1395
Moderate

Located in a high-ceilinged historic building in downtown Wilmington, Caffe Phoenix combines great atmosphere with excellent Mediterranean cuisine. It features a coffee bar in the morning.

Caprice Bistro
10 Market Street, Wilmington; 910-815-0810
Moderate

This small, informal restaurant features authentic French cuisine, including homemade pâté, *steak au poivre* with hand-cut *pommes frites* (French fries), rabbit stew, and an excellent selection of desserts.

Circa 1922
8 North Front Street, Wilmington; 910-762-1922
Moderate

Located right next door to Caffe Phoenix, the equally stylish Circa 1922 specializes in tapas—small portions of creative dishes meant to be shared among friends. Selections range from "Pad Thai" to "Lamb Shank Confit" to shrimp and grits.

Deluxe
114 Market Street, Wilmington; 910-251-0333.
Moderate to expensive

From the initial serving of dill bread to the chocolate crème brûlée dessert, every dish at this restaurant is delicious. The entrées include filet mignon, herb-rubbed salmon with lobster cognac sauce, and rosemary-seared duck breast.

Elijah's
Chandlers Wharf, Wilmington; 910-343-1448
Moderate

For those looking for an informal spot to sit by the water and enjoy a beer and a plate of oysters, this is the place to go. Located on the Cape Fear River, Elijah's has plenty of seating and a diverse menu. This is a good place to bring the family. Don't leave without trying the crab dip.

Lodgings in Wilmington

Wilmington has numerous excellent motels, inns, and bed-and-breakfasts. Below is a small sampling of those in the downtown area.

Best Western Coast Line Inn
503 Nutt Street, Wilmington; 910-763-2800
Moderate to expensive

Located at the historic Coast Line Center, a former railroad depot on the Cape Fear River, this motel offers 53 rooms, each with a river view. It is on The Riverwalk and close to The Cotton Exchange. The on-site Grouper Nancy's Restaurant offers indoor and outdoor seating by the river.

Catherine's Inn
410 South Front Street, Wilmington; 800-476-0723 or 910-251-0863
Moderate to expensive

Located in a beautiful 1883 home on a shady street, Catherine's Inn offers five elegant rooms, each with its own decor. A two-story screened porch in the rear and a spacious private lawn overlook the Cape Fear River.

Front Street Inn
215 South Front Street, Wilmington; 800-336-8184
www.frontstreetinn.com
Expensive

Lovers of fine art and architecture will enjoy staying at this historic inn, which has arched windows, metal railings, and maple floors. Each of the 10 rooms is individually decorated and full of natural light. The second-floor rooms have river views and balconies. The Sol y Sombra Bar and Breakfast Room serves healthful breakfasts, beer, wine, and champagne.

Hilton Wilmington Riverside
301 North Water Street, Wilmington; 910-763-5900
www.wilmingtonhilton.com
Expensive

A fixture on the Wilmington waterfront since its construction in the early 1970s, this nine-story hotel offers fantastic views of the Cape Fear River and a prime location on The Riverwalk. The poolside cabana bar is a popular gathering spot that features live music on Friday evenings in summer.

The Wilmingtonian
202 Nun Street, Wilmington; 910-251-2212
www.verandas.com
Expensive

Surrounded by historic homes and churches in the heart of downtown Wilmington, this inn consists of five buildings of various ages and styles. The 40 suites are individually designed and furnished, some with kitchens for long-term stays (favored by actors at the nearby film studios). Guests have the privilege of dining at the Wilmingtonian Club in the historic de Rosset House.

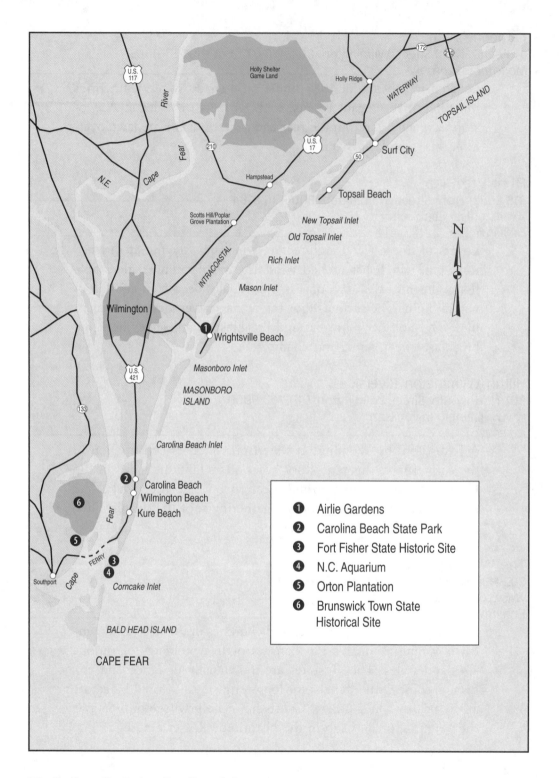

Holly Shelter
Game Land

U.S. 117

River

Fear

Cape

N.E.

210

Hampstead

Holly Ridge

WATERWAY

TOPSAIL ISLAND

172

210

U.S. 17

Surf City

50

Topsail Beach

New Topsail Inlet

Old Topsail Inlet

Scotts Hill/Poplar
Grove Plantation

INTRACOASTAL

Rich Inlet

Mason Inlet

N

Wilmington

① Wrightsville Beach

Masonboro Inlet

MASONBORO
ISLAND

U.S. 421

133

Carolina Beach Inlet

② Carolina Beach
Wilmington Beach

Kure Beach

⑥

Fear

⑤

FERRY

③

④

Southport

Cape

Corncake Inlet

BALD HEAD ISLAND

CAPE FEAR

① Airlie Gardens
② Carolina Beach State Park
③ Fort Fisher State Historic Site
④ N.C. Aquarium
⑤ Orton Plantation
⑥ Brunswick Town State
   Historical Site

Wrightsville Beach

Due east of Wilmington lies one of the oldest beach resorts in the state. Incorporated in 1899, the town of Wrightsville Beach occupies a five-mile-long island of the same name. For more than a century, it has been the principal retreat for residents of the Wilmington area. A trolley once ran from the downtown area to Wrightsville Beach, bringing riders to the famed Lumina Pavilion for a day of beach games, bowling, and dancing in the enormous ballroom. The trolley was discontinued in 1940, and the Lumina was torn down in 1973. The history of Wrightsville Beach, including a scale model of the town as it looked around 1910, is nicely captured in the **Wrightsville Beach Museum of History** (910-256-2569) at 303 West Salisbury Street.

Today, Wrightsville Beach is densely developed, yet it retains a certain charm, owing to the age and traditional wood-shingle style of many of its cottages and the relative lack of commercial establishments. Most houses are owned by longstanding residents and have been passed on from generation to generation. Boating is extremely popular here, as evidenced by the ever-busy marinas clustered around the bridge over the Intracoastal Waterway. Visitors can charter powerboats and sailboats and rent jet-skis, kayaks, and more. Those towing their own boats can launch them via a free public ramp at Harbour Island, which lies between Wrightsville Beach and the mainland.

The public can access the beach at numerous points along the island, though parking spaces are limited. During peak season, visitors are advised to arrive early in the morning if they want to find a space.

Pier fishing is available at **Johnnie Mercer's Pier** (910-256-2743) at the foot of East Salisbury Street. This new concrete pier replaces a wooden one destroyed by Hurricane Floyd.

FOR MORE INFORMATION
Cape Fear Coast Convention and Visitors Bureau, 24 North Third Street, Wilmington, N.C. 28401 (910-341-4030; www.cape-fear.nc.us)

Restaurants on Wrightsville Beach

Bluewater, An American Grill
4 Marina Street, Wrightsville Beach; 910-256-8500
Moderate

Located just over the bridge from the mainland, this two-story restaurant offers great views of the boat traffic along the Intracoastal Waterway. Local seafood is the specialty. Steaks, chicken, and barbecued ribs are also served.

Brown Dog Grill
7105 Wrightsville Avenue, Wrightsville Beach; 910-256-2688
Moderate

Its menu prepared by L'Académie de Cuisine graduate Paul Hornung, the Brown Dog Grill offers gourmet fare in an intimate setting. Dinner specialties include pan-seared and mesquite-grilled meats and seafood, served with fresh vegetables and innovative sauces.

Dockside Restaurant and Marina
1308 Airlie Road, Wrightsville Beach; 910-256-2752
Moderate

The Dockside offers a superb view of the Intracoastal Waterway. Guests have the option of dining indoors or out. Specialties include seafood marinara, shrimp Creole, and seafood lasagna.

Oceanic Restaurant
703 South Lumina Avenue, Wrightsville Beach; 910-256-5551
Expensive

Voted "Best Seafood Restaurant" and "Best View" by *Encore* magazine in 2000, the three-story Oceanic offers excellent food and a superb view of the ocean. Specialties include pan-seared grouper in a crust of cashews and sesame seeds, served over mashed potatoes. Outdoor dining on the pier is available in summer.

Blockade Runner Resort Hotel

275 Waynick Boulevard, Wrightsville Beach; 800-541-1161 or 910-256-2251
www.blockade-runner.com

Expensive

This 150-room hotel sits right on the ocean. All rooms have either an oceanfront or a sound-side view. Amenities include a restaurant and lounge, free entertainment, and a sailing center. Free limousine service is offered to Wilmington International Airport.

Carolina Temple Apartments

550 Waynick Boulevard, Wrightsville Beach; 910-256-2773
www.capefear.nc.us/CAT/

Moderate

Consisting of two Plantation-style cottages built in the early 1900s, Carolina Temple Apartments offers modern comforts with a link to the past. All 16 units are air-conditioned and have kitchenettes, private baths, and large porches. Rooms rent primarily by the week from June through August.

Masonboro Island

Situated between Wrightsville Beach and Carolina Beach is an eight-mile-long undeveloped island that is protected as part of the North Carolina Estuarine Research Reserve system, also known as the North Carolina Coastal Reserves. Masonboro Island is the largest undeveloped barrier island on this part of the coast. Accessible only by boat, it consists of a beach-and-dune complex that fronts a wide salt marsh. The narrow line of dunes is continually being overwashed and is retreating into the marshes as the sea level rises.

Masonboro Island is a favorite place for surfing and swimming away from the crowds. It is also a good site for birding. Wilson's plovers (*Charadrius wilsonia*) nest here. Dick's Bay at the south end of the island is a good place to see marbled gotwits (*Limosa fedoa*) and perhaps piping plovers. From autumn to spring, the salt marsh harbors large numbers of sharp-tailed (*Ammospiza caudacuta*) and seaside (*Ammospiza maritima*) sparrows.

Masonboro Island can be accessed from public boat ramps on the Intracoastal Waterway off U.S. 74/76 or from Wrightsville Beach or Carolina Beach. You can land anywhere the draft of your boat allows. Overnight camping is permitted except on the frontal dunes. There are no facilities of any kind, so be sure to bring everything you will need.

FOR MORE INFORMATION

North Carolina Coastal Reserves, 135 Duke Marine Lab Road, Beaufort, N.C. 28516 (252-728-2170; www.ncnerr.org)

Pleasure Island

Pleasure Island is a chamber-of-commerce-derived name for the 12-mile-long island/peninsula running from Carolina Beach Inlet in the north to Fort Fisher Recreation Area in the south. It is separated from the mainland by a man-made cut for the Intracoastal Waterway. Pleasure Island supports a mixture of developed and natural areas, all easily accessible via U.S. 421, which runs the length of the island.

Immediately after crossing the bridge over the Intracoastal Waterway, you'll arrive at the town of **Carolina Beach**. Until recently, Carolina Beach was considered a party town that appealed primarily to a young crowd. Many beach cottages were poorly maintained, and the landscaping was sparse. However, the town underwent a transformation in the 1990s to become more family-oriented. Today, it is a mixture of upscale single-family homes and condominiums interspersed with 1950s-style beach cottages and motels.

Carolina Beach's chief drawing card is that its beach, boardwalk, motels, shopping, and entertainment all lie within walking distance of one another. The town is centered around a municipal yacht basin (910-458-2985) that is home to numerous charter fishing boats and a fleet of cruise ships operated by **Winner Cruise Boats** (910-458-5356). During the summer, Winner offers regularly scheduled 90-minute excursions on the Intracoastal Waterway. The cruise boats are a popular form of nightlife, featuring dinner, dancing, and alcohol. The town's boardwalk fronts the ocean on one side and a multitude of arcades, shops, and nightclubs on the other. The blue-collar environment appeals primarily to those who like to walk right off the beach to a barstool or pinball machine.

A typical day's catch for a Pleasure Island charter fishing expedition

The **Carolina Beach Fishing Pier** (910-458-5518) at 1800 Carolina Avenue draws anglers and sightseers in droves. It has a snack bar, a grill, a game room, and a tackle shop. The **Jubilee Amusement Park** (910-458-9017) at 1000 North Lake Park Boulevard is a major family attraction featuring three water slides, three go-cart tracks, bungee jumping, and an arcade. The town's famous Beach Music Festival, held each June, features big-name shag music bands.

For those wanting to get close to nature, **Carolina Coastal Adventures** (910-458-9111) offers guided kayak and motorboat trips to numerous destinations in the area. One popular outing for kayakers explores the nearby Fort Fisher Basin, approximately 8,000 acres of protected marsh and shoals loaded with shorebirds. Carolina Coastal Adventures also offers inshore and near-shore fishing and sightseeing trips in its powered skiffs.

Just south of Carolina Beach is the town of **Kure Beach**. Incorporated in 1947, Kure is primarily a residential community of modest beach cottages. Zoning prohibits structures taller than 35 feet. Kure bills itself as a family-oriented beach and has lifeguards on duty during the summer season. Aside from the beach itself, the **Kure Beach Pier** (910-278-5962) at Avenue K is the main attraction. The pier has a snack shop, a tackle shop, and an arcade.

FOR MORE INFORMATION
Cape Fear Coast Convention and Visitors Bureau, 24 North Third Street, Wilmington, N.C. 28401 (910-341-4030; www.cape-fear.nc.us)

ᴄᴏCarolina Beach State Park

Just south of Snow's Cut at the northern end of Pleasure Island lies Carolina Beach State Park. This 1,773-acre park may seem unimpressive at first glance. The scrubby forest bordering the entry road lacks the grandeur of Nags Head Woods or the Green Swamp. But the park contains a remarkable diversity of plant species—some 240 in all, according to one recent study, including 30 that are rare in North Carolina. It also offers one of the few public campgrounds on this part of the coast and a marina providing access to the Cape Fear River.

Carolina Beach State Park has six miles of trails winding through a variety of habitats. Be sure to stop at the park office to pick up a trail map, as the crisscrossing network of footpaths—both official and unofficial—can be confusing. The "headliner" is the **Fly Trap Trail**, an easy 0.5-mile loop named for the insectivorous plant that grows here. The trail starts out along an impene-trable pocosin, thick with wax myrtle, gallberry, and red bay. It then opens on to a grassy savanna shaded by longleaf and pond pines. The waterlogged soil of the savanna is deficient in nitrogen, a key ingredient for plant growth. To survive here, plants must get nitrogen from another source. The insectivores—the sun-dew, the Venus flytrap, and the bladderwort—obtain nitrogen by capturing and digesting insects. Insectivorous plants are frequently poached and are thus not identified by signs. However, by examining the drawings provided in the Fly Trap Trail brochure, you should be able to find some of the plants hidden amongst the bracken ferns and wiregrass. Beyond the savanna, the trail enters a plant commu-nity known as a dry sand ridge (or xeric sand-hill scrub). Since the sandy soil dries out quickly after rain, the plants growing here—longleaf pines with an un-derstory of turkey oaks (*Quercus laevis*) and bear grass (*Yucca filamentosa*)—have deep taproots and, in the case of the latter two plants, leathery leaves suited to holding precious moisture.

The other signature trail in the park is the **Sugarloaf Trail**, a three-mile loop that begins and ends at the marina parking lot. The trail passes along the Cape Fear River and crosses tidal marshes on boardwalks before reaching Sugarloaf Dune, a 50-foot high relict sand dune rising above the forest canopy. For centu-ries, the dune has been used as a landmark by ships navigating the Cape Fear River. The trail continues through dry sand ridges interspersed with freshwater wetland communities, including several ponds and a rare cypress savanna.

The park's campground has two bathhouses with showers and 82 drive-in campsites available on a first-come, first-served basis. Most offer full or partial shade. The full-service marina has two boat ramps. There is a handicapped-accessible fishing deck on the Cape Fear River.

DIRECTIONS
From U.S. 421 south of the Snow's Cut bridge, turn west on Dow Road. Follow the signs to the park entrance.

ACTIVITIES
Hiking, camping, and boating are allowed, but swimming is not.

FACILITIES
Campground, marina, picnic area, park office with restrooms

DATES
The park is open year-round.

FEES
Admission to the park is free. A fee is charged for camping.

CLOSEST TOWN
Carolina Beach is one mile away.

FOR MORE INFORMATION
Carolina Beach State Park, P.O. Box 475, Carolina Beach, N.C. 28428 (910-458-8206; www.ncparks.net)

Fort Fisher State Historic Site

Visitors to Fort Fisher may be disappointed to find that a series of earthen mounds is all that is to be seen of this once-formidable defensive work, which ran for a mile along the Cape Fear River. However, Fort Fisher is highly significant for the role it played in the Civil War and is well worth a visit for those who enjoy history. This fort was the centerpiece of the Confederate army's Cape Fear defenses, designed to keep the port of Wilmington open to ships able to run the Union blockade. Unlike older forts built of brick and mortar, Fort Fisher consisted mostly of earth and sand, which made it ideal for absorbing the shock of cannon fire.

Union forces made two assaults on Fort Fisher. The first, in December 1864, was repulsed with heavy loss of life. Union forces returned in January 1865 with

Fort Fisher occupied a key position guarding the mouth of the Cape Fear River.

an armada of 50 warships and more than 3,000 infantry. Ships bombarded the fort for two and a half days. The infantry followed with an attack that lasted another day. After fierce hand-to-hand combat, the fortress fell. Within weeks, Union forces occupied Wilmington, and the last Confederate supply line was severed.

Today, you can stroll the earthworks and climb a reconstructed battery. The visitor center, renovated in 2002, offers a 15-minute audiovisual program, displays depicting the original fort, a fiberoptic map describing the battles, and artifacts from the fort. The Cove, a grassy area beside the fort shaded by picturesque live oaks, provides a great place for kids to run.

Naturalists will want to take a stroll down to the water to look at the unusual "hard-ground" habitat visible at low tide. The rocks off Fort Fisher are of a type rarely seen above the sea's surface. They represent the near-shore edge of a series of sandstone and mud-stone ledges that occur across the continental shelf and along the topographic change in seafloor slope known as the shelf-slope break. These subsurface ledges support diverse communities of algae, soft and encrusting coral, sea anemones, sea whips, and finfish.

DIRECTIONS
Fort Fisher is located on U.S. 421 south of Kure Beach.

ACTIVITIES
Touring fort and museum

FACILITIES
Museum with restrooms, a gift shop, and a 15-minute audiovisual program

DATES
From April through October, the site is open from 9 A.M. to 5 P.M. Monday through Saturday and from 1 P.M. to 5 P.M. on Sunday. From November through March, it is open from 10 A.M. to 4 P.M. Tuesday through Saturday and from 1 P.M. to 4 P.M. on Sunday.

FEES
None

CLOSEST TOWN
Kure Beach is one mile away.

FOR MORE INFORMATION
Fort Fisher State Historic Site, 1610 Fort Fisher Boulevard, Kure Beach, N.C. 28449 (910-458-5538; www.ego.net/us/nc/ilm/tts/ftfisher.html)

North Carolina Aquarium at Fort Fisher

Reopened in 2002 after a $17 million renovation, the Fort Fisher aquarium is a state-of-the-art facility. After walking through the entrance, you'll find yourself in a half-acre greenhouse filled with artificial rock ledges and trees depicting the headland of the nearby Cape Fear River. Jets of water vapor moisten the live plants in the understory. A tumbling waterfall feeds a tank filled with sturgeon, carp, and perch native to the upstream reaches of the river. A second tank holds alligators and turtles common to the blackwater swamps of the coastal plain.

The Coastal Waters exhibit features a touch tank similar to those found in the other state aquariums. Here, you can handle horseshoe crabs and conchs under the eye of aquarium staff. This is one of the best ways for children to gain an understanding of these creatures' physiognomy and habits. The show-stopper of the aquarium is the Cape Fear Shoals Open Ocean Tank, a two-story aquarium filled with stingrays, sharks, and moray eels, among other creatures. Divers periodically give narrations from inside the tank, answering questions via audio systems built into their masks. And don't miss the jellyfish tank, lit by a blue light against a black background. Jellyfish ordinarily seen washed up on the beach are here revealed in all their graceful beauty.

The Cape Fear Shoals Open Ocean Tank at the North Carolina Acquarium at Fort Fisher

DIRECTIONS

The aquarium is located on U.S. 421 south of Kure Beach. Follow the brown road signs.

ACTIVITIES

Touring museum

FACILITIES

Museum, gift shop

DATES

The aquarium is open daily from 9 A.M. to 5 P.M. It is closed Thanksgiving, Christmas, and New Year's Day.

FEES

An admission fee is charged.

CLOSEST TOWN

Kure Beach is one mile away.

FOR MORE INFORMATION

North Carolina Aquarium at Fort Fisher, P.O. Box 1, Kure Beach, N.C. 28449 (910-458-8257; www.ncaquariums.com)

Fort Fisher State Recreation Area

This four-mile stretch of undeveloped beach and tidal marsh provides the public with access to the Atlantic Ocean. Four-wheel-drive vehicles are allowed on the beach here, making this a popular destination for surf fishermen and off-road enthusiasts. A small visitor center provides basic information on the area. A bathhouse and a concession stand are also on the premises.

DIRECTIONS
The recreation area is located on U.S. 421 south of Kure Beach. Follow the brown road signs.

ACTIVITIES
Swimming, fishing, beachcombing, four-wheeling

FACILITIES
Visitor center, bathhouse, concession stand

DATES
The recreation area is open daily from 8 A.M. to 5 P.M. It is closed on state holidays.

FEES
None

CLOSEST TOWN
Kure Beach is one mile away.

FOR MORE INFORMATION
Fort Fisher State Recreation Area, 1000 Loggerhead Road, Kure Beach, N.C. 28449 (910-458-5798)

Fort Fisher-Southport Ferry

This half-hour ferry ride is extremely useful for getting to and from the many attractions on opposite sides of the Cape Fear River. It allows travelers to conduct what is known as **The Circle Tour** of Wilmington, Southport, Pleasure Island, and points in between. The ride offers excellent views of the Price's Creek

Laughing gulls trail the Fort Fisher ferry.

Lighthouse, Zeke's Island, The Rocks, and the Sunny Point Army Terminal. Travelers are also likely to see giant freighters traveling the river on their way to and from Wilmington. Reservations are not required. Call 800-BY-FERRY for fare and schedule information.

RESTAURANTS ON PLEASURE ISLAND

The Cottage
1 North Lake Park Boulevard, Carolina Beach; 910-458-4383
Moderate

Located in a 1916 Bungalow-style dwelling listed on the National Register of Historic Places, The Cottage offers a handsome environment and excellent food. Gourmet seafood dinners such as "Masonboro Fish in Foil," soft-shell crabs, and Wanchese scallops are offered, as are a variety of pastas with homemade sauces.

The Deckhouse
205 Charlotte Avenue, Carolina Beach; 910-458-1026
Moderate

The Deckhouse comes highly recommended for its seafood, steaks, and chicken. A specialty of the house is grouper piccata, sautéed in lemon butter, white wine, and capers. The restaurant has a large bar area.

Michael's Seafood Restaurant & Catering
1018 North Lake Park Boulevard, Carolina Beach; 910-458-7761
Moderate

Voted "Restaurant of the Year" in 2001 by the Wilmington Chamber of Commerce, Michael's is best known for its seafood chowder, a rich mix loaded with crabmeat, clams, scallops, and vegetables. The restaurant sends its chowder all over the country. Kids will enjoy the aquariums containing tropical fish, alligators, and a giant eel.

The Lighthouse
113 Avenue K, Kure Beach; 910-458-5608
Moderate

Featuring both a restaurant and a raw bar, The Lighthouse offers a choice of dining in either an intimate or a lively environment. Its signature entrée is "The Lighthouse Bucket," which includes shrimp, scallops, oysters, mussels, and clams, served with steamed corn and red potatoes.

LODGINGS ON PLEASURE ISLAND

Atlantic Towers
1615 South Lake Park Boulevard, Carolina Beach; 800-BEACH-40 or 910-458-8313
www.atlantic-towers.com
Moderate

This 11-story facility offers 137 condominiums, all with ocean views and private balconies. It has outdoor and indoor swimming pools, a game room, and a conference room. It is open year-round.

The Savannah Inn
316 Carolina Avenue North, Carolina Beach; 910-458-6555
www.thesavannainn.com
Moderate

"We Cater to Picky People," announces the sign outside this small oceanfront motel. The rooms are individually and tastefully decorated, the grounds immaculately landscaped. An outdoor swimming pool fronts the beach.

Darlings by the Sea
329 Atlantic Avenue, Kure Beach; 800-383-8111 or 910-458-8887
www.darlingsbythesea.com
Expensive

> Darlings offers five impeccably furnished suites "for romantic couples," complete with whirlpool baths, king-sized beds, and private terraces facing the ocean. A gourmet continental breakfast is included with the price of the room.

Ocean Princess Bed and Breakfast
824 Fort Fisher Boulevard South, Kure Beach; 800-762-4863 or 910-458-6712
www.oceanprincess.com
Expensive

> Bordered by a grove of wind-swept live oaks and sporting distinctive lavender siding, the Ocean Princess offers a quiet retreat for adults only. The inn has 10 rooms, two suites, and two cottages, all with private entrances and patios. A swimming pool, a whirlpool, and hammocks grace the shady backyard.

Orton Plantation

People who have visited Middleton Plantation outside Charleston, South Carolina, will note some striking similarities to Orton Plantation on the banks of the Cape Fear River. As with Middleton, a sandy bluff graced with ancient live oaks and elaborate gardens overlooks the marshy edges of a river and what appears to be a series of man-made ponds.

Orton Plantation is located at the northernmost extent of the rice-growing region that thrived in the low country of the Carolinas during the 18th and 19th centuries. The low-lying margins of coastal rivers were diked off and alternately flooded and drained to allow the growing and harvesting of rice. The backbreaking work of planting and harvesting was done by slaves. Upon the elimination of slavery after the Civil War and upon facing competition from areas of the Deep South better suited to mechanization, the rice culture in the Carolinas came to an end.

Orton was founded in 1725 by Roger Moore, who came to the Cape Fear region from England with a large and influential group of settlers. The Moores founded nearby Brunswick Town and several other plantations. His dominance of the region earned Roger the nickname "King" and led the Moores to launch the first armed resistance to the British rule of the colonies.

Orton House, the lone survivor of the great plantation homes that once lined the Lower Cape Fear River, graces the center of the gardens. Moore's original brick house is believed to constitute the core of the present structure. Dr. Frederick Hill purchased the house in 1826 and enlarged it in the Greek Revival temple form, an unusual architectural style in North Carolina. In 1910, James Sprunt and his wife, Luola, added the Colonial Revival wings, making this an icon of antebellum Southern architecture in the eyes of many.

Today, Orton House is closed to the public, but **Luola's Chapel** and **Orton Plantation Gardens** are open. This is a truly romantic location, especially during the first two weeks in April, when the camellias and azaleas are in bloom. A footpath traverses the bluff along the river, offering views of the gardens and the old rice fields. The latter are good places to see wading birds and the occasional alligator. The lake beside the entrance road is also a good bird-watching locale.

DIRECTIONS

Orton Plantation is located on Plantation Road off N.C. 133 approximately 18 miles south of Wilmington and 10 miles north of Southport.

ACTIVITIES

Touring gardens

FACILITIES

Visitor center

DATES

The plantation is open daily from 8 A.M. to 6 P.M. during the spring and summer and from 10 A.M. to 5 P.M. in autumn. It is closed December 1 through February 28.

FEES

An admission fee is charged.

CLOSEST TOWN

Southport is 10 miles away.

FOR MORE INFORMATION

Orton Plantation Gardens, 9149 Orton Road S.E., Winnabow, N.C. 28479 (910-371-6851; www.ortongardens.com)

Brunswick Town State Historic Site

Lying just north of Orton Plantation, Brunswick Town was once a thriving colonial port and the residence of the Royal governor. It was laid out in 1725 by Maurice Moore, brother of Roger Moore of Orton Plantation. Governor William Tryon resided here in a house called Russellborough until he completed Tryon Palace in New Bern.

Brunswick Town was the site of early resistance to British colonial rule. To extract more money from the colonies, the British imposed the Stamp Act, which levied a tax on goods unloaded at colonial ports. In 1765, a group of local colonists surrounded Russellborough to protest the Stamp Act, holding Governor Tryon under house arrest. This ended enforcement of the act in the Cape Fear region.

Brunswick Town was short-lived, however. Wilmington, located 15 miles upstream, became the preferred port for the Lower Cape Fear River. The population further dwindled when the Royal governor relocated to New Bern in 1770. When the British burned the town during the American Revolution, they found few residents.

During the Civil War, the Confederates built an earthen defensive work called Fort Anderson over part of the town. That fort was abandoned in 1865 after bombardment by the United States Navy.

Except for the ruins of **St. Philips Church**, whose 22-foot-tall brick walls dominate the site, little remains of either Brunswick Town or Fort Anderson today. However, the site is well worth a visit. Rangers bring the town and the fort to life through guided tours. The visitor center contains a cannon recovered from the Spanish privateer *Fortuna*, which attacked the town in 1748 and was subsequently blown up.

DIRECTIONS
Brunswick Town is located on St. Philips Road off N.C. 133 south of Wilmington. Follow the brown signs to the site.

ACTIVITIES
Touring ruins

FACILITIES
Visitor center

Southport

Graced with historic homes and businesses, shaded by ancient live oaks, and offering a superb view of the Cape Fear estuary, Southport is one of the most delightful towns on the North Carolina coast. This is a great place to go for a quiet retreat, especially if you enjoy walking, visiting historic sites, or shopping for antiques.

First named Smithville, the town dates to the late 1740s and the construction of Fort Johnson at the mouth of the Cape Fear. Smithville served as a home to the river pilots who guided ships up the Cape Fear. It later became a summer retreat for Wilmington residents seeking to enjoy the ocean breezes. The town was renamed Southport in 1881 in anticipation of its becoming a major seaport, though it never reached the status of Wilmington. Today, Southport hosts recreational boaters and a handful of fishing boats and charters.

You should first stop at the **Southport Visitor Center** (910-457-7927) at 113 West Moore Street. Here, you can read a history of the town and pick up maps for a self-guided walking tour. The one-mile loop encompasses 25 historic sites, including the **Adkins-Ruark House** (1890), boyhood home of author and journalist Robert Ruark; the **Fort Johnson Officers Quarters**, the oldest surviving component of the military complex, dating to 1748; the **Brunswick County Jail**, now home to the Southport Historical Society; the **Old Smithville Burying Ground**; and **Franklin Square Park**, laid out in 1792 with walls constructed from the ballast stones of old sailing ships. You'll also want to tour the **North**

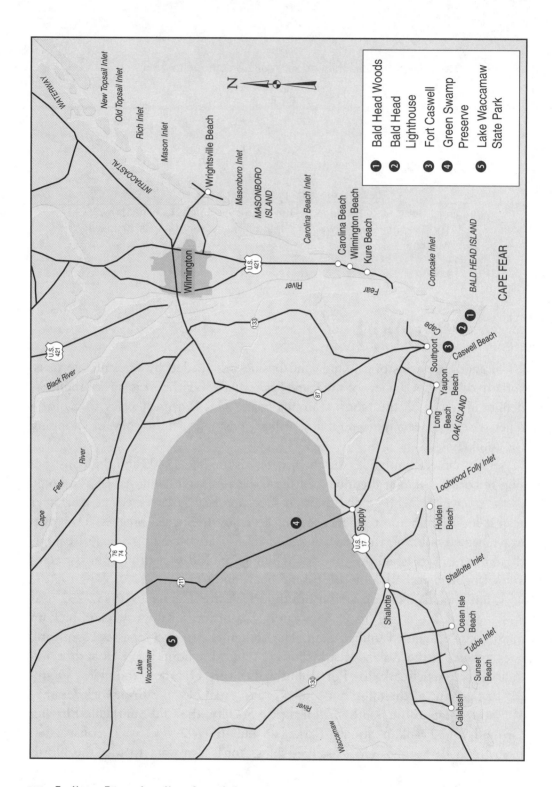

N

Bald Head Woods

Bald Head Lighthouse

Fort Caswell

Green Swamp Preserve

Lake Waccamaw State Park

New Topsail Inlet

Old Topsail Inlet

Rich Inlet

Mason Inlet

Wrightsville Beach

INTRACOASTAL WATERWAY

Masonboro Inlet

MASONBORO ISLAND

Carolina Beach Inlet

Carolina Beach
Wilmington Beach
Kure Beach

Corncake Inlet

BALD HEAD ISLAND

CAPE FEAR

Wilmington

U.S. 421

Fear River

Cape

Southport

Caswell Beach

133

U.S. 421

Black River

Yaupon Beach

Long Beach

OAK ISLAND

87

Lockwood Folly Inlet

Cape Fear River

Supply

U.S. 17

Holden Beach

Shallotte Inlet

76 74

211

Shallotte

Ocean Isle Beach

Tubbs Inlet

130

Sunset Beach

Lake Waccamaw

Calabash

Waccamaw River

White ibis gather by the thousands on Battery Island off of Southport.

Carolina Maritime Museum of Southport (910-456-0003) at 166 North Howe Street. This small museum is packed with interesting exhibits, including scale models of ships that have plied the Cape Fear region, artifacts from area shipwrecks, and information on local pirate Stede Bonnet.

The most popular gathering point in Southport is **Waterfront Park** on Bay Street. From here, you can see the lighthouses on Bald Head Island and Oak Island, crab off the city pier, and watch the sun rise. It is also an excellent spot for birding. Boat-tailed grackles stalk the lawn. Pelicans, gulls, and terns patrol the tide line offshore. In winter, double-breasted cormorants, red-breasted mergansers, and other migrating ducks are frequently sighted.

During spring and summer, visitors to the Southport waterfront see flocks of large white birds with pink, curved beaks passing overhead. These are white ibises, flying to and from their nesting grounds on **Battery Island**, a low-lying spit of land located half a mile offshore. Battery Island is home to some 10,000 nesting pairs of white ibises, as well as black and snowy egrets, black-crowned night herons, and little blue and tricolored herons. A National Audubon Sanctuary, the island is off-limits to the public. However, you can view the birds from the waterfront using binoculars or see them up close by boat. The dawn and sunset flights to and from the island can be spectacular, especially in late summer.

Another popular gathering spot is **Southport Marina**, located at the west end of town. The marina is home to a host of guide services that will take you inshore, near shore, or offshore to fish for flounder, speckled trout, red drum, king mackerel, and more. Located across from the marina, the Adventure Company (910-454-0607) offers bike rentals and guided kayak trips to area creeks and marshes. Brunswick County is blessed with great paddling opportunities, including **Town Creek, Rice Creek**, and the **Lockwood Folly River**, which are little known to anyone besides local fishermen. Lined with cypress trees, prowled by alligators and water moccasins, these blackwater creeks are a nature lover's paradise. The free *Canoe and Kayak Access Guide* is available from the **Brunswick County Parks and Recreation Department** (800-222-4790 or 910-253-2670). The guide will enable you to explore these streams on your own. However, first-time visitors are encouraged to go with an outfitter, who can arrange for drop-offs and pickups and point out natural features that might otherwise be missed.

FOR MORE INFORMATION

Southport-Oak Island Area Chamber of Commerce, 4841 Long Beach Road S.E., Southport, N.C. 28461 (800-457-6964; www.southport-oakisland.com)

RESTAURANTS IN SOUTHPORT

Mr. P's Waterway
317 Bay Street, Southport; 910-457-0801
Moderate

The entrées at Mr. P's include seafood specials like shrimp, oysters, and Andouille sausage in brown gumbo sauce over grits, plus beef dishes like slow-roasted prime rib.

Provision Company
Yacht Drive and Bay Street, Southport; 910-457-0654
Moderate

This restaurant occupies the same dockside location as Mr. P's Waterway. At the Provision Company, you can step up to the counter, order your blackened tuna, get a beer out of the cooler, and ease out on to the deck for a great view of Oak Island. This is casual coastal dining at its best.

Thai Peppers
115 East Moore Street, Southport; 910-457-0095
Moderate

This restaurant offers a welcome break for those who've had too much seafood. Here, you can expect all your Thai favorites—beef, chicken, and pork, cooked with red and green curry to your preferred level of spiciness.

Lodgings in Southport

Lois Jane's Riverview Inn
106 West Bay Street, Southport; 800-457-1152 or 910-457-6701
www.sppilot.com
Expensive

This historic home, constructed around 1890, was built by the present owner's grandfather and restored by her children. It is furnished with period furniture and family heirlooms. The accommodations include two rooms with private baths and two that share a bath. Considering the great view of the waterfront and the easy walking to downtown Southport, the location couldn't be better.

Riverside Motel
103 West Bay Street, Southport; 910-457-6986
Inexpensive

This eight-unit motel offers well-kept rooms with an excellent view of the water. It is within easy walking distance of several restaurants and downtown Southport.

Sea Captain Motor Lodge
608 West Street, Southport; 910-457-5263
www.seacaptainmotorlodge.com
Moderate

This 96-unit motel is conveniently located next to Southport Marina. Amenities include an outdoor swimming pool and the adjacent Sea Captain Restaurant, which serves breakfast, lunch, and dinner.

Constructed in 1817, the Bald Head Island Lighthouse is the oldest in North Carolina.

Bald Head Island

Bald Head is the largest island in the patchwork of high ground and marsh collectively known as Smith Island, located at the southern tip of the Cape Fear region. Unless you have your own boat, Bald Head is accessible only by private ferry from Southport. This controlled access, combined with a near total absence of cars and commercial establishments, makes this resort island ideal for those seeking solitude in a laid-back, albeit tony, atmosphere. It's a great place if you want to explore the coastal environment or indulge in a week of golf, croquet, or tennis. It's not a good choice for kids who want to hang out at the arcade or meet their peers on the beach.

Bald Head Island remained unknown to tourists until the mid-1970s, when Texas oilman George Mitchell purchased and began to develop it as an exclusive resort community. Today, Bald Head stands as a model of tasteful development, its houses and community buildings crafted in coastal vernacular architecture and carefully situated among the dunes and maritime forest. Commercial development has been limited to a few stores and restaurants, mostly clustered around the marina. Except for construction vehicles, cars are banned from the island. Travel is done primarily by electric golf cart along narrow roads known as "wynds."

Day visitors to Bald Head will want to rent bicycles or golf carts to get around the island. These are available from **Island Passage** (910-457-4944), located at 1 Marina Wynd. Island Passage also rents canoes for exploring Bald Head Creek, a three-mile-long tidal creek that is frequented by a variety of wading birds and the occasional alligator. The company will arrange to pick you up at the far end of the creek, so you can paddle with the tide at a leisurely pace.

Another option for day visitors is to take the **Bald Head Island Historic Tour** (910-457-5003). This guided tour, available from Tuesday through Saturday, includes parking, a round-trip ferry ride, visits to key historic sites, and lunch on the island for one price. The tour departs on the 10:00 A.M. ferry from Indigo Plantation, spends three to four hours on the island, and departs for Southport at 2:30 P.M. Advance reservations are required.

The most popular destination for day visitors is the **Bald Head Lighthouse**, affectionately known as "Old Baldy." Constructed in 1817 of brick and faced with stucco and brownstone, Bald Head is the oldest lighthouse in the state. It has a distinctive octagonal shape and a weathered appearance. The lighthouse is conveniently located a short walk from the ferry landing and is open year-round. For a small donation, you can enter the darkened interior of the lighthouse and climb the 110 feet to the top. Only trim adults will be able to fit through the narrow opening into the lamp room, from which the original light has been removed. The view from the top is spectacular.

A second site of historical interest lies at the opposite (southeast) end of the island. **Captain Charlie's Station** consists of four bungalows built in 1903 to house the keeper and family of the Cape Fear Lighthouse. That lighthouse was deactivated in 1958 and has since been destroyed, though the foundation is still visible. The buildings making up Captain Charlie's Station are not open to the public, though they are available for rent. Their commanding view of the sea makes them worth a visit.

On the way out to Captain Charlie's along Federal Road, you'll pass through a lush maritime forest known as **Bald Head Woods**. George Mitchell donated approximately 200 acres of this land to The Nature Conservancy. It is now part of the North Carolina Coastal Reserve. Bald Head Woods is unique in that it contains tropical plant species such as the cabbage palmetto, as well as more northerly trees such as the red maple. The Bald Head Island Conservancy, an independent nonprofit organization, has constructed several miles of trails through the forest. The trails are close (don't expect grand views) and buggy, but they will give you an appreciation of the lushness and variety of a healthy maritime forest. Trailheads are identified by signs and by small wooden parking decks along Federal Road.

The Bald Head Island Conservancy is headquartered in a complex of buildings known as **Turtle Central** (910-457-0917), part of the old Cape Fear Lighthouse complex. Turtle Central includes a small gift shop and a classroom. During spring and summer, the conservancy hosts a variety of educational programs in this classroom that introduce visitors and residents to the natural wonders of Bald Head Island. Outdoor activities include kayaking Bald Head Creek, beachcombing, and birding.

Starting in June and running through August, conservancy members have the unique opportunity to accompany a naturalist on a nightly turtle walk. Spotting a giant loggerhead lumbering across the beach to lay her eggs is a truly unforgettable experience. Spaces on the turtle walks are limited and fill very quickly. Call 910-457-5786 for membership information and reservations.

The conservancy also offers a week-long camp for rising second through sixth graders, junior naturalist activities for rising seventh through 10th graders, and thrice-yearly fishing schools. These activities are designed for those staying on Bald Head, rather than for day visitors. Other activities available to renters and residents include tennis, swimming, croquet, and golf at the **Bald Head Island Club**. The club's 18-hole golf course is considered one of the most beautiful in the South and is worth playing for the views alone.

A final spot worth visiting on Bald Head is **Cape Fear**, the southernmost point in North Carolina. The land literally disappears in a point and runs offshore for some 20 miles in a network of treacherous sand bars known as Frying Pan Shoals. Like the other two capes in the state (Hatteras and Lookout), Cape Fear is a dramatic spot where waves collide from different directions. Shorebirds gather here in considerable numbers. During the cool months, this is a good spot to see Northern gannets and scoters, as well as the occasional jaeger.

> ### FOR MORE INFORMATION
> Bald Head Island Information Center, 5079 Southport-Supply Road S.E., Southport N.C. 28461 (800-432-RENT; www.baldheadisland.com)

RESTAURANTS ON BALD HEAD ISLAND

Eb and Flo's
Bald Head Island Marina, Bald Head Island; 910-457-7217
Moderate

One of the few legitimate "hangouts" on the island, this casual eatery offers good food and a commanding view of the harbor. Specialties include the "Bald Head Island Steam Pot," featuring shrimp, little-neck clams, king crab legs, and local oysters, served with new potatoes and corn on the cob.

River Pilot Café
Bald Head Island Marina, Bald Head Island; 910-457-7390
Moderate

Also located on the harbor, the River Pilot is open for breakfast, lunch, and dinner. It is famous for its buffet breakfast. She-crab soup and crab burgers are among the favorites for lunch and dinner.

LODGINGS ON BALD HEAD ISLAND

Except for the bed-and-breakfasts listed below, lodgings on Bald Head are strictly multi-day house rentals. Call 800-432-RENT for reservations.

Marsh Harbor Inn and Conference Center
Bald Head Island Marina, Bald Head Island; 800-432-RENT
www.baldheadisland.com
Expensive

Located at the marina, Marsh Harbor offers easy access to the ferry and restaurants, as well as superb views. The 15 rooms all have private baths. Some open on to private porches. Guests enjoy breakfast at the River Pilot Café.

Theodosia's Bed and Breakfast
Bald Head Island Marina, Bald Head Island; 800-656-1812 or 910-457-6563
www.theodosias.com
Expensive

Boasting an ornate Victorian design and a trademark lavender color scheme, Theodosia's offers luxury accommodations with an emphasis on romance. All guests receive a golf cart for transportation and privileges at the Bald Head Island Club.

Oak Island

Oak Island is a 13-mile-long strip of land fronted by the Atlantic Ocean on one side and the Intracoastal Waterway on the other. Three incorporated communities—Caswell Beach, Yaupon Beach, and Long Beach—abut each other in a more or less continuous line of development. However, the shady canopy of oaks for which the island was named softens the impact of the development and gives this island a distinctive appeal. Some 5,000 people, including numerous retirees, have made Oak Island a permanent home. Thanks to its numerous public beach access points and its wealth of houses for rent, this is also a popular destination for vacationers.

Caswell Beach is the easternmost community on the island. It is home to 200 permanent residents and many more vacationers in summer. Aside from the beach, the principal recreational attraction at Caswell is the **Oak Island Golf and Country Club** (910-578-5275). One of the vintage courses in the area, it is open to the public. The town also contains several sites of historic interest, including Fort Caswell (see below) and the **Oak Island Lighthouse**, both located at the eastern end of N.C. 133. Built in 1958, the Oak Island Lighthouse is identified by its three horizontal bands of gray, white, and black. The colors are actually part of the pigment of the cement, rather than being painted on the exterior. At 2.8 million candlepower, it is the most powerful lighthouse in the country. Maintained by the United States Coast Guard, it is open for visitation on Tuesday and Saturday from 10 A.M. to 2 P.M. Call 910-278-1133 for information.

Yaupon Beach has the look and feel of a mainland residential community. Contemporary ranch homes and bungalows nestle beneath the oaks along a grid of numbered streets. Yaupon caters to tourists by offering several beach access points, motels, and the **Yaupon Pier** (910-278-9400), located on Ocean Drive at the end of Womble Street.

Boasting a year-round population of approximately 4,500, **Long Beach** is the largest community on Oak Island. It is densely populated yet heavily wooded. Rental housing is available in abundance; a handful of motels and restaurants are also open for business. Long Beach has numerous beach access points and two fishing piers. At 1,012 feet, **Long Beach Pier** (910-278-5962) at 2729 West Beach Drive is said to be the longest pier in the state. The **Ocean Crest Pier** (910-278-6674) at 1411 East Beach Drive is only slightly shorter. Both are popular gathering points. The **Long Beach Parks and Recreation Department** (910-278-5518) maintains an excellent canoe trail system. Four trails varying in length from four to seven miles have been laid out along portions of the Intracoastal Waterway and various creeks and sloughs. This is a good place to observe wading birds and, in Lockwood Folly Inlet, the occasional school of dolphins. Stop by the Long Beach Parks and Recreation Department at 3003 East Oak Island Drive to pick up a trail map.

> ### FOR MORE INFORMATION
> Southport-Oak Island Area Chamber of Commerce, 4841 Long Beach Road S.E., Southport, N.C. 28461 (800-457-6964; www.southport-oakisland.com)

Fort Caswell

Located at the eastern end of Oak Island overlooking the mouth of the Cape Fear River, Fort Caswell played an integral part in coastal defenses both during and after the Civil War. This 200-acre complex of abandoned fortifications and former military barracks is now owned and occupied by the North Carolina Baptist Assembly, part of the Baptist State Convention of North Carolina. The assembly uses the grounds and buildings for training events and retreats. At its discretion and for a small fee, it will allow members of the public to tour the grounds. It's a visit well worth making.

Scattered along the eastern shoreline is a series of bunkers and fortifications dating to 1826. The original Fort Caswell was a pentagonal structure of brick and masonry surrounded by earthen ramparts. Confederate forces occupied the fort during the Civil War and incorporated it into the Cape Fear defense system. When Union forces took nearby Fort Fisher in 1865, the Confederates abandoned Fort Caswell, detonating the powder magazine and destroying much of the interior. However, a substantial portion of the fort remains intact and is an impressive sight.

Fort Caswell was neglected until the 1890s, when the military saw the need to shore up its coastal defenses. It embarked on a large-scale building program that continued through World War I. The site now includes concrete bunkers and a handsome collection of wooden barracks, mess halls, and administrative buildings. It was sold to private concerns in 1925 and repurchased by the United States Navy at the start of World War II to serve as an island patrol communications base.

Having outlived its usefulness as a military base, the entire complex was sold to the Baptist State Convention of North Carolina in 1949 for $86,000. The Baptist organization has since restored all of the buildings on the site and added a few more to accommodate its recreational and educational activities. Facilities are available for rent by Baptist and other religious groups. The fortifications are essentially untouched and lie in various states of disrepair. Visitors are cautioned against entering them. Fortunately, they are easily viewed from the grounds.

DIRECTIONS
Fort Caswell is located on Oak Island at the terminus of N.C. 133. Entry is through a manned gate.

ACTIVITIES
Touring ruins

FACILITIES
A wide variety of facilities is available to those renting the complex but not to the visiting public.

DATES
The fort is open to visitors after Labor Day and before Memorial Day during business hours on weekdays.

FEES
An admission fee is charged.

CLOSEST TOWN
Southport is 10 miles away.

FOR MORE INFORMATION
North Carolina Baptist Assembly, 100 Caswell Beach Road, Oak Island, N.C. 28465 (910-278-9501; www.fortcaswell.com)

RESTAURANTS ON OAK ISLAND

Fish House Restaurant
57th Place, Long Beach; 910-278-6012
Moderate

Located at Blue Water Point Marina, the Fish House specializes in fresh seafood, including "Grouper Oscar" and stuffed flounder. It boasts a fine view of the marina and the Intracoastal Waterway. It is open for lunch on weekends and for dinner in season.

Table One Bistro
1407 East Beach Drive, Long Beach; 910-278-4777
Moderate

Table One offers fine dining in a casual atmosphere with an ocean view. The food here is cooked on a mesquite grill. Specialties include mahi-mahi, shrimp, and scallops baked on a cedar plank. The restaurant is open for dinner only.

LODGINGS ON OAK ISLAND

Driftwood Motel
604 Ocean Drive, Yaupon Beach; 910-278-6114
www.driftwoodnc.com
Inexpensive to moderate

Located six blocks from Oak Island Golf and Country Club and adjacent to the Yaupon Pier, this 14-unit motel offers a convenient location at an affordable price. Amenities include an outdoor pool, a children's play area, a basketball court, and outdoor grills.

Blue Water Point Marina and Resort Motel
57th Place, Long Beach; 910-278-1230
www.bluewaterpointmotel.com
Moderate

Located on the sound side of Oak Island, Blue Water caters primarily to recreational boaters but is an appealing choice for anyone looking for an attractive place to stay. The motel offers rooms with waterway views, an outdoor pool, and a nearby public boat launch. The marina rents floating docks, slips, pontoon boats, and johnboats. It is home base to several charter boats and head boats. Motel guests get a 50 percent discount on head-boat tickets and boat rentals.

The beaches of the South Brunswick Islands are among the best in the state.

South Brunswick Islands

Three islands make up the chain collectively known as the South Brunswick Islands. These are Holden Beach, Ocean Isle Beach, and Sunset Beach.

Holden Beach is the longest of the three, at 11 miles. Like Oak Island, it has a sizable year-round population made up largely of retirees. Holden Beach is a quiet, family-oriented beach town. It offers little in the way of nightlife, restaurants, or motels. Public parking along the beach is limited. However, numerous houses are available for rent. The **Holden Beach Pier** (910-842-6483) has a game room, a grill, and a snack bar.

In contrast to Holden Beach, **Ocean Isle Beach** is almost exclusively oriented toward tourism. The island is covered from sound to shore with bungalows, condominiums, and even a high-rise hotel. It has a number of restaurants, an excellent museum, and plenty of places to buy or rent surfboards, fishing gear, and the like. The **Ocean Isle Beach Water Slide** (910-579-9678) provides a fun recreational option.

Last in the chain of islands is **Sunset Beach**. At only three miles in length, Sunset is tiny, but it is favored by many North and South Carolinians for its lack of commercial development and its expansive beaches. While longshore currents and storms regularly strip many islands of their sand, Sunset's beaches have been growing over the years. "Oceanfront" homes may be a hundred yards or more from the water, located behind several ridges of dunes and lush thickets of wax myrtle. The trek to the beach appeals to many people but may be tough on parents with young children who need to be regularly escorted back to the house. As of this writing, Sunset Beach was accessible only by a single-lane floating bridge across the Intracoastal Waterway. Crossing it can entail a wait of 15 or 20 minutes while the bridge opens and closes to allow the passage of watercraft. Some view this bridge, the last of its kind in North Carolina, as part of Sunset's charm. Others see it as an annoyance. The floating bridge is scheduled to be replaced by a high-rise bridge in 2004. Vacationers on the South Brunswick Islands have access to top-notch public golf courses on the mainland; some 36 are within a 15- to 20-minute drive. These include **Lockwood Golf Links** (910-842-5666), a William Byrd-designed par-72 at the confluence of the Lockwood Folly River and the Intracoastal Waterway; **Brick Landing Plantation** (910-754-5545), rated one of the top 50 golf courses in the Southeast by *Florida Golf Week* magazine; **Oyster Bay Golf Links** (910-579-3528), a challenging par-70 voted among the top 50 golf courses in the country by *Golf Digest* in 1990; and **Sea Trail Golf Resort**, featuring three par-72 courses.

Birders will be interested to know that the two large ponds known as **Twin Lakes**—located on N.C. 179 just west of the mainland town of Sunset Beach— are the only sites in North Carolina frequented by wood storks (*Mycteria americana*). After nesting in Florida and Georgia, a flock of storks usually moves to these ponds around mid-July and stays to the end of September. The grounds are owned by Oyster Bay Golf Links, so the birding public must view the ponds from the roadside.

Another good birding spot is the appropriately named **Bird Island**, located across a shallow inlet at the west end of Sunset Beach. Bird Island was purchased by the state in 2002 and is now part of the North Carolina Estuarine Research Reserve system. The sand flats beside the inlet are a good place to see shorebirds, especially at high tide. This is also one of the state's best sites for reddish egrets (*Egretta rufescens*), one or more of which are often seen here between July and September. The island can be reached by canoeing or wading the inlet at low tide; if you take the latter approach, make sure you keep an eye on the water level so you can wade back. The shrubby interior of Bird Island is a good place to see painted buntings. The jetties at the western end of the island are a good spot for viewing cormorants and a variety of ducks in fall and winter.

FOR MORE INFORMATION
South Brunswick Islands Chamber of Commerce, P.O. Box 1185, Shallotte, N.C. (910-754-6644; www.sbichamber.com)

Museum of Coastal Carolina

Vacationers on the South Brunswick Islands may be surprised to learn that a first-rate natural-history museum is located at the beach. Housed in a white, windowless building just across the bridge on Ocean Isle Beach, the Museum of Coastal Carolina houses a treasure trove of dioramas and exhibits on the natural history of coastal North and South Carolina. The Reef Room features life-sized models of marine life positioned as if swimming over and under the viewer. The floor of the exhibit contains part of a Civil War-era shipwreck that washed ashore during Hurricane Hugo. A case of rifles and additional Civil War artifacts recovered from sunken blockade runners are showcased in other displays. The Shell Room features an impressive collection of seashells, including samples of most of the 200 different species found along the Carolina coast. Other attractions include sharks' teeth and jaws and a popular sea-turtle exhibit. A large addition that opened in 1996 houses a spectacular waterfowl diorama that displays ducks, geese, and swans of the coastal wetlands, along with the remains of a 2,000-year-old dugout canoe. The museum offers a Tuesday-evening lecture series, as well as field trips and workshops related to coastal ecology and history.

DIRECTIONS
The museum is located at 21 East Second Street just across the bridge on Ocean Isle Beach.

ACTIVITIES
Evening lectures, field trips, workshops

FACILITIES
Gift shop

DATES
From Memorial Day through Labor Day, the museum is open Tuesday, Wednesday, Friday, and Saturday from 9 A.M. to 5 P.M., Monday and Thursday from 9 A.M. to 9 P.M., and Sunday from 1 P.M. to 5 P.M. After Labor Day, it is open Friday and Saturday from 9 A.M. to 5 P.M. and Sunday from 1 P.M. to 5 P.M.

FEES
An admission fee is charged.

⌒Ingram Planetarium

Another cultural attraction was added to the South Brunswick Islands when the Ingram Planetarium opened in 2002. Located on the mainland side of Sunset Beach, the planetarium is named in honor of the late Stuart Ingram, who helped found both this and the Museum of Coastal Carolina. It features star shows and multimedia presentations in an 85-seat theater topped by a 40-foot dome.

DIRECTIONS
The planetarium is located behind the Food Lion shopping center on N.C. 179 in the mainland town of Sunset Beach.

ACTIVITIES
Watching star shows

FACILITIES
Museum, gift shop

DATES
The planetarium is open Tuesday through Saturday from 3 P.M. to 9 P.M.

FEES
An admission fee is charged.

CLOSEST TOWN
Sunset Beach

FOR MORE INFORMATION
Museum of Coastal Carolina, 21 East Second Street, Ocean Isle Beach, N.C. 28469 (910-575-0033)

There are 36 golf courses within a 20-minute drive of the South Brunswick Islands.

Restaurants on the South Brunswick Islands

Sharky's
81 Causeway Drive, Ocean Isle Beach; 910-579-9177
Inexpensive

Alive with music and offering a great view of the Intracoastal Waterway, Sharky's is one of the favorite gathering spots for families and 20-somethings on Ocean Isle. Salads, sandwiches, and pizzas are served for lunch. Dinner entrées include steaks, chicken, and seafood. Boaters can tie up for lunch or dinner at the restaurant's dock.

Stars Waterfront Café
14 Causeway Drive, Ocean Isle Beach; 910-579-7838
Moderate

Stars has the ambiance of a nightclub—linen napkins, astral motif, cool colors. It offers a welcome break from the harsh light of the beach. The food is also refreshingly out of the ordinary. Among the favorites are "Fried Green Tomato Napoleon," made with Louisiana crawfish, corn ragout, and chipotle remoulade, and "Low Country Shrimp over Grits."

Sugar Shack
1609 Hale Beach Road, Ocean Isle Beach; 910-579-3844
Moderate

With reggae music wafting from loudspeakers and tropical art-work on the walls, Sugar Shack brings the flavor of Jamaica to the North Carolina coast. It specializes in such entrées as jerk chicken, "Brown Stewed Fish" (slowly cooked red snapper), and curried goat.

Twin Lakes Seafood Restaurant
102 Sunset Boulevard, Sunset Beach; 910-579-6373
Moderate

Twin Lakes may have the longest menu of any restaurant on the coast—11 pages. But quality is not sacrificed for quantity. While enjoying a wonderful view of the Intracoastal Waterway and Sunset Beach's famous floating bridge, diners are treated to such specialties as blackened yellowfin tuna, served with pineapple-mango salsa, and flounder stuffed with feta cheese, spinach, and garlic.

LODGINGS ON THE SOUTH BRUNSWICK ISLANDS

Most visitors to the South Brunswick Islands stay in one of the many vacation homes available for rent. However, the area also offers a number of motels, most located in Ocean Isle Beach.

The Islander Inn
57 West First Street, Ocean Isle Beach; 888-325-4753 or 910-575-7000
www.IslanderInn.com
Expensive

Advertising itself as the "Coastal Carolinas' Golf Package Specialist," The Islander Inn caters to vacationers seeking bargain rates at area golf courses and proximity to the beach. Amenities include an oceanfront pool and deck, an indoor pool and hot tub, and spacious rooms, most with an oceanfront view and a balcony.

Ocean Isle Inn
37 West First Street, Ocean Isle Beach; 800-352-5988 or 910-579-0750
www.oceanisleinn.com
Expensive

Located next to The Islander Inn, this motel offers an oceanfront pool and sun deck, an indoor pool with a Jacuzzi, complimentary continental breakfast, and business amenities such as data ports and telephones with voice mail.

The Winds Oceanfront Inn
310 East First Street, Ocean Isle Beach; 800-334-3581 or 910-579-0750
www.thewinds.com
Moderate to expensive

Beautifully landscaped with palm trees, banana trees, and subtropical gardens, this inn offers a wide range of accommodations, from one- and two-bedroom suites to six-bedroom resort houses. Amenities include two outdoor pools, an indoor pool, whirlpools, an exercise room, shuffleboard and volleyball courts, and free bicycles for guests.

Calabash

Calabash is the last town along the coast before the South Carolina state line. The town's main claim to fame is its wealth of restaurants serving "Calabash-style" seafood—meaning seafood that is breaded and fried and served with hush puppies, more of both than most people can eat. The restaurants are virtually indistinguishable from each other in terms of menu. Diners looking for a view along with their food may prefer one of three restaurants overlooking the Little River, where the fishing boats bring in their catch. These are **Beck's Seafood Restaurant** (910-579-6776), **Captain John's Seafood House** (910-579-6011), and **Captain Nance's Seafood Restaurant** (910-579-2574).

Calabash is also home to **The Hurricane Fleet** (843-249-3571), which operates out of the marina at the end of River Street. This company offers daily adventure cruises aboard the 90-foot *Hurricane II*. The cruise boat follows working shrimp boats, giving passengers an up-close view of dolphins and sharks feeding off the by-catch as the nets are hauled out of the water. The Hurricane Fleet also offers full-day and half-day fishing trips aboard three sportfishing vessels.

> ### DIRECTIONS
> Calabash is located on U.S. 17 approximately 25 miles north of Myrtle Beach, South Carolina, and 45 miles south of Wilmington.

Green Swamp Preserve

Inland from the heavily populated coastline of Brunswick County, development tapers off, then stops altogether north of U.S. 17. Much of this land is the Green Swamp, a 140-square-mile block of bay forests, pocosins, longleaf pine savannas, and loblolly pine plantations. The Green hardly resembles the cherished vision of a Southern swamp—tall cypress trees rising out of tannin-stained waters. Most of the swamp's big timber was logged in the last century and its waters drained by a grid of canals. Timber companies still own and manage a large part of the Green. In 1977, Federal Paper Board generously donated some 14,000 acres to The Nature Conservancy to set aside as a preserve.

The Green Swamp Preserve protects a broad array of lower-coastal-plain ecosystems that are fast disappearing as development and commercial pine plantations spread across the land. Approximately 12,700 acres of the preserve are covered by dense evergreen shrub bogs, while longleaf pine savannas and white cedar swamps comprise another 500 acres. The wetter savanna communities support an amazing abundance of plants. More than 14 species of carnivorous plants grow here, including Venus flytraps and four species of pitcher plants. In springtime, orchids, irises, and the federally endangered rough-leaf loosestrife (*Lysimachia asperulaefolia*) carpet the savanna floor. The Green also supports three federally endangered animal species—the American alligator, the Eastern diamondback rattlesnake (*Crotalus adamanteus*), and the red-cockaded woodpecker.

The plant communities of the Green Swamp's pocosins and savannas evolved in the face of periodic forest fires and are dependent upon fire to survive. The cones of pond pines, for example, release their seeds only after exposure to very high temperatures. Wiregrass flowers vigorously only after burning. In place of wildfires, The Nature Conservancy now conducts prescribed burns to maintain these plant communities and to keep wax myrtles and other aggressive shrubs at bay.

The Nature Conservancy's preferred method of granting public access is to conduct periodic tours of the preserve. The poaching of Venus flytraps has led it to discourage casual visitors. However, the conservancy also maintains a parking area and a short network of trails off N.C. 211. These trails lead through a pocosin forest into a longleaf pine savanna, where you'll stand a good chance of seeing a red-cockaded woodpecker. Look for this small, rather drab-colored bird going to and from resin-streaked nesting cavities in old-growth pines.

Lake Waccamaw State Park / Waccamaw River

At the north end of the Green Swamp lies one of the most unusual bodies of water in North Carolina. Lake Waccamaw is the largest of the water-filled Carolina bays, a series of oval-shaped depressions scattered across the Atlantic seaboard from Maryland to Georgia but most prevalent in North Carolina. The origin of these bays is a mystery. Because they are only several thousand years old and exhibit a nearly uniform orientation, some scientists speculate that they were created by a meteor shower—perhaps by a meteor that exploded in the earth's atmosphere, creating a series of shock waves but leaving no trace of meteorites.

Most Carolina bays are highly acidic, which limits the diversity of aquatic life they can support. Lake Waccamaw, however, is acid-neutral, owing to the limestone bluffs that line its north shore. This unique combination of factors has

A giant bald cypress dwarfs canoeists on the Waccamaw River.

allowed a remarkable diversity of aquatic plants and animals to develop, many of which are endemic to the lake—meaning they are found nowhere else in the world. These include three species of fish (the Waccamaw silverside, the Waccamaw killifish, and the Waccamaw darter), a mussel called the Waccamaw spike, and two snails (the Waccamaw amnicola and the Waccamaw siltsnail).

If you're a casual observer, you're unlikely to see these creatures in the wild or to appreciate their slight genetic differences. However, there is a good chance you'll observe a variety of wading birds along the shore, an alligator or two in the lake, and songbirds such as the bright yellow prothonotary warbler in the surrounding woods.

Lake Waccamaw State Park, which occupies 1,732 acres on the southern rim of the lake, provides public access to the lake and its surrounding woods. Three nature trails, a 700-foot handicapped-accessible boardwalk, and a 375-foot pier allow visitors to explore different habitats. The park has a primitive group camping area and an attractive picnic area shaded by live oaks. There are no public boat ramps in the park, but two can be found on the east and west sides of the lake.

If you're longing for a true wilderness experience, consider taking a canoe trip down the Waccamaw River. From the south end of the lake, this narrow stream winds through some of the wildest reaches of the Green Swamp. Red-shouldered hawks, water moccasins, and alligators are frequently seen along the river. Black bears and bobcats also prowl the swamp, though they are rarely observed. Approximately six miles south of the lake, the river passes the community of Riverview, once known as Crusoe Island. Though now connected to the outside world by a paved road, this once-isolated place is thought to have been settled in the 1790s by French citizens who fled Haiti during a war between the French and black slaves. Some members of this community still make canoes out of cypress logs in the fashion of traditional swampers.

You can enjoy a good day trip by starting at the lake and paddling 11 miles to the S.R. 1928 bridge east of Old Dock. The Waccamaw River Outdoor Center maintains a takeout and put-in here. Another good day trip is to begin at this bridge and paddle the 12.9 miles to the N.C. 130 bridge. If you want to make this an overnight excursion, it is possible to camp on the sand bars and bluffs along the river. Before venturing out on either of these sections, call the ranger at Lake Waccamaw State Park and ask about river conditions. Low water and downed trees may considerably lengthen the time of your trip or make the river altogether impassable. Likewise, extremely high water will send the river out of its banks and into the surrounding forest, making it difficult to follow the channel. Assuming the water level is decent, the best months to paddle the river are April and May, when temperatures are mild, trees and flowers are in bloom, and reptiles and birds are active.

DIRECTIONS
Heading west on U.S. 74/76 at the town of Lake Waccamaw, turn left on Council Avenue. Turn left on Lake Shore Drive, then right on Bella Coola Road. Follow the signs to the park.

ACTIVITIES
Hiking, picnicking, canoeing

FACILITIES
Visitor center, handicapped-accessible picnic area, boardwalk, pier

DATES
The park is open from 8 A.M. to 5 P.M. November through February; from 8 A.M. to 6 P.M. during March and October; from 8 A.M. to 7 P.M. during April, May, and

Black River

North of Lake Waccamaw in the swampy lowlands of the Cape Fear River Basin lies one of the most magical of eastern North Carolina's blackwater rivers. The Black River flows 66 miles through portions of Sampson, Pender, and Bladen Counties before emptying into the Cape Fear 14 miles upstream from Wilmington. The Black is lined by a dense forest that includes the oldest known trees east of the Rocky Mountains—a stand of 1,700-year-old bald cypresses. You will need a guide to point out these trees, as their size is not commensurate with their age. The nutrient-poor river has constrained their growth, and storms have knocked off their tops. However, laying hands on a tree that was alive when Constantine the Great ruled the Roman Empire is a moving experience.

The best time to canoe the Black is during spring, when the swamp roses are in bloom and migratory songbirds fill the trees. Fishing for bass, sunfish, and bowfin is good in both spring and summer. Fall offers excellent colors, especially among the red maples and bald cypresses. Water levels fluctuate significantly over the course of the year. During periods of low flow, you may have to maneuver or portage around fallen logs and trees.

All the land along the Black is privately owned, so overnight camping is not recommended. Day trips are possible by putting in at the North Carolina Wildlife Resources Commission's public boat landing on Ivanhoe Road about 0.5 mile south of the community of Ivanhoe, then canoeing down to Beatty's Bridge on S.R. 1550. This nine-mile stretch runs through bottom-land hardwood forests and cypress swamps. Below Beatty's Bridge, the river runs 14 miles to a North

Carolina Wildlife Resources Commission boat ramp 1.5 miles south of the N.C. 11/53 bridge. This stretch contains Larkin's Cove and Three Sisters, the sites where the oldest known bald cypresses are found. To reach this spot, you can also paddle upstream from the latter takeout.

To locate and enjoy the often subtle natural wonders of the Black, it is recommended that you take a guided canoe trip. Guide services may have access to private campsites as well. Trips are offered by **The Adventure Company** (910-454-0607) and **Rock Rest Adventures** (919-542-5502), among others.

DIRECTIONS
From Wilmington, drive north on U.S. 421 to the intersection with N.C. 11/53. Go south on N.C. 11/53 for approximately 10 miles to the bridge over the Black River. Turn left on Kelly Road (S.R. 1547) just past the bridge and drive 1.5 miles to the boat ramp. Consult DeLorme's *North Carolina Atlas* for the best routes to the various put-ins.

ACTIVITIES
Canoeing, fishing, bird-watching

FACILITIES
Boat ramps

DATES
The river may be run year-round.

FEES
None

CLOSEST TOWN
Wilmington is approximately 25 miles away.

FOR MORE INFORMATION
The Nature Conservancy, Southeast Coastal Plain Office, Building 4, Unit E, Old Wrightsboro Road, Wilmington, N.C. 28405 (910-762-6277; http://nature.org/wherewework/northamerica/states/northcarolina/preserves/art5589.html)

$\mathcal{B}$ibliography

Alexander, John, and James Lazell. *Ribbon of Sand: The Amazing Convergence of the Ocean and the Outer Banks*. Chapel Hill, N.C.: Algonquin Books of Chapel Hill, 1992.

Bannon, James, and Morrison Giffen. *Sea Kayaking the Carolinas*. Asheville, N.C.: Out There Press, 1997.

Barefoot, Daniel W. *Touring the Backroads of North Carolina's Upper Coast*. Winston-Salem, N.C.: John F. Blair, Publisher, 1995.

Bartram, William. *Travels of William Bartram*. 1791. Edited by Mark Van Doren. New York: Dover Publications, 1928.

Bishir, Catherine, and Michael Southern. *A Guide to the Historic Architecture of Eastern North Carolina*. Chapel Hill: University of North Carolina Press, 1996.

Carson, Rachel. *The Edge of the Sea*. New York: Signet Books, 1955.

Cecelski, David. *A Historian's Coast: Adventures into the Tidewater Past*. Winston-Salem, N.C.: John F. Blair, Publisher, 2000.

DeBlieu, Jan. *Hatteras Journal*. Winston-Salem, N.C.: John F. Blair, Publisher, 1998.

Farb, Roderick M. *Shipwrecks: Diving the Graveyard of the Atlantic*. Hillsborough, N.C.: Menasha Ridge Press, 1985.

Fields, Margaret, and Ida Philips Lynch. *A Guide to Nature Conservancy Projects in North Carolina*. Durham: The Nature Conservancy, North Carolina Chapter, 2000.

Frankenberg, Dirk. *The Nature of North Carolina's Southern Coast*. Chapel Hill: University of North Carolina Press, 1997.

————. *The Nature of the Outer Banks*. Chapel Hill: University of North Carolina Press, 1995.

Fussell, John O., III. *A Birder's Guide to Coastal North Carolina*. Chapel Hill: University of North Carolina Press, 1994.

Lawson, John. *A New Voyage to Carolina*. 1709. Edited by Hugh T. Lefler. Chapel Hill: University of North Carolina Press, 1967.

North Carolina Coastal Plain Paddle Trails Guide. Seven Springs, N.C.: North Carolina Division of Parks and Recreation. Available at http://ils.unc.edu/parkproject.nctrails.html.

Simpson, Bland, and Ann Cary Simpson. *Into the Sound Country*. Chapel Hill: University of North Carolina Press, 1997.

Teal, John and Mildred. *Life and Death of the Salt Marsh*. New York: Ballantine Books, 1969.

Ward, H. Trawick, and R. P. Stephen Davis, Jr. *Time Before History: The Archaeology of North Carolina*. Chapel Hill: University of North Carolina Press, 1999.

*I*ndex